Love's Fire

Living the Awakened Journey

More Praises for Loves Fire: Living the Awakening Journey

Loves Fire: Living the Awakening Journey grippingly draws the reader into Dr. Conte's painful journey as she heals from the loss of her life partner, William. We follow her through despair, confusion, acceptance, back into despair and finally into the joyful realization that our loved ones never leave us. They are available for us in spirit, if not in body. As a counselor for many who have experienced great losses, I would highly recommend this book as a guidebook for traversing the rocky path of grief and as a road map for healing.

> Patricia Sherman, Ph.D., LCSW
> Author of *From Tragedy to Triumph: How to Heal from Trauma and Start Living a Happy and Wonderful Life*

This is a poignant guide to infinite possibilities. Tianna's insightful and heart-felt journey takes the reader to places that count - to your soul. Devour this book and help heart and soul soar.

> Jill Lublin
> International speaker and best-selling author of *Get Noticed... Get Referrals, Networking Magic,* and *Guerilla Publicity* and host of "Do the Dream" radio show

True happiness is not something we stumble across in life, it's about making a real connection with yourself and the Universe to unveil your purpose through your passion. Tianna's remarkable and beautiful love story embodies this truth. Enjoy it whilst you embrace your own heavenly journey.

> Alexandra Watson
> Best-selling author of *The Happiness System: 7 Easy & Effective Steps to Creating a Wonderful Life!*

A most amazing love story that pierces the mystery of a bond so strong that it transcends death and illumines the miracle of everlasting life. Truly inspirational.

> Sharon Lund
> Author of *The Integrated Being: Techniques to Heal Your Mind- Body-Spirit,* and producer of *Dying to LIVE NDE*

Tianna and Janet with William have provided an excellent guidebook for people who are grieving. Through her personal journey we learn what to do to get out of the depths of abject depression and connect with the infinite realm of life's beauty.

> Alexandra Leclere
> Author of *Seeing the Dead, Talking with Spirits*

Not a story you'd want to miss-we can all benefit from the magical mystical adventures (and lessons) of Tianna while processing her grief. Say, "Tianna, thank you for sharing!"

> Katie Toomey, RN
> Certified sexual assault nurse examiner and hypnotherapist

More Praises for Loves Fire: Beyond Mortal Boundaries

Love's Fire is a highly personal story of love that transcends all barriers. Neither cultural taboos nor death are able to break this bond of true chemistry. Deeply moving and full of intrigue, *Love's Fire* shows that real life, when lived with love, is often stranger (and more interesting) than fiction!

Randy Hurlburt
Author of *Love Is Not a Game (But You Should Know the Odds)*

Tianna bares her soul in a most beautiful love story of time. A true tale of love, sexuality and spirituality in one. A must read.

Carmel Greenwood
Author of *Letting Go* & *Loving Life*

Love's Fire is a book of wonder; those who will be blessed by reading it cannot help but be touched   by grace and wrapped in the arms of everlasting love. Thank you for your courage to speak your truth, to honor the roots and wings of your love, and for opening your readers to life's infinite *possibilities. Is there a greater destiny than to be a love- bridge between the seen and the unseen worlds and a channel of the great Love-Energy that is here to heal and uplift this world? Your courage to love without boundaries and without fear restores us to Beauty and Wholeness.*

Paula Voelkel
Holistic Practitioner

A special thank you from William for a review, found on Amazon.com, that he claims captures the essence of both books and purpose of their love journey:

This is an uplifting and inspirational story of twin soul love and tran-scendence. Tianna and William are definitely at the forefront of pioneering work concerning twin souls and ascension. Tianna's very optimistic writing style reflects her Sagittarian nature. She offers her view of how to live and love at a very high level by opening your heart and being conscious in each moment. She does not lecture about this but very openly and honestly reveals it through her life story.

Also revealed in the end is not tragedy but hope that looks like an ending is really just another beginning into a bigger adventure. If you live life on the spiritual cutting edge, this book will make you stand up and cheer.

Joy Star
Infinite Possibilities Productions
New York

Infinite Possibilities Productions
New York

Love's Fire

Living the Awakened Journey

Book Two: Quantum Leap

Tianna Conte-Dubs, N.D.
Janet Cunningham, Ph.D. with
William

Lyrics to the song "How Could Anyone," with words and music by Libby Roderick, are from the recordings "How Could Anyone" and "If You See a Dream," copyright 1988 by Libby Roderick Music. These lyrics appear on page 170 and are reprinted with permission, which we gratefully acknowledge. Recordings are by Turtle Island Records, P.O. Box 203294, Anchorage, AK 99520.

Infinite Possibilities Productions, Tianna Conte-Dubs, and Janet Cunningham have designed this book to provide information in regard to the subject matters covered. The purpose of this book is to educate. It is sold with the understanding that the publisher and authors are not liable for the misconception or misuse of information provided. Every effort has been made to make this book as complete and as accurate as possible. Infinite Possibilities and the authors shall have neither liability nor responsibility to any person or entity with respect to any loss, damage, or injury caused or alleged to be caused directly or indirectly by the information contained in this book.

Published in the United States of America

Infinite Possibilities Productions
2005 Palmer Avenue #181
Larchmont, NY 10538-2421

Visionary concept for cover: Tianna Conte-Dubs
Artist: Elyse Sgandurra

ISBN: 978-0-9724008-8-6
Library of Congress Control Number: 2005935907

Free Gifts To Jumpstart Your Self Awakening
"Are you ready to be initiated?"

These mystical words, spoken intimately in a hot tub nearly three decades ago, launched our eternal love journey. You have honored us by taking your precious time to read our story. Now it's our turn to give back in a R-Evolutionary™ way. We want to gift you with something special and innovative to empower and enrich your life.

Our deepest desire is to illumine the possibility that love never dies and neither do we. We are aware that most people identify solely with the physical body and have a difficult time trusting anything beyond their physical senses. This perception keeps the fear of death prominent.

Everything is energy, and everyone has a unique frequency. In his own way, William has broken the illusion that life ends with death. All consciousness is connected in energetic unity. Partnering with Tianna, he has demonstrated the possibility of bridging the visible and invisible worlds.

Each one of us is an infinite being of Light so much greater than we appear to be. As promised, as our way of passing on the torch of this message that both love and life are everlasting, we invite you to enjoy innovative gifts designed to give you an experiential awareness of reality beyond your five senses.

Now, we ask ... are *YOU* ready to be initiated?

Our complimentary gifts for your personal evolution (valued at $250):

➤ *Quantum Energy Healing-* Enjoy one month of daily energy transmission per your intention. This allows for the release stress and raises your frequency. **www.yourgpscode.com**

➤ Video of choreographed GPS Salutation/Yoga Body Prayer Practice... Start and end your day in an empowered way. **www.spiritualitymadepractical.com**

➤ PDF for Sleep – 5 Simple Solutions to Getting a Good Night's Rest. Sleep is the foundation of a healthy immune system. **www.5simplesleepsolutions.com**

Dedication

To all those who have experienced a deep love in any relationship, and the grief that loss brings. I salute the courage and compassion that it takes to move through such a journey. For me, four women embodied the nurturing that it took to sustain me through my darkest hours:

My mother, Adele Conte
My mother-in-law, Veronica Dubs
William's former wife, Rebecca
My angel, Willie Mae Morgan

Tianna Conte-Dubs

On behalf of William,

To the divine feminine within all beings and for me, especially, my beloved twin, Tianna, who is the ideal embodiment of this energy.

William

To the feminine energy, in both men and women, that is being re-awakened in its wisdom and power.

Janet Cunningham

Contents

Foreword

Who better than Tianna Conte to tell an intimate personal story of death's upheaval- an upheaval not for those who pass, but for those left behind. Like Tianna, I know from personal experience as well as from my research that no amount of inner work and spiritual understanding can prevent the inevitable grief patterned into our physical human minds and triggered by the loss of a loved one.

Driven by the death of her beloved William and supported by her many years of work as a psychospiritual therapist, Tianna offers important insights into: 1) the grieving process with its unbearable depression and sleeplessness; 2) the nature of love as the ultimate means of union between souls; 3) the importance of friends helping us to emerge from the darkness; and 4) the fascinating and gratifying rapport that can develop across the veil when soul mates are separated by death. That rapport manifests in many ways, from the sense of our loved one's invisible presence, to silent, playful dialogs in the mind and heart. From CD players and radios and lights turning on and off by themselves to other-worldly networking and matchmaking, our invisible loved one guides us to people who would be good for us to know.

Tianna takes us not only to psychic mediums and afterlife seminars where we learn a lot about life and death, but also on trips to sacred places around the world where one chance meeting after another leads her (and us) to deeper spiritual insight and the real meaning of love and eternal life . . . all choreographed by invisible forces that certainly include William, with his infectious laugh.

That message comes through clearly in this book. Tianna, together with co-author Janet Cunningham, a specialist in regression therapy and researcher in Ancient Egyptian mysteries, with William's guidance from beyond, fuse a union that tells the story of the possible immortality of humankind.

Through my own research I know that the fear of death, so widespread on this planet, is the result of our mind having cut itself off from our higher self. Day to day we live under the notion that security is bound up in this physical body and our material possessions-a security that our mind is afraid to lose. Through spiritual growth we learn that real security is in that timeless part of us that generally stays hidden away in our unconscious mind, coming out to play during our dreams and meditations, and ultimately survives the death of the physical body. True security is really bound up in the real you and me- the spirit.

Mark Macy

www.worlditc.org

Works include:

Spirit Faces (Red Wheel/Weiser, 2006)
Beyond this World (Fall, 2006)
Bridge to Paradise (guided visualization CD with Hemi-Sync® technology)
Miracles in the Storm (NAL/Penguin Putnam, 2001)
Conversations Beyond the Light (Griffin Publishing, 1995)

Acknowledgements

All artistic endeavors begin as inspiration. The authors wish to express deep gratitude to God/Divine/ Universe, by whatever name one calls the *Source of all that is,* from which all creation comes. Most especially we acknowledge as a special blessing the presence of the Divine Feminine in the form of the Black Madonna. This trilogy exists as a result of collaboration between dimensional worlds.

The magic words Thank You best speak the feelings of our hearts and souls. Many persons touched our lives in the writing of this trilogy, yet certain people stand out as having made a significant difference. We express our gratitude to the following friends, family members, colleagues and clients who have offered their invaluable input.

The co-authors collectively wish to thank:

- Dianne Purdie - the person most responsible for bringing the authors together as speakers of Dreamtime Journeys. Dianne's belief in and encouragement of our partnering has been a treasure.
- Rebecca Dubs - the person whose spiritual awareness allowed for such a love story to transpire and this story to be shared. Her courage and open heart are an inspiration.
- Adele Conte - Tianna's mother, who gave her complete blessing and permission to reveal long-kept family secrets.
- Linda Conte - Tianna's sister, whose consummate cheerleading has offered unwavering assurances that empowered this story to be told and inspired an epilogue to be written.
- Joanne Garland - our copy editor, whose compassionate identification with the spirituality of our story filled our collaboration with grace and ease. Her wisdom and support were extraordinary in bringing forth this book.
- Elyse Sgandurra - our artist, who took Tianna's vision into manifestation with great care and beauty, capturing the essence of its message.
- Jessica Sigman- our graphic artist, whose brilliance and creativity brought forth colors that enrich the cover of Book Two.
- Alyce Domenitz -long-time friend whose proficiency in proofreading was invaluable.

➢ Amtrak - our railroad system that facilitated transportation between the two earthbound co-authors. Writing this story without easy access between homes would have been an extreme challenge.

➢ Last, but not least, Tootsie Rolls® and hot chocolate, which sustained our human cravings for treats during long hours of writing.

Tianna specifically wishes to thank:

➢ Joe Sugarman- dear friend, whose recognition and encouragement of the spiritual message contained within this story planted the seed that evolved into a trilogy.

➢ Mary Azima French Jackson - best friend, whose presence was cherished throughout the unfolding events of the story and whose listening and feedback earned her the endearing title, *godmother for the trilogy.*

➢ T. Harv Eker - mentor whose wisdom and workshops provided "the quantum leap" I needed to re-ignite my soul's passion and purpose and the courage to share once again my work and these books.

➢ Bennett Brooks - long-time friend whose skill with a camera and knowing of me captured the essence of my photograph for this book.

➢ Jonathan Dubs - my stepson, whose understanding and acceptance made a difference in publishing this story.

➢ Nazy Massoud - good friend and colleague whose perception of possibilities and potentials has been enthusiastic in promoting the trilogy.

➢ Willie Mae Morgan- friend and angel assistant whose devotion and ceaseless caring has been a constant blessing for William and me during the most trying of times.

➢ Sally Kane and Bea Sandford - angel friends whom I honor for single handedly launching my career and infinitely supporting my life.

➢ My many friends whose open hearts and insights after reading all or part of this story sustained my writing and provided constant tweaking to its fullest expression: Claudia Abruzzo, Gail Marie Del Balzo, Natalie Edelman, Denice Galicia, Joyce Gioia, Judy Jewel, Ian Lobb, Jacqueline Low-Canaleti, Krystalya Marie, Loria Raiola, Divya Schnirring, Katie Toomey, and Rabbi Shohama Weiner.

➢ Last, but not least, Starsky, my Shih Tzu puppy. He was a gift from William after completion of Book One. Born February 15, 2003, Starsky has been an endless source of affection and playfulness, and he continues to be my ultimate stress buster.

iv

William specifically wants to thank:

- ➤ Rebecca and son Jonathan, without whose love and generosity this story would never have unfolded and without whose blessings it could never have been told.
- ➤ Janet specifically wants to thank:
- ➤ My family members, who have always encouraged my writing.
- ➤ The numerous friends and colleagues who kept pleading for our book to be published.

Introduction

The last transcendent kiss with my beloved William, a kiss that rocked my world and shattered my dreams, continued to haunt me long after his memorial. My prior illusion, one that I had savored briefly, of dying together passionately as one, had now been stripped from me forever. The shock that had enveloped me since our last kiss, and being ripped from the Light, had replaced the certainty of my cherished reality. I was spiraling into chaos and could hardly catch my breath. In that moment, no one could have cursed both life and self more forcefully than I did. Why had I come back? What purpose remained for my life to continue? Was its destiny in its perfection that I could not foresee, or free will gone amuck?

Devastated and disillusioned, I found myself plagued by these questions, most especially, *How can I go on?* Merely waking up from under bed covers seemed close to impossible, yet my life continued. Gone was my blissful union with William, gone was my fulfilling life's work, and gone were my many dreams for the future. In short, gone was all hope. All of the fire in my life, a fire that had filled my heart with limitless joy, had now been extinguished.

If ever I had to summon all of my mystical gifts, and the expertise and resources of my therapeutic and shamanic training, now was the time. Even though I knew and taught that everything that transpires in life is for our evolutionary good and higher purpose, nothing seemed to make sense anymore. Bathing in the ecstasy of the Light one moment and plunged into the agony of a grieving body the next sent me reeling. The idea that I had more to offer life, or more to receive from it, seemed a cruel joke. The alternative that of giving up on life, felt equally unacceptable to me. So many questions remained unanswered, and these questions challenged both my destiny and my free will.

Trying my best to emerge from the depths of despair became a daily struggle. Taking baby step by baby step, no matter how small, became my initial task. I sought any thread of hope and nurturing that might help me move through the abyss of emptiness. No plans for a future beckoned to me, and no blueprint lay before me. I felt sustained solely by a spiritual force greater than my shattered ego.

Perplexed, I pondered over many questions. If we indeed create our reality, or at the most, co-create it with God, or at the very least, attract it into our experience, who had created this script? Surely it could not have been me. In my anguish these truths that I had held dearly, had taught and lived for so many years, seemed preposterous. All seemed meaningless: To think that I had specialized in releasing stress and training others to live passionately and love life to the fullest. I even embodied this way of being. How ironic it all seemed to me now. I grappled with feeling this firestorm of pain. Talk about being tested; this seemed the ultimate "exam."

Now how was I going to be true to myself and still walk my talk? Could I do it? The word "responsibility" resonated within me. I often translated that word as the ability to respond from my heart rather than react to outer circumstances. How could I honor that truth now? To me, perception colored all reality. Nothing happened by coincidence. Reason and meaning existed in everything. What meaning could possibly exist in this emptiness? I had espoused living one's dreams and had done so for many years. Now my dreams had been dashed! What would be next?

I vowed that if God had a dream for me, a dream that was bigger than I could see, or if God had a purpose for this body, then it was God's job to do it. No longer could I rely solely on my conscious self in creating my reality. I was too tired and drained of any mental efforting. No more affirmations, visualizations, treasure mapping or other techniques that I used to defer to. The only power left within me was the desire to die quickly and/or awaken my soul's blueprint encoded in our DNA.

I dared God to reveal His/Her plan to me, if there even was one. As for my part, I would stay open despite the pain and never give up. I would engage in no self-destructive behaviors, despite the temptation. Finally, I would listen for inner guidance and take the steps that my intuition directed. Never would I have believed that such a daring plea would stir powerful forces and synchronicities to summon the answers. All I knew was that I wanted a rewrite.

My terror at being alone, alone to integrate the daunting reality of having ushered my beloved into the Light, only to be catapulted back into a body wracked with pain. This became more than I could bear. Little did I realize that when I cried out to God for mercy, and to William for comfort, my prayers to return to wholeness had begun to be answered in ways beyond human comprehension. Unbeknownst to me, surrender to and trust in the unknown became the key element that would blaze a trail through the darkness. Tempted as I could have been to give up, I knew that surrender leads the way to new possibilities whereas giving up ends all options.

In the deepest recesses of my mind I vaguely recalled the life review from my near-death experience (NDE). Its major messages that had inspired me then could perhaps sustain me now. Foremost among them was to accept agony and integrate and move through it as soon as one is capable of doing. William's death and my return from the Light clearly qualified as agony greater than anything I could consciously move through.

Not once, but twice going into the Light and coming back? What was the purpose? My NDE had foretold that I was to pass on some message. What could it be? To me, the only idea that filtered through my pain was to write something titled, *Rejected by the Light*. I questioned whether it's true that moments which cause the greatest pain can also contain the seeds of our spiritual awakening. Now I was forced to rely on my NDE as a blueprint for my continued existence.

Taking stock of my inner and outer resources, I was determined to press on. My lifelong way of living already included multisensory and multidimensional awareness. Would this perception become an extraordinary survival mechanism as well? Could it fuel me to draw from the wellspring of my inner wisdom?

To that end, I couldn't help being plagued and strangely encouraged by the memory of the last time I had been so devastated emotionally. At that time, I was only 13 years old with no one and nowhere to turn, having recently lost my father to cancer and my virginity to sexual violation. It was spending time in nature and communicating with what I believed was God in heaven that somehow, over time, transformed these tragedies into triumph. I recalled the words I heard so long ago that resonated within me, "Surrender, day by day and step by step, you will be shown the way." Would that same innocence and faith sustain me again? Would my sense of urgency to draw from higher sources provide a beacon of light to illumine a path through the void of my brokenness?

Relying on intuition as my compass, I was drawn toward brilliant spiritual teachers and remarkable experiences. In and of itself, this path brought amazing support and validation to my instinct to trust the mystery.

Nothing happens by accident. Never could I possibly have envisioned what my climactic turning point would ultimately be. To be blessed and redirected in my destined purpose by a mystical encounter of divine magnitude would prove to be beyond anything I could hope for. My limited mind could never have fathomed the endless possibilities of my infinite mind. I dare say, this is true for everyone.

In addition, through my mystic gifts, which fortuitously remained intact despite life's traumas, William and I began to forge an evolutionary union. Ever a consummate communicator, William through countless antics demonstrated how the invisible world could serve as a worthy ally to the visible world. The progression of his contact illuminated the message, *Love never dies and neither do we.* Gradually and relentlessly this message unfolded.

Despite my own hesitancy to accept the truth that William remained with me, repeated confirmations by mediums, spiritual masters, and ultimately technology proved overwhelming in convincing me of his continued presence. The daily presence of our deceased loved ones, angels, and spiritual guidance is not an illusion. Yes, their presence is subtle, yes, it is enhanced by a belief system that invites contact, and yes it requires both listening within and trusting the occurrences that might otherwise be dismissed. Hesitantly I came to embrace a reality beyond the scope of my senses.

Finally, by resting on the laurels of my invisible relationship with William, I sensed that all seemed well. Destiny once again surprised me. The discovery of a skin cancer lodged in my upper lip, curiously enough, at the spot where we last kissed, initiated my next quantum leap into the unknown. This cancer set the stage for a surfacing of buried secrets that would promote either evolutionary expansion, or my ultimate physical demise.

Clueless as to how to resolve the cancer issue, I called forth both mystical and medical knowledge. Again, a journey unfolded that extended beyond mortal boundaries, facilitated and blessed by an encounter with the Black Madonna. Her message through me, to humanity as a whole, is one of compassion for the shadow side of our nature at a time when we unearth the wounds from our past for our higher evolution.

My grieving literally took me to the ends of the earth. Travels to exotic lands that span the globe, from Bali to the North Pole, from Costa Rica to Tibet, and teachings from spiritual masters and renowned experts in their fields, became the backdrop for my leap into the unknown. Each person, each encounter, each experience provided a piece of the puzzle that brought much needed insight and unraveled the meaning in all that had transpired.

At the same time, whisperings of Ancient Egypt wafted through my memory. Triggered by a friend's response, a grander identification emerged. In my personal story I felt a kinship with the archetype of Isis, known as the goddess of immortal love. Her inconsolable grief at the death of her husband, Osiris, rivaled my own. In the ancient myth, Osiris' body had been dismembered and strewn throughout Egypt. The determination of Isis to make love with him one last time summoned her divine powers to bring Osiris to wholeness for that final consummation. She did so, and through that union produced the baby Horus, the sun god of light.

I felt an eerie connection with both of these mythic figures: Isis in her grief, Osiris in his brokenness. Reflecting on my own saga, I recognized what an appropriate 21st century twist it beheld. Metaphorically I had felt dismembered, and it would take William's intervention to ultimately reawaken me to the divine power of love and rebirth.

We, the authors, acknowledge that the earth is right now going through such rapid changes and paradigm shifts that many people are being catapulted into chaos and life challenging situations. As it was for me back in 1997, when darkness enveloped my world, I could neither see nor fathom what the future of my personal evolution would hold. Although giving up or languishing in despondency would have been a far easier choice, I knew enough not to linger on those options.

We believe that each person is significant in the larger scheme of life and is being called to his or her divine best. No one is alone. To this end, accessing and utilizing both inner and outer resources is a necessary step and can provide welcome respite. Trust is a key factor that can unfold this power with grace, ease, and inspired action.

Divine support and internal wisdom are available to all who seek to develop further awareness and guidance. We affirm not only that the earth is evolving, and that every human being is also evolving, toward heights greater than the limited human mind can imagine. The story that forms this trilogy is a mere prelude to further possibilities. I am a mere forerunner to what we believe will be commonplace as the earth's vibrational frequency continues to rise. We offer the suggestion that as you read about my love journey, let it speak intuitively to the message as it relates to your own life.

The dance of the masculine and feminine, in empowered oneness, is what we believe is needed if the illusion of separateness is to be healed in the world today. Our trilogy is a product of that union. Through awakening the heart and living live based on love, not fear, we bring the message as it relates to immortal love that is eternal.

Indeed, we are poised at a time in history where sages and scientists can finally agree that, viewed from a quantum level of awareness, we are all connected. Transformation is taking place at an accelerated rate. Even the word *transformation* can be translated into *going beyond form*. Could "death" be the ultimate transformation that ushers immortality in spirit as a way of living?

What had begun within me as a longing to die, to join my beloved, ultimately shifted into the awesome realization that our love continues. Only the forms have changed. Love never dies, and consciousness is eternal. From this truth emerges a re-membering of the ultimate beloved within, that part of us which is everlasting, the *God Self.*

Tianna Conte Dubs and Janet Cunningham
with William

December 7, 2010

Highlights of Book One of the Trilogy

We the authors are sensitive to the awareness that not everyone has read our Book One, *Love's Fire: Beyond Mortal Boundaries*. It covers:

- ➤ the early mystical roots reflected throughout Tianna's childhood
- ➤ her father's teachings, which become a backbone for her life after his early death
- ➤ sexual violation at a tender age
- ➤ transformation of the *sacred wound* into self-mastery and expertise in an emerging field of healing
- ➤ living life successfully while longing for deep love
- ➤ the unusual and controversial way that Tianna and William forged their romantic union
- ➤ the sexual and spiritual experiences of the two lovers
- ➤ a life-altering near-death experience for Tianna and a life-threatening illness for William
- ➤ a cancer journey that embraced ancient healing traditions with modem treatments in alternative and conventional medicine
- ➤ a transcendent farewell kiss at the moment of William's passing that left Tianna torn between two worlds
- ➤ a memorial service celebrating William's life and contact beyond belief.

For anyone who is interested in reading Book One, please visit our website:

www.loves-fire.com

CHAPTER ONE

Humpty Dumpty

∞

By sheer force of will, I had made it through the memorial. One would think that the hardest part was over. The truth is that the hardest part had just begun. Stark reality now set in and I had to face my worst fear, that of living without my beloved William. Despite the power of William's cremation and the beauty of his memorial service, once they were over, I began to sink deeper and deeper into sorrow.

My body, which ached to be with him, was racked by the pain of his absence. Never again would I gaze into William's sparkling eyes, bathe in the radiance of his smile, or hear his sensuous voice and contagious laughter. Never again would I feel the warm embrace of his loving arms. For ten years I had hardly been able to bear being apart from him for a day. Now it was to be forever? How could I go on? How could I live without him? This would be not just for a day, a week, a year, but a lifetime. He was gone forever! He was really gone! All attempts to console me proved futile.

Indeed, words meant to comfort me I found agonizing. Especially when anyone said, "I know how you feel." No, they did not. They didn't have a clue. I knew they meant well. However, that was not enough. William and I had been as close as two people could be. How could any other person know what was going on inside of me, inside my mind and my heart?

I also cringed at other statements. "The happiness and love that you and William experienced in a few years was more than most people know in a lifetime." Yes, we had been blessed to have such a love. Hearing those words only accentuated the void inside me.

Others would say, "I'm thinking about you." Well, that was fine except that mere thoughts didn't reach me. If anyone wanted to make a difference, they could have called or visited. That rarely happened. I longed to hear the words, "I'm here for you, tell me what you need."

What I needed, and I dare say what all people grieving need most, was compassionate listening. Under the weight of overwhelming grief, even though I knew I needed support, I found it extremely difficult to ask for it. The words, "I'm here for you, tell me what you need", would have brought me great solace. Instead I found mere mention of "moving on" or "getting over this loss" to be too horrific even to entertain.

My life as I had cherished it had now vanished. That was the simple truth of it. I would never again feel the warmth of William's lips and physical touch. All things precious and valued in our life as a couple had been taken away. How could I think of a future when the future of which I dreamed and had been living was now permanently gone?

I had committed to spending the rest of my life with William. Although I knew better, it seemed unfair that I had so little precious time with him as my husband. Even the miracle of his remission had further strengthened my certainty that our marriage would last through my lifetime. I truly believed that my search for my destined soulmate was over. We were in our forties, with an unlimited future before us, anticipating that the best was yet to come. We even teased each other about how we could make growing old together fun and exciting. Never had I prepared for this marriage to be cut so short. From ecstatic bride to grieving widow in less than two months was more than I could bear.

To most people, the mere mention of imagining life without their mate strikes terror. I was supposed to accept this reality and know that I'd get over it? "Getting over it" did not even feel like an option. How does one get over that oneness in heart and soul that had made William a part of me? I had experienced amputation, in a metaphorical sense. All that remained was a phantom feeling. At best, all I could do was move through that feeling.

I acknowledged fully that grieving is an individual process, unique for each person, both in its journey and in its timing. I remained aware that the grieving cycle has its ups and downs, often on a day-to-day basis, and sometimes on a moment-to-moment basis. I had even taught on the subject. I remembered from my shamanic training that living in the present could be an antidote to the agonizing memories of the past and the fearful projections of the future. Yet staying in the present seemed an impossible feat.

I was forcing myself to implement what I knew. I had valued the fact that a support network of caring people can make a significant difference. In the grip of such devastation, turning to other people can cushion the loneliness and pain of loss. Now it was my turn. Even with all of this knowing, I felt trapped in a morass of despair.

After the funeral, it seemed as if everyone disappeared just when I needed them most. Finally, I could understand the depth of pain that William had experienced when he had been pronounced in remission. Assuming that he would be fine, people suddenly began attending to their own needs. He wasn't fine then, and I wasn't fine now. William had meant everything to me, and now I found myself alone again. It was an eerie aloneness, a haunting reminder of my father's death so many decades earlier. I didn't know how to reach out. I felt that all hope was lost.

I had risen to the occasion for the memorial through both my love for William and my innate training as a professional. However, the memorial was over. From that point on, I grew more and more depressed. My heart started to experience real pains that grew more and more intense, yet I didn't care. Secretly I wanted to have a heart attack. I longed for death to set me free.

Every day became darker and more painful. Each night I'd go to bed and plead not to wake up. Yet each morning the inevitable happened, another day dawned. This nightmare was all too real. I cried as if I couldn't stop. I sobbed into what seemed like an abyss where my heart had once resided. The emptiness inside felt overwhelming. The pain was never-ending. I wondered if it would ever stop. I once heard in a play the phrase, "an ocean of endless tears." I related intimately to that image.

All I wanted to do was die, yet I didn't dare tell anyone. I couldn't eat anymore, I couldn't sleep, and I couldn't care less. Even my rituals, which had been cornerstones in my life and had always sustained me, seemed meaningless and almost laughable. Rating my day, as I often had, on a scale of one to ten as a gauge of how my life was going and if improvements were needed seemed preposterous now.

To think I had once regarded going to sleep each night as a little death. My ritual had been to review the day, give thanks for its blessings, and bring closure, as best I could, to its upheavals. How could I ever bring closure to this?

To think I used to wake each morning and think of the day as a new beginning and a new opportunity. Now I felt like groaning, *Good God, it's morning. How do I go on from here?*

My pains grew worse, and hardest was the depression. All of the light had gone from my life. Knowing that a light shone at the end of the tunnel meant nothing to me. All that lay before me was the tunnel. Everything seemed black, black, and black. The joy and passion that had once filled me had been extinguished like the flame of a candle. Not only was William's fire gone. I felt that I had lost my own fire as well.

It is believed that God does not send anyone more than they can bear. From my darkness I cried out to the Universe, "God, what you think I can bear and what I think I can bear are extremely different. Help me, if I am to go on."

No longer could I innocently, and without ire, mouth the words, *Thy will be done* from my favorite daily prayer, the Our Father. Inwardly I began to shriek, *Thy will is always being done!* I transformed my prayer to, *God grant me the strength, patience, and wisdom to accept Your will.*

My tirade barely over, I received a response in a form that made no sense to me. Obsessively a nursery rhyme began to play inside my head. It was Humpty Dumpty. Yet I believed that Humpty Dumpty had nothing on me. Humpty was just a shattered egg, while I was a shattered human being with a shattered heart. What was the connection? I mouthed the words of that nursery rhyme over and over and tried to extract some meaning from them.

Humpty Dumpty sat on a wall,
Humpty Dumpty had a great fall,
All the king's horses and all the king's men
Couldn't put Humpty together again.

What was happening to me? The nursery rhyme refused to stop. I had no choice. I had to take Humpty apart, piece-by-piece. I felt cracked wide open. So, what did I have in common with Humpty? I needed to see if this child's rhyme held a clue that my inner guidance wanted me to have.

I knew that sometimes rhymes, cartoons, and songs were means by which my wisdom could express its knowing. Was this one of those times? Was it a return to the innocence of my inner child that was illuminating the way? Otherwise, what was going on? Whom could I tell about this, a child's rhyme that wouldn't stop repeating itself inside my head?

4

Humpty had been a big egg who suffered a great fall. I started with it as a metaphor:

Humpty Dumpty sat on a wall. Humpty Dumpty had a great fall...

Humpty Dumpty had been a big egg. Who am I in relationship to this? I reflected that we are more than our physical form, and each of us has an aura that expands, so it can look like an egg. Humpty had been made of a shell, as is an egg. I am human and yet I have an energy field around me as a cosmic egg. Okay, that worked.

Now the words, "sat on a wall," what was I sitting on? The image of meditation came up. Meditation is usually done sitting upright. Meditation involves expanding to the oneness, knowing that we are much greater than our physical form. Humpty had a boundary consisting of his eggshell. As a human, I had a boundary of a body, and was so much bigger. William used to meditate. Often, we would sit together in meditation and each of us expand into the oneness, which felt like bliss. First individually and then as we shared together, our energy would expand.

In our private intercourse style, we had merged either sexually or verbally through an interchange of experiences, ideas, and knowing. The resulting bliss would intoxicate us. We'd laugh that people talk about falling in love. They don't have a clue that love is a rising process.

Look at the words "falling in love." You fall on your face. With rising in love, you look into the face of your beloved. You see your own reflection in the mirror that they hold. Sometimes the mirror is clear, and two people see each other's beauty. Sometimes the mirror needs polishing because people see each other's flaws. However, people still see their own reflection, and we knew that.

William captured the highest of this truth in his wedding vow to me, "You are the divine reflection of myself." When we looked into each other's eyes we saw both the lightness and the shadows. As spiritual mates, we accepted all. This full acceptance is valid and available for everyone. We would rise in love, not just for ourselves. We would feel the oneness that is the greater union. In that blessed moment, we did not feel separateness. We felt infinite lightness, as if we were levitating. This knowing also helped us in our ministry and in performing weddings.

Oh, now I've got it.

Humpty had sat on a wall. His fall was limited. Humpty had also been just that physical form. Our bodies have accidents, and everyone can see when the physical body is broken. People allow time for physical healing, and they help that broken body to heal itself.

I had risen in love with William to an ultimate union that had gone beyond a body. Indeed, a spiritual union needs no body, so no one could see the extent of how broken I now felt. The fall from oneness, in my mystic knowing, is illusion. However, that fall feels real on this physical plane. So does the sense of separation. A fall from oneness is like a fall from grace. Such a fall is more devastating than any physical fall could be, both in its pain and in its experience of the abyss.

Okay, I've got that piece now.

All the king's horses and all the king's men
Couldn't put Humpty together again.

I knew now that I had to be on the right track. Wisdom had begun to unfold a depth of knowledge and training that I hadn't realized was within me. Of course, all the king's horses and all the king's men are the people and experts who lie outside of oneself. They may be well meaning or they may be brilliant, and they can help. However, they can't fix anything. Fixing is an inside job. If they were sensitive enough, and present and loving, they could assist the fixing process. However, they couldn't do it for me. I knew this.

I did find myself blessed with a handful of people who remained present for me. As best they were able, they gave their all. To this day I cherish them for it, especially Willie Mae, Mary, my sister Linda, and Rebecca. I could call whenever I needed them. Sleeplessness overtook me at night, with the pain often climaxing around three in the morning. The one person I could call who stayed consistently there for me was William's former wife, my dear friend Rebecca. However groggy, she would pick up the phone and listen compassionately to my extreme distress, then offer words of comfort. In addition, Rebecca and I formed what we lovingly called the "Wives of William Support Group" to help each other through our pain.

Still, even with this support, how could I put myself back together on my own? No one outside of myself could return wholeness to me. This was the question that I pondered. Even Humpty could probably have put himself back together. Unfortunately, the rhyme ends there.

I felt like a shell of the woman I had once been, in that I felt completely shattered and broken. Again, I dared the Universe to put the pieces together again so that I could feel my wholeness. To me, repair seemed an impossible task. It was a journey that I couldn't fathom.

I knew that any great loss, pain, or brokenness is a crack in one's reality. One might say it's one's egg. Such a loss becomes an opportunity for Initiation. I mused that in ancient days, the call to the ultimate Initiation was mastery in knowing that life is eternal. Did I have, inside me, what it would take to embrace this challenge of spiritual expansion as my Initiation? Would the grieving journey become that portal for me?

How does one begin to make sense of or find meaning in something that is incomprehensible? Even though it's human nature to want to figure it out, I knew that my finite mind could at best spew out conditioned beliefs or limited thinking. All I could do was surrender to a higher force. I hoped would contain some answers and reveal them in a timely fashion.

Through my pain of that time, I could not have known that the Universe had accepted my dare and had already begun to unfold its answers. Only much later did I realize that my beloved was even then attempting to reach me through the darkness, to assure me of his presence. At that time, however, I dismissed everything.

Then little things began to happen. Every evening at nine the CD player would start to play our love song, "Destiny." Family and friends convinced me that William, ever the trickster, had probably put the CD player on a timer before he had died. How could be have managed to do that while bedridden? The answer eluded me.

Then, almost as if William had been listening to my talk of this phenomenon, the audio system would switch from CD to radio to tape and switch its start-up time to eight o'clock in the morning. How could this be explained? No one knew, yet everyone rationalized. Finally, my cousin Peter exclaimed in exasperation, "Enough of this!" Vehemently he pulled the plug.

By Christmas Eve of 1997 my depression had grown so black that I found myself being sucked into a whirlpool of darkness. In an attempt to pull myself out of that suction, I called some of my dearest friends to be there for me. All did their best. However, I found that no one and no words could make a difference. Finally, I called my therapist in California who had been instrumental in helping William and me through his groundbreaking work via audiotapes. I expressed to him what I understood, and then I lamented, "I don't know what's happening."

He answered, "You know what's happening. You are a therapist, what would you say to a client?"

I replied, "You need to go into the pain and see where it's going to take you. Let go of the resistance."

"Well, go for it, and let me know what happens when you're done with that." Little did I realize, until hours later, that his unspoken assessment was that I would either make it through the pain and live, or he would learn that I had died.

It was time for the inevitable. I could no longer avoid going into my pain. I knew how important it would be to set up a safe space for myself. I instructed Willie Mae that no one was to disturb me for any reason, under any conditions. I needed total privacy and I knew that I could trust her completely. The stage was set. I secluded myself in my office and shut the door.

I got down on a pad on the floor, covered myself with a blanket, and curled into a fetal position. My depression felt ominous and my heart pains had grown strong. I was determined to let go into the pain to see where it would take me. I sank down, down, down, into an awareness of the darkness. Then I spiraled further down into a dark tunnel that came right through me. It was so dark that I saw no light. I moved into the experience. I stopped feeling my physical body. I followed that tunnel to its edge, where it remained dark. The only light I could see lay far off on the horizon as a sliver.

All of a sudden, I sensed a presence in the darkness, as if William had come to me. Indeed, I felt him standing next to me. However, I couldn't see him. I could hear his words telepathically.

Beloved, I made the choice that was right for me. My journey was complete for the fulfillment of its destiny. Now you need to make the choice that is right for you and the fulfillment of your destiny and determine what your journey will be.

When I heard these words, a strange sensation coursed through my non-physical being. I was awareness, and before me I saw two choices, stay, or *go into the Light.* A child-like rhyme expressed it best:

Eeny meenie miney mo, do I stay, or do I go?

Going would be easier. Staying would mean that I'd have to move back through the darkness, into the void, through the pain, and start over. Going would be so easy. William stood right there for me. I could just join him.

The "I" of which I was aware moved easily toward wanting to surrender into death. Suddenly a force ran through me that felt greater and larger than this "I." This force entered my "so-called" ability to choose with a power to live.

Once this determination came forward, the compassion of the energy unfolded three visions. In the first vision, William had experienced his own version of a similar process. For him, the Light had been right there, much closer, beckoning him to step into it. For me, the Light remained off in the distance, as a sliver. A seeming translation for this difference is that it had been his time, and this was not mine.

The second vision included everything that had unfolded during the week prior to William's passing. I saw the irritation, the judgments, the TV being on too loud. All that we had gone through turned out to be perfect for what was intended. These irritations had provided time for our personalities to disengage so that our spirits could move on. No judgments or blame were needed. All was well.

The third and final vision was of all that I remembered from my NDE, through my journey with William, to his conscious death, our last kiss, and my entering the Light with him and beyond. All of this experience became part of the reason that I had stayed behind. It was a purpose that needed to be shared. This is so others could be part of the knowing of their true self, and that death as an end, is an illusion.

With that realization, my visions disappeared. William embraced me and whispered, *Beloved, I will love you forever and be there eternally.* Mentally I whispered in kind, *Beloved, I will love you forever and be there eternally.* He moved back into the Light, and once again I entered the dark spiral. Then I opened my eyes and noticed the time. It was five o'clock on Christmas morning. I heard the words, *Merry Christmas to your rebirth.*

I was back, from where? I had no idea. What had happened? I couldn't be sure. Anxiously I waited until the appropriate hour to call Joe in California. Since it was Christmas, I called him at home to share my experience and ask his opinion.

Upon hearing my voice, he remarked, "You're back. I knew that either you would make it through, or you would die. There was no other option. You were mourning to die, and not grieving. Now you can begin to grieve and move on."

These words rang through me as true. Yet I didn't have a clue as to how to begin the process. I hated to hear the words, "move on." What did these words mean? How could I do it? Where would I go? I felt so alone, and it was Christmas.

One of my dearest friends, Loria, reached out to me through my darkness. Generously she offered to spend her holiday with me because she felt that I needed her more than did her family. She assured me that I didn't have to be strong. I could just feel whatever I was feeling. She wanted to be with me just to provide comfort. She even offered a massage. Her love and support touched me deeply. Since she was someone who could see through the shell to the real me, I accepted her generous offer with gratitude. She added that she would have vacation time in February and asked if I wanted to go somewhere. Thus, the first seed was planted to travel. Yet I wasn't ready to act on it.

Even my own mystic visions, which had just illumined so much spiritual truth, I could not yet absorb. Nothing and no one seemed to be able to penetrate my darkness. I realize now that no shortcuts exist, even with the knowing. I had received illuminations. Pieces of the past had been revealed, the present was clear to me in its darkness, and I had seen pieces of possibilities of what lay ahead.

Looking back, I can understand that this experience of receiving illumination didn't lessen or bypass one bit of my emotional or physical pain. All I knew was that I missed William every single day, more and more. I cried for more time with him. His memory remained imprinted in every inch of my skin, every fiber of my heart, every fragment of my mind and, it seemed, every cell of my body.

I even had a revealing dream: In it, I sat on William's lap with my arms around him, imploring, "Stay with me. Don't go. Don't leave me." As I held onto him, his long hair and beard disappeared and revealed the face of my father. When I woke from that dream, I realized the depth of the grief that I carried. It was not only for William. My grief had its roots in the tears that I had never shed for my father. Now I realized that this overlapping of memories and trapped emotions could be true for everyone else who experiences great loss.

As my earlier NDE had revealed to me, one must experience and move through each moment of agony. I decided that I would start, step by step, day by day, and let the process take me. I knew that I had no outside anchor, no children on whom I could focus my love and attention, and no work in which I could bury myself. Death had shattered the identity that I had always known in my various life roles. Further, I intentionally closed all escape routes that drugs or alcohol could have offered.

Looking back, I now realize that William, as my spiritual mate, had been a mirror who had empowered me to view the reflection of myself. With that mirror gone, I no longer saw a reflection outside of myself and I needed to turn within to find that beloved. That was the challenge that I faced.

I knew that first I needed to leave the surroundings of my home and the people who knew me. Such people reflected back my history and memories, which I found too painful. I knew that everyone meant well. However, they could not possibly understand what I was experiencing. I had always been the strong one; most people had never had any idea of what was going on inside of me.

I felt pressured by their projections of, "Time will heal, you'll meet a new man, go back to work." I knew that time alone would heal nothing. Only by engaging my spirit could I find that pathway. I wrestled within myself as to what that pathway could be. I didn't have a clue.

Again, I turned to God for an answer. *You sent me my divine partner. He healed through the power of our love. I thought that was the message. Now he is dead. How do I go on? What's the meaning to this mystery?* Again, I heard, *In time, truth will be revealed.* This time I labeled the answer unacceptable. It sounded like a cruel joke.

I sought refuge in one of my favorite spots, my hot tub. What I really wanted was to go to a spa and take a mud bath to release the toxins that I held in my body and my emotions. However, I was alone at home. I had become sheltered. Going to a spa would have been too much for me. I couldn't leave. I was housebound, not functioning as me. I had no will to get up in the morning, get dressed, or eat. I just wanted to waste away.

That day while everyone was out, I decided, *enough of this*. As I sat in the warm water of my hot tub, I felt safe enough and skilled enough to let my emotions come up fully. I had begun to shut down. Suddenly my grieving came up with a fury. I started to howl, wailing out loud, yelling at my own spirit, my soul, me, God-whoever might be listening. "How could you set me up for such pain? You knew the destiny you assisted, and you didn't let me know! You let something happen that has shattered me! I choose it. I will it. I'm ready. I have no fear! I'm ready to go. I want to die." Even though I was indulging in images of how easy it would be to slowly slip under the water, I would not do it of my own physical hands. I pleaded, "Take me out!"

Startled, I felt a peaceful and loving energy respond, *This is not your time.*

11

My ego retorted, "Just do it, who cares about time?"

Let's work together, it replied.

I decided that my ego needed its own expression, needed to talk back, so I let it rip. "I can't see how we can work this out!"

The energy responded, *Let's start by telling me what your needs are.*

My ego shot back, "That's an unfair question. I've been living in bliss with the man I adore. He is gone and now I want to leave. I can't listen to someone else's problems anymore. The only thing that gives me a sense of pleasure is to travel. I want to travel the world." The energy listened compassionately and replied, *Fine, with one condition: You can travel and go to sacred places with groups in a kind of pilgrimage, not just idle vacations. Go to where you can be guided and nurtured to reconnect with your power.*

My ego agreed and continued, "Now, I want to go to spas."

The energy acquiesced. *Fine. The condition is, remember your own claim that the word "spa" stands for "soul personality alignment," so allow yourself to become still after your treatments, and learn to listen within.*

"I want to shop, shop till I drop," I added.

The energy cautioned, *One condition: As long as you have the money, enjoy yourself. Just don't go beyond your limits.*

Ego complied. "I'm willing to give you six months to follow this pattern without longing to die. Then we'll renegotiate."

The bath was now over, and the energy withdrew. For the first time since losing William, I began to feel an interest in re-engaging in life. Knowing that my agreement would be for only six months, I could give it my all.

One factor I soon became aware of was how could I afford financially to uphold this promise. The answer came immediately. What savings I had left, after I had paid William's devastating cancer bills, were worth nothing in the bank. I began to see that if I were to have a life, it was time to put myself and my life first. I thought, *Save for a rainy day? This is torrential downpour and flooding. What is the use of having savings and no life?*

It was time for me to trust that the same wisdom that had expressed itself in dialogue would somehow provide. the "how" was a mystery. Looking back, I now realize that in a creative fashion, my soul and personality had engaged in this dialogue. My soul's energy exemplified compassion and acceptance, while my ego let its demands be heard. The two aspects of myself were doing their best to team up and put Humpty

Dumpty together again. This realization became the first step in a journey that would lead me into the unknown. It would be by leaps of faith, toward a distant inner healing that I did not yet imagine was possible.

CHAPTER TWO

Leap of Faith

∞

Christmas, being a holiday that felt more like a hurdle, was now over. The New Year was fast approaching, and I couldn't wait for 1997 to be done. It isn't that an arbitrary date makes a difference. However, the date seemed symbolic, and that symbolism of a new beginning has always carried significance for me.

Lost as to how to pursue my journey toward wholeness, all I knew to do was begin where I was. Yet *"where was I?"* I needed an assessment. It seemed a simple enough task, although the prospect of carrying it out felt immense.

It was natural for me to automatically perform my usual ritual for the end of an old year. I seemed to need it this year more than ever, yet this year it felt more arduous. Originally, I had designed the ritual for myself, and it carried deep meaning for me. I had since shared it with countless people, as a way of cleansing and starting anew.

The ritual had its roots in an encounter I'd had 35 years earlier with a female shaman in her nineties. I had met her during the time of my import-export business. The wisdom that she shared at that time sustains me to this day. So much so, that I created a ritual to anchor that knowledge. I had performed this ritual every year, without fail. This year would be no exception.

In reflecting back to one particular conversation with her, I realized that this truth she had communicated to me I now had to embody. We had talked about life and perception. I remembered asking her to share her wisdom. She was an elder, a woman of power in her community. I was always eager to ask the questions that would elicit that deeper knowing.

Since we had a great rapport, she imparted, "Perception in life is everything. If one perceives events that happen in life as a curse, then it will forever remain so. Instead, if one perceives so-called curses as blessings in disguise, then the job becomes removing the disguise. That way at least one might have the gift of seeing its blessings. One may see it in a week, one year, ten years, a lifetime, or never. An open state of mind can make the difference."

For me now, with her wisdom and the knowing from my own NDE, my challenge would be to embrace the "death" of my beloved. I would need to see William's passing as a blessing in disguise, rather than as the curse that I had felt it to be. It seemed a task too overwhelming to imagine, yet it was surely mine to do.

I would start with my own ritual. After all, I had designed this process as a physical expression to retain the knowledge that this wise woman had given me. I knew that it would be ideal to perceive every life experience from the lens of this wisdom. However, I was also practical and knew that the demands of everyday life would preclude frequent reflections. Once a year would be my aim. The annual ritual would be more important now than ever.

I sat down with several sheets of paper and prepared to do my meditative year-end review. The ritual works in either of two ways. After closing your eyes, take in a deep breath, breathing in the new and exhaling the old. Either start in January of the old year and move forward in calendar months or start at December of that year and move back in calendar months, whichever works best in jogging one's memory. One month at a time, recall and review two basic categories. One category is that of blessings, seen as gifts through people and experiences. The other category is challenges, otherwise known as blessings in disguise, and could even be viewed as curses, through people and experiences.

Usually one starts with a minimum of two pages, each page labeled appropriately with (1) Blessings/Gifts and (2) Challenges/Curses. With eyes softly opened, you then records from each month the people and experiences that stand out in each category. Feel free to let the memories flow spontaneously and jot them down on the appropriate pages.

Once this is done, silently appreciate the process. Looking at the entire year, you will see and gain an intuitive feel for the balance between the two categories. The purpose is not judgment, just awareness. It is especially relevant for remembering the blessings. It's easy to remember the "curses." You will use those lists for the next section.

With both lists complete, look at them and form your dream list for the New Year by seeing which blessings to continue and which challenges you wish to transform. Also, on your dream list, add any other desires that come to mind.

Midnight on New Year's Eve is the power hour. As close to midnight as possible, burn both lists, the blessings and the challenges. The idea is to give thanks for all of it and then let it all go. This ritual serves as a type of baptism by fire, so that you can receive the dream list with an open slate. As close after midnight as possible, sprinkle the dream list very lightly with water as a christening for the New Year. Place the dream list under your pillow, inviting a dream that can access your inner wisdom for its realization.

The year 1997 had been one of my most unbalanced years ever. Still there were blessings. It felt good to note these blessings along with all the challenges. I admit that I didn't do as thorough a job as I usually had. However, I did the best I could under the circumstances. The new list seemed like an impossible dream. I did do it, and I slept on it. That night, I received a profound dream that involved William. I didn't realize its full meaning at the time.

In the dream, we were on a plane and William was standing by an open exit. He was joyfully happy, fully healthy and beckoning me to join him. I was sitting in a passenger's seat when he attracted my attention. He had his arms outstretched with a look of, *Come here, come join me.* The plane was nearing its destination and I expected to wait until it landed to disembark. I would leave the plane, standing in line with everybody else. However, I could never resist William, not even in a dream. So, even though the action made no sense to me, I rose to follow his lead.

I started to reach for my carry-on baggage, when he gave a gesture to leave it behind. I hated to leave my baggage behind. Even though it was only filled with "stuff," I was attached to it. I complied with William's wishes and let it all go. I stood up and quietly walked over to him. I didn't want to cause any commotion.

William took my hand and led the way. We leaped out of the open exit into the unknown that was the sky. I awakened at that moment to a sense of wonder. I let the meaning marinate within me. It felt like one of those special dreams that my father talked about. I invited its meaning.

What I came to understand from the dream was two-fold. First, I felt William encouraging me to travel and to trust him to lead the way. I didn't quite know what that meant. Yet that was the intuitive sense that I had. Second, and this was the more intriguing, it seemed that he was showing a way to exit graciously and effortlessly.

17

In doing so, I would need to leave "baggage" behind, to lighten up. I conjectured that this "moving on" had something to do with a more aware or conscious death. So many people face exiting with fear and a heavy heart. William, through this dream, seemed to be saying, *Let go. It's a leap of faith into the unknown.*

In many ways, facing life without William was that leap for me. I knew that I needed now to leave my home and my memories of the past few months. Everything I looked at, everything I touched, reminded me of William and our precious love. I couldn't even sleep in what had been our bed. In effect, I became bed-less in my own home. I roamed the various rooms seeking a refuge, yet there seemed to be none. There were only painful memories of the shared dream that was gone forever.

With William by my side in our ecstatic love and a career that had filled me to the core with purpose and prosperity, I had been living my dream. As sung by Bette Midler, William had been my hero and *the wind beneath my wings.* Now I needed to fly solo.

The daunting question now facing me was how to rebuild myself. I now had to leave behind the familiar and loving routine of sharing life with a beloved partner and forge a new routine alone. Yes, alone again without the security of being desired and cherished by my ideal man, as I had become accustomed to enjoying. I was in my mid-forties. As a woman I was no longer the maiden of youth, but neither was I the crone of elder years. Suddenly single, I dreaded the mere idea of starting over. I posed to myself the questions of who, what, when, how to begin. I knew that the answers were buried inside of me.

With my intuition as a compass, I heard whisperings that to start a new life I needed to focus on something that would nurture me and reveal meaning in what had transpired. Finding even a thread of comfort and support, let alone enjoyment, is quite a task during grieving, yet a necessary one. For me, that task would be soul searching and include travel, new experiences, inner learning, and personal mastery.

My first step to renew myself was going to "Wizards," a course in consciousness that was taking place in Florida during January. It was there that its founder addressed reinventing oneself. Something about that word resonated within me. I felt that he was speaking to me directly. I knew that what I needed to do was reinvent myself. Intuitively I had come to the right place.

In particular, one of the course's trainers was especially helpful when she reminded me that I had never lost my wholeness. I was complete. In embracing this experience of loss, I would be a bigger person for it. At that time I had no clue as to how it could come to be. However, I knew she spoke truth, and it was reassuring.

To further aid in removing grief from my body, I had massages with a sensitive healer. Even though the pain was still deep, and my longing to join William remained intense, she spoke words that touched me deeply. She comforted me with the words, "One day, you will realize why you are still here. There is a greater purpose for you. When you recognize that moment, you will know it and be ecstatic for it."

"That will be the day," I replied, though I appreciated her words.

I used to remark jokingly that as long as we're breathing, we have a purpose. Yes, I was still breathing so I must have a purpose. Despite my misgivings, I felt determined to remain open to the possibility.

I returned home, inspired and ready to take whatever steps were needed. I didn't anticipate that upon my return, William would be actively welcoming me. By that, I mean, as I walked through the door I was greeted by our love song, "Destiny." I naturally assumed that someone in the house had turned it on. Well, not quite whom I would have expected!

Both my mother and Willie Mae agreed, "Yes, the song started playing, but that no one here had anything to do with it. Remember, Peter pulled the plug, and it hasn't been touched since then." I was mystified, and chuckled, "So what else is possible?"

No sooner did I ask, that I felt a strange tingling in my right ear. It was then that the first sound of William's voice broke through. I heard, *emotions are static. When you're still, it's easy to communicate.* Literally I couldn't believe my ears! Yet I did hear it. I couldn't deny it. William's voice and message also felt strangely comforting.

Still, hearing his voice disoriented me. I decided I wanted to consult with a professional on how I was doing, and what was happening. In my own opinion, I knew that in addition to grieving, I was suffering from post-traumatic shock disorder. I needed to be sure that these strange events were not just my mind playing tricks.

I hadn't felt the need to go to a bereavement specialist. I was trained in that myself and was doing fine on my own. Some suggested a psychiatrist. Even though I honor the profession, I didn't need the drugs that would inevitably be prescribed.

Knowing my own innate gifts since childhood, I wanted to be true to myself. Yet I also wanted to be reasonable and explore all avenues. I needed to know what I was feeling, and how to work with these thoughts and messages in a trusting process. I needed reassurance that I wasn't losing it. As fate would have it, the healer I chose was "tuned in" and "right on."

The person I went to see proved uniquely qualified for my needs. So much so, that Willie Mae would drive me one and a half hours each way to see her. Helen was a healer in her mid-70's who had awakened psychic awareness through her own NDE. She had also worked with William and me prior to his death.

My first session was even more dramatic and illuminating than I could ever have imagined. Helen confirmed what I had been hearing as accurate without my telling her. She then proceeded to do laying-on-of-hands to balance my energy. What happened next amazed both of us.

As she placed her hands on me, her touch felt like William's. I remained silent and said nothing. I thought I was just feeling healing energies that brought up memories of William's touch, a touch that I longed for and missed so dearly.

I was surprised when she exclaimed, "Oh, he's being so pushy. He's pushed his hand right through mine to touch your shoulder." Now I was speechless. Yet I uttered, "What?" She laughed, and replied, "Don't you feel him? He's right here, and quite strong."

I stammered, " Yes but I thought it was the healing." She responded, "Yes, but it's not my hands doing the healing." Her words simultaneously stunned and relieved me.

Later she went on to inform us that she also has the gift of mediumship. With awakened spirits, such as William, it was easy to feel them and let them come through. She assured me that William was fine, that I was fine, and that all was well. I thanked her and asked to see her on a weekly basis for as long as I needed. She said she was okay with that and acquiesced. It wasn't necessary. It would be beneficial only if I wanted to deepen my own skills of receivership.

That was a concept I had not considered, since the Brazilian healers had warned me never to do that. However, this was William, and I felt quite safe experimenting. Again, following my intuition and working with this woman proved strengthening in my personal healing. It was an incredible confirmation of the mystery that was yet unfolding.

During that month of sessions, I learned to trust that this communication with William was real. It was not my imagination. My doubts gradually gave way to trust with discretion, as the contact continued and deepened. Over time, this contact with William became a delightful and dependable source of guidance. One of my most amusing confirmations came after a dinner that I had attended.

William and I had always shared little rituals. One of them was that we never drank without toasting each other, or the moment. I had a glass of wine in my hands and thought, *Beloved, wherever you are, this one is for you.* I didn't tell anyone. Helen, the medium hesitantly commented, "This is unusual. I see him holding up a glass of red wine and he is saying, 'Back to you for the other night.'"

These validations happened, time and time again, on a frequent basis. It seemed that in my weekly sessions with Helen, that week's antics were confirmed without my saying a word to her beforehand. One of the most confrontive validations for me involved my favorite candy, Tootsie Rolls Whenever I was stressed, and this was definitely one of those times, I would overindulge eating them. William, when he was alive, would often tease me to cut it out because my face would break out. Little did I expect that his reprimand would continue after his passing.

I walked in for one of my sessions and the first words out of Helen's mouth was, "William is upset at all the Tootsie Rolls you are eating. He says, your complexion is a mess." Some admonitions never change.

In an especially profound session with Helen, one of his demonstrations showed his sense of humor. Her left hand started hurting and she grasped it. In a bewildered state, she commented, "He is showing me his left hand and I'm feeling pain. He is proclaiming, 'You could have killed me!'

She continued, "What does that mean?" I couldn't contain my laughter, and neither could Willie Mae. I pointed to Willie Mae and exclaimed, "It was her fault." She defended herself and quipped, "I apologized to my baby."

On the evening of his transition, she had inadvertently slammed the hospital bed railing on his lifeless hand. My friend Sally, in her desire to offer comfort, had dismissed this action by saying, "Oh it's okay, Willie Mae, he's dead, he can't feel it." William now indicated otherwise. However, he was laughing, as he complained, so we took this it as his way of teasing us and confirming his awareness that he knew what was going on at that time.

These are some of his amusing antics. On a more serious note, and one communication that touched me deeply involved his mother. It shows how our deceased loved ones are watching out for us. Now, in her 70's, with her husband and son gone, she was facing a financial challenge regarding her home. I was at a loss as to how to help her.

Suddenly I heard, *reverse mortgages* in my right ear. I, myself, had never heard of the term and was puzzled as to what it was. Inquiring further, a reverse mortgage was the solution to his mother's problem. It worked brilliantly. I was moved by how he continued to support his mother as best he could.

Not relying solely on William's support, I was following my own passions. This exploration included studies in consciousness. Friends mentioned a workshop by Gregg Braden called, "Awakening to Zero Point: The Collective Initiation." I had never heard of him and his work. However, something inside me urged, *"Go."* In February, I attended a weekend that was exceptional in its presentation and awakened a deeper truth inside me.

Particularly, something dramatic happened when Braden spoke about "Initiation in the 21st century." In this regard, he was discussing relationships and the mirror that they hold. At that moment, a strong vibrational feeling that left an unforgettable impact coursed through my body. It was a sensation that seemed like every cell of my body was electrically popping like kernels of corn.

It was clearly an energetic response that stunned me. Even though I didn't understand it at the time, I knew that my response was relevant to what I was going through. I was grateful that I had stretched myself to go to such a workshop, while still feeling vulnerable.

At the end of the workshop, I briefly shared with him what I had experienced. I also told him of William's passing, and of our last kiss. I shared my experiences because I knew Gregg was sensitive to NDE's, having had two himself. As he expressed appreciation for our love and union and the energy that it had brought to the earth, his compassion and presence were very moving.

I had now found two more pieces to the puzzle: my relationship with William had been a mirror, and our union had brought energy to the earth. Internalizing these two months, I continued with my leap of faith. The next two adventures would take me to a tropical honeymoon paradise, then to a portal into an entirely new realm.

I couldn't wait to share with Helen about my weekend in the Gregg Braden workshop. Since her sessions also included bodywork, somehow, I felt that the new puzzle pieces held a mystery that she could help me decipher. I had come to count on my sessions with her to expand my own awareness. In addition to communication with William, her bodywork with me was very renewing, It helped me to move through the grieving.

In one session, I told her that I felt like I needed to get away and a friend suggested we travel to an island. No sooner had I spoken this, that she started hearing William talking to her of where I should go and what I should do. Specifically, he first mentioned an island with a B.... Guess which one? Bali, again, the same island that William had suggested through another medium shortly after his passing.

Again, I emphatically I shrieked, "No way!" I mentioned to Helen, "Loria [my friend who had offered to go away with me] and I were thinking more along the lines of a Caribbean island." I addressed him directly. "Hear me, William, I am not considering any of the islands that we went to."

Helen laughed, and continued, "He is insisting Jamaica. There are villas with private pools that he had researched before he left." I was flabbergasted. Of all places, he dared suggest the island where we had intended to go for a honeymoon after he grew stronger. I exclaimed, "Absolutely not, it's none of his business. I'll pick the island, and it will have a spa on it." Helen agreed and wished me well. I wouldn't see her again until I returned.

Upon reaching home, I called Loria and told her about the session. She laughed and announced, "Any island that you want is fine with me. I trust you completely." With that, I told her I'd be back in touch with details after I found out which island. I also wanted to double check that she still wanted to go, "I don't know what kind of companion I'll be." She assured me and replied "Even if you want to cry and sob, it's okay. You don't have to be any way with me. I know you and even in your deepest despair you're more fun to hang out with than most people who whine about life."

One logical way to find the right island was to look for the one with a good spa. Knowing my passion for spas, William had given me a subscription to *Spa Finder* magazine. It was my favorite source for scouting locations of the best spas. In this particular issue, St. Lucia seemed to be the island of choice. It had all the ingredients that were alluring. It had primal rainforests, sulfur springs, and an inviting spa called LeSport.

Loria and I made arrangements to travel that February. Neither of us had been to this island so we just booked LeSport for a few days. We thought if we liked it, we would extend our stay. If not, we'd explore another inviting place on the island.

The island of St. Lucia was truly beautiful and the LeSport spa we went to was exquisite. We were treated like royalty. *I'm crying my way through paradise,* I thought. We enjoyed daily treatments. We even found that the top of the center had a rooftop lounge where one could sunbathe nude. We were nurtured, we talked, Loria did her yoga, and we gave each other the space we needed. She mingled freely with people, while I kept to myself.

We were both happy to be there and decided to extend our stay. That's when we learned that they were already booked. Sad to hear this, we just replied, "Tell us another place where we can go."

The receptionist retorted, "There are no hotels available on the entire island. Didn't your travel agent tell you that this week is Mardi Gras?"

"No, how about a motel, a B&B?"

"Everything on the island has been booked for weeks."

"A tent?"

"No, I don't know what to offer you."

All of sudden I heard laughter and the words, *Ask for the Jalousie Plantation.* I was puzzled, and it was difficult even to pronounce the name. I had never heard of the place, yet I trusted the voice that had spoken in my right ear. I did so, and timidly asked, "How about the Jalousie Plantation?" She responded that they had gone out of business many months ago.

Curiously, I thought, Hmmm...*Why did I hear a name that no longer existed? Was there a reason why I Heard "Plantation" instead of "Hilton"?* Since it wasn't listed by that name in any literature, perhaps this communication was to let me know that this information came from beyond the normal range of perception. "Then please get us a reservation at the Jalousie Hilton.

The receptionist replied, "They're very expensive, and I'm sure they're booked."

Loria chuckled. "Traveling with you is an adventure, so it's okay with me. Check it out. If it's available, it's a sign."

The receptionist came back and reported, "It's amazing. They have one room available." She repeated, "It's very expensive." Quite high, even for my exorbitant tastes. However, Loria and I agreed to book the room. I thought nothing more of it until Loria inquired, "How did you know about the Jalousie?"

"A voice," I replied.

Loria affectionately stated, "Thanks, William." Then she smiled and asked coyly. "Do you think he had a hand in this?"

The driver who came to take us from LeSport to the Jalousie Hilton seemed like an angel. The drive itself was like something out of an Indiana Jones movie. Hairpin turns over the mountains followed one right after the next, on the edge of a cliff. Not slowing down an iota, the driver further delighted in recounting the tales of many mishaps along that road.

Loria became nauseated and murmured, "I feel like I'm going over Niagara Falls in a barrel." To top it off, when we finally arrived at our destination, we discovered a place that resembled a honeymoon haven. I was ready to die when I took one look at it.

After he regained his health and strength, William and I planned a honeymoon escape to Jamaica. The villa at the Jalousie Hilton could have been that place. Loria and I were taken to a lovely little villa, private, with its own small pool. With all the trappings of a romantic cottage, it was painful beyond belief.

I told myself I didn't care, and would make it work. As night fell, I slipped into the robe they had provided. I walked to the edge of the pool. There, I sat down with just my legs dangling in the water. Sulking, *Here it is, a beautiful starry night, and I am alone in the kind of place that William and I would have savored.*

I started lamenting aloud and ad nauseam. "How could you do this?" It's bad enough that I'm alone, but alone in a honeymoon palace that reminds me of what we planned. Loria is my friend, but this is not what I wanted...." I carried on and on and on. It was a private villa, so I felt free to drop my robe and sit there naked.

I was interrupted in my whining by what felt like a pair of hands on my naked body. I turned around. There was no one there. I thought I had been too loud, and I started lamenting privately. I felt the hands again. Again, there was no one. I was the only one there. All of a sudden I felt the hands more strongly. This time I was pushed, bodily, into the pool's icy cold water.

Everyone who knows me knows that I don't plunge into cold water willingly, if at all. I heard, *Jump up and down, it will get you warm.* William, when physically alive, would often come from the front and pull me into the water. He would then urge me to jump up and down to stay warm.

I beseeched, "William, could that be you? Are you here? If this is contact, give me a sign."

I heard laughter and the words, *Look up, look up at the sky now.*

At that precise moment, I saw a brilliant shooting star crossed the darkness. I heard, *I'm your guiding star now.*

I exclaimed, "Oh my God! We were guiding lights, could this be?" I continued pleading, "I'm in this freezing pool. If this is contact, I need another sign. Please, if this is really you, if this is really contact, give me another sign."

Suddenly all the lights in the resort had a blackout. I was startled, and my body was visibly shaking..

By one comer of the pool in front of me, I saw a shimmering form, no face or body. "Is that you? "I asked. "I need a sign. William, if it's you, please manifest now! Show your body, show your face, I'll stop grieving. I'll do my work, whatever you want! Please, please, please!"

The lights switched back on. I heard the words, *Your Initiation is now complete. It's time to move on. You need to do what you need to do. Step by step, I'm with you all the way, but it's time to move on.*

I was ecstatic! I went from depression and exhaustion, to a state dramatically different. I began to believe that I had contact. This was different. I was physically touched! Also, the night sky gave me quite a show. It was etched into my memory. Loria peered from the doorway, took one look at me and exclaimed, "What just happened out there? You're radiant. You're lit from inside out." I told her the story. I could tell by the expression on her face that she was spellbound by its wonder. "Would you believe...could it be?"

"Of course, leave it to you both, anything's possible." At that point Loria believed contact had been made.

I had now shifted and my ego and emotions were out of the way. In a millisecond, I had felt loved. I'd had my first contact that resulted in my physical body being visibly moved.

The next day, Loria and I went to Carnivale. It was held near the spa that we had left. However, we would never go by car. That afternoon, we took a wonderful water taxi ride.

I was sitting in the boat relishing the tropical beauty of the island. Suddenly, I felt my hair being brushed and hands placed on my face. It was as if William was with me. I felt expanded enough to be joyous without thinking.

I was feeling the sun against my skin and telepathically hearing fragments of a song in my right ear. *...Our love is brighter than the brightest star that shines every night above....* I was somewhat familiar with the lyrics, believing it to be Petula Clark. However, it was not a song that I ever sang. Curiously. when he was alive, William would always play songs or sing to me when he wanted to get a message across. Was he still up to his old tricks?

When Loria and I returned from Carnivale that evening, we heard of a manager's party for the guests. Remember, I had asked for one more sign. It came while speaking to the Middle Eastern man who was the manager. I commented, "This place is magnificent, and the energy here seems so spiritual that it reminds me of the Andes in Peru."

He responded, "I think I can share this with you. People have remarked that the energy of the mountains and the land here is such a spiritual place that it allows contact with other dimensions to be made easier."

I didn't tell him my story. I simply replied, "Oh yes, I totally believe that." Inside myself, I knew I had received my sign.

The Universe was telling me that the environment of this place helped people to make contact. I now knew that I had changed. The challenge came immediately. There were honeymooners all around me. I thought I would have been in pain, in "honeymoon hell."

Specifically, one couple in particular reminded me of William and me. I offered to them in conversation, "I wish for you what I had with my husband, that every day is a honeymoon." They thought that was wonderful. I continued, "For a lifelong journey, make love count every day." I knew, by sharing like that, something big had shifted inside of me. My contribution to them came from a place of power.

It was time to return to New York. I was counting the minutes until I could share with Helen what had happened. She beat me to the punch. The first words out of her mouth were, "I'm so glad you're here. William has gotten so pushy, he pushed me out of bed. He is excited that you were coming. I've never seen such a strong spirit."

I registered the word "pushy "and questioned, "What was he so excited about?"

She replied, "He wanted to let you know that he has been initiated to another level of his mastery, and so have you." Again, the word "initiation" It seemed to resonate within me of a theme, common to our relationship. William had used that word upon our first lovemaking, and now he used it again during a powerful demonstration of contact. Could there be a deeper meaning that I was not yet aware of?

Helen was laughing as she repeated his words. "He wants to know how you enjoyed the honeymoon that he provided. Under the circumstances, it was the best he could do. He called in all the favors he could."

I was mystified and responded, "It was wonderful for one, yet it was not quite the honeymoon I had anticipated in physical form."

"It's the best he could do," is how Helen ended the session.

When I returned home, my longing for William grew intense. Thoughts went to our cherished time together. I decided to view our

27

wedding videotape. I searched all over and it was nowhere to be found. Finally, I heard, *it's in the messy pile, over there.* I would never call it a messy pile. However, William would.

I went to the designated pile and thought, *Great; which tape?* There were about 35 video tapes there. One fell down. Guess which one? Yes, it was the very one that I had tried so hard to find, the one in which we had expressed our eternal love. Willie Mae wanted to watch it with me, so we did. While watching, I telepathically heard the message, *For now, that's the best I can do in the physical.*

March was approaching and I had been invited by Raymond Moody to attend his training for professionals in facilitating afterlife communication. Moody is the leading authority on near-death experiences and is a world renowned best-selling author. I admired him for his humanity and compassion as well as for his research.

A year previously, William and I had met Raymond and Cheryl, his wife, on what we called our " honeymoon cruise." We became close and had much to share. As I had told him the story of my own NDE, he looked at me and alluded to a living bridge. "Okay, whatever that means." He smiled and left it, not responding. As an aside, I later discovered that he and Helen were friends. It's a small world.

When the Moodys heard that William passed, they reached out to me in a very touching way that I cherish to this day. Cheryl called and asked if I would be interested in experiencing the psychomanteum that her husband had created to access communication with those who had passed over. I queried, "Tell me more."

That is when she invited me, as their guest, saying, "You come in the physical and William in the non-physical, to take this training."

"I'm honored, but I'm a mess."

"That's exactly why you need to come."

The day of my departure was an eventful one. It was the first time I was to fly out of Newark Airport alone, from the same airport William and I had always used. Crying my way through the terminal and toward the gate, I missed my flight. Fortunately, I was able to call the Moodys and reschedule my arrival for later that day.

They were magnificent and could not have been more gracious. They even met me at the airport and drove me to their home. I arrived a few days prior to the start of the training, so we could spend some personal time together, and I could experience the psychomanteum.

In ancient Greece, the psychomanteum was fashioned in underground caverns called "halls of visions." Standing in front of a shining metal surface or caldron, grieving people saw and spoke with deceased loved ones. In today's world, Moody has drawn upon this wisdom and created a replica in accessible form.

The psychomanteum is a totally darkened chamber, so black that one cannot see any light penetrate from the outside. I sat inside the chamber, alone. A tiny lightbulb behind me revealed a mirror in front of me. I was told to focus upon that mirror with soft eyes. In this mirror would appear the vision or apparition of the person in spirit with whom I wished to communicate.

The first vision that I received was not contact, as I think of it. Naturally, I longed to visually see William in the physical. Instead, the image that appeared was clouds. Between the clouds spanned a jeweled bridge. It was magnificent and covered with gems of all kinds, such as diamonds, sapphires, and emeralds.

Suddenly, a figure of light started dancing on the bridge. It was in the form of a human, yet it had no face. It was only light. The figure extended its hand and another figure of light from the other side of the bridge came to join it. Together they danced a love dance. At the end of which, the two figures embraced and merged into union. They became one body of light and manifested as a single flame.

I breathed through that image and accepted it without under-standing. The next image that emerged was a torch, similar to the one used in the Olympics. A figure of light carried this torch and ran toward another figure of light facing it. The one holding the torch passed it over to the other. Those were my initial images in Raymond Moody's psychomanteum.

As I contemplated the meaning of these figures and visions, I felt as if they held an importance that I did not fully comprehend. However, I filed them in my memory. Years would elapse before their message would crystalize, both literally and figuratively. For now, it was time for the training portion to take place. Other professionals joined us and we were to facilitate each other in working with the psychomanteum. This training included conducting a verbal interview before one of us entered the chamber, and then eliciting feedback after the experience.

During my turn, once again in the darkened chamber, another amazing event caught me completely off guard. Suddenly, as I was gazing into the mirror, it was as if someone shone a spotlight on it. In the mirror's center, directly toward me, came the face of my father. Clearly, I heard the words through my father, *It was his time! It was his time!* Nothing else.

As abruptly as he entered, my father left. I cried and cried and cried. The experience shook me to my core.

Still in a tearful state, I related this vision to the group. Moody asked, "Do you understand the message of your father?"

As best I could, I explained the message. I told them, it meant that it was William's time and there was nothing I could have done differently to prevent it.

Moody asked, "Why do you think it was your father who came to you, and not William?"

I easily responded, "Great question. I believe because my father had the kind of authority that I would listen to. He always spoke truth to me. I imagine, that the message had to come from him or I would not have accepted it. I can picture the two of them colluding that if William came, I would argue with him. I would not speak back to my father."

Moody explained, "See, it's like a telephone. You want to call up X but they're not always there to take the call. Occasionally, someone else comes who can better answer your call. It's the same way between the worlds."

There was no better messenger than my father to deliver these words. Even though my father had died physically when I was 13, I shared with the group that my father always showed up during the key moments of my life when I needed him most. He had been there during William's illness. Again, this was one of those times.

I returned home filled with gratitude to the Moodys for the portal they opened for me. Despite the fact that I remained clueless as to where all of these new experiences were heading, the mystery was gradually unfolding. Upon looking back, with the Moodys' support, Helen's support, William's antics, and most especially following my own intuition, my leap of faith had begun to find ground under my feet.

CHAPTER THREE

Spiritual Odyssey

∞

BALI

Four months had now elapsed since William's passing. During those months, intuitively I had found courses and destinations that sustained me. I pressed on, despite family admonitions that I appeared to be running away from my grief. The notion of running away seemed preposterous, since I recognized that grief remains inside. Wherever I went, this grief would stay with me and I could never run away from it. I felt instead that I ran *with* it toward an unknown future that continued to beckon.

Now the steps that I heard William whisper to me began to turn into leaps. Ever since the trip to St. Lucia I had heard William's messages telepathically. Now I heard them more regularly, with more contact, and he grew insistent. Travel seemed to be the theme of his promptings. Either he was picking up on my passion for travel to heal me, or he knew something greater than I could see. In either case, I honored our union enough to trust his lead. Never could I have realized that the many lands and the many masters I would visit would contribute a piece of the puzzle that would ultimately complete my grief journey and uncover universal truths.

Go to Bali, go to Bali. Again, Bali! I had first heard this message through a medium soon after William's passing, and again through Helen, two separate mediums at two separate times. Now William told me directly; this was my next step.

My resistance began to wear thin. I asked the Infinite for a sign.

After all, Bali lay on the other side of the world and I was still grieving. Yet if I received a clear enough sign, I would stay open to the suggestion.

That very week a brochure arrived from Power Places Tours and it mentioned a trip to Bali. The same brochure described a group tour to Tibet. I felt a pull inside of me because I admired Gregg Braden, the speaker who would lead the Tibet tour. However, I recognized that a trip to Tibet would be too strenuous for my weakened body. As I examined this brochure from cover to cover and considered other trips, the energy continued to move me toward Bali.

In my own mind the deal was sealed when, as I flipped TV channels mindlessly, I landed on a show about Bali. This program focused specifically on Bali's spirituality. It mentioned how the Balinese understand that death is part of life, and that life continues.

Okay, I'd go. Then I had a dream that I was not to go alone, so I invited Sally to come along as my guest, as our special thank you. She had done much for William and me in so many ways.

The flight to Bali felt endless. Twenty-eight hours after departure, and thoroughly exhausted, we landed at Bali's airport. My luggage was nowhere to be found. I concluded that my belongings had gone to a destination unknown. After my initial disappointment, I decided to embrace this loss as a metaphor that alluded to my dream. *Leave the baggage behind and be in your innocence.* I mused that all I needed to buy were sarongs and halter tops. I'd probably find them easily. I put the matter out of my mind. It was off to the hotel.

Our car traveled up a long driveway lined with palm trees, where we beheld paradise. The hotel appeared to be a palatial structure with oceanfront accommodations and a lighted swimming pool. In my bedraggled state I felt as if I were viewing a mirage. Yet it was real. This place contained everything of which fantasies are made. Even the hotel shop offered all of the clothing that I needed. Interestingly, I had previously envisioned myself looking as if I had lived there. When we met our tour group the next day, I showed up in a brightly colored silk sarong and halter top. It was just as I had envisioned.

Seminars would be part of this adventure. During one session, when talk turned to the topic of death, a strange thing happened. I, who resist microphones, felt as if someone had pushed me to grasp it. Trembling as I spoke, I began to share a bit of my experience of the previous year. The participants listened graciously and attentively. They seemed to identify with the points that I made in my story.

Later, two of the tour leaders approached at different times. One, a shaman herself, held her hands in a prayer position and told me, "You are a deathwalker." I didn't have a clue what that meant. Later I learned that a deathwalker is one who walks through the illusion of death and leads the way for others.

This was the first time I had received a message telling me that I had to do something about illuminating death. My first thought had been to wonder if I could live through my loss and survive the experience, never mind be able to teach about it. In my state of grief, talking about it seemed impossible.

The body does die. I knew the emotional pain of physical loss for those left behind. This loss leaves a void that hurts like hell. I often observed that death occurs not only for the person who passes over. It is also for the person who grieves and has lost his or her old identity. That person faces a life-challenging choice: remain stuck, metaphorically climbing into the grave, or embrace this pain and grow further into the next step of life.

I knew all too well how seductive the thought of giving up could be. Yet if death is the grandest illusion of them all, what would giving up really mean? At this point I was open to anything.

My "anything" arrived through an incredible medium named Stephan. This flamboyantly dressed man approached casually and surprised me with a challenge. He eyed me with intensity. "I have a question for you, and I know I can ask it." Curious, I nodded for him to go ahead and ask. He continued, "Who is that very handsome man in spirit who looks like James Brolin and follows you everywhere you go?"

If ever someone wanted to get my attention, this was it! I exclaimed, "Oh my God! You can see him?"

"Yes."

"You can see William?"

He replied, "Oh yeah, I can see him, I can hear him. It's a gift I've had since childhood."

Stephan turned out to be a professional medium from Switzerland. "You have to give me a session," I told him excitedly.

He replied, "Not while I'm on vacation."

"Okay, right after this journey," I added quickly, unflustered.

"I live in Geneva, Switzerland," he explained.

"I don't care, I'll be there."

My intensity moved him. "It seems that you have a burning need for me to speak to William for you."

"Yes! I'll do whatever you want, name it."

33

He paused and looked straight at me, evaluating. He offered, "I'll grant you a favor. You can ask me one burning question for him, just one. I'm not doing a reading here. I'll just ask him the question that you long to have answered."

With tears in my eyes I took a deep breath. "Okay, my question to William is, *Why? Why when we were living our dream, did you leave me? You were in remission and we were at the point of fulfilling our dream together. Why did you drop your body? Why did you go?"* Even in asking this question, I trembled.

"You are not going to like my answer," Stephan responded.

I braced myself, "Tell me, because I need to hear it. I have so much going on that's eating at me inside. I need to know."

Stephan hesitated before commencing, "OK. William claimed it was an act of aggression. There was no longer any quality of life, being trapped in a body that couldn't move. He was so frustrated in a body with ebbing life force that he wanted out."

Though I found it painful to receive this statement, I heard William's truth. I understood how well William had worked with energy. In his mastery, he had used that aggressive energy to achieve release from his body.

Stephan continued, "He could push for life, but only with time and a lot of hard work. He didn't need to be in that body to fulfill his destiny. Since he was complete, the only reason he would want to stay was to enjoy your love in the physical. He knew that you had the gifts to hear him mystically and communicate once you got over grieving him. Your love would continue. Remember, he promised that the two of you could never be separated. Without the body, he could continue his work through you. He knew you'd be okay, and he'd be free."

Startled by this revelation, yet soothed by its accuracy, I fell silent. I had received my answer to the question of *Why?* This answer did not feel good, because it validated that William had left me consciously. That fact hurt me deeply. At the same time, I had compassion for William's pain, and that compassion brought me the beginning shreds of peace of mind. I had tortured myself with endless questions. *Why now? Did our love falter? Did I fail him? Was he angry? Could having the chemo sooner have made a difference?* William had now answered me through a medium and had addressed all of my concerns in his simple truth. These questions would never gnaw so fiercely at me again.

34

I felt both flabbergasted and relieved. My sense of knowing had now been confirmed. I had been driving myself crazy with *could have, should have,* things. I knew better, but I couldn't help it. I had hung onto a mixture of compassion and pain. I was the one who had been left behind. Death didn't scare either one of us. Still, William hadn't died. He had experienced an aware departure with full awakening.

My compassion soon grew stronger than my agony as I processed Stephan's words. To clarify this message in my own mind I continued, "What you're saying is that yes, we're here to fulfill our destiny. He could have done that in the body, and with much work and time out from the mission itself. He found it easier at that point to let go of his body than to do the rehabilitation?"

"Yes, he would have been physically healthy in a few years. However, at that point, enough was enough. His piece was fulfilled."

I had traveled all the way to Bali to receive the message that I needed to hear. I acknowledged that this message had come through Stephan. I thanked him with heartfelt appreciation for setting me free. William's message had been difficult for me to hear, yet its truth rang throughout my being. My belief that we could have had more years together had not been just my imagination. Through mediums I had now received the healing that William had promised. I had also honored the strength of our union.

From that point on, I would welcome William's wisdom and communication, and would do so with an open heart and less resistance. The two of us had reached a turning point. Again, we hadn't traveled to Bali the way I had dreamed, yet we were indeed in Bali together.

One evening after a workshop about raising frequencies, William came to me in a dream. In that dream he explained another piece of the puzzle. It was a piece that had caused me so much anguish. Intuitively he had known or felt that his purpose had been to radiate light through his body. He had done this through the joy that emanated from his presence. That was what most people had felt from him.

William had experienced great pain at watching his father die from chemotherapy. Therefore, even if chemotherapy could heal and save his physical body, he had feared that it would deaden his life force. His light, and his ability to express that light, remained his priority. He wouldn't compromise his purpose for the sake of his physical body.

William had succumbed to chemo when his awareness of the loss of life had become so great and so real that he thought it would allow him to remain in physical form. His initial intuition had been right. Although the chemo had brought his body into a state of remission, his body had not grown strong enough to sustain his full life force. At that point, he found it easier to focus on the purpose of ascension. He chose to do so while he still had the strength. Stephan's reading told me this truth, and my dream confirmed it.

Following my time with Stephan, revelations abounded in Bali.

Another came through a speaker named Barbara, who addressed specific concerns that each of us had. My concern involved grieving, and her response helped me to better understand the depths of my pain. Barbara explained that many times when the grieving person experiences overwhelming emotions, these emotions could be due to sensing the energy presence of the departed loved one. Yet our senses are limited in their ability to perceive, and the mind cannot understand what's happening. What is most obvious is the pain of loss. The body reflects this pain through grief.

Could it be that my bouts of emotional release and crying had been the most intense when William had been around? Barbara illumined the fact that during such moments, our loved ones could be beside us in the very same room. Although this notion didn't change my process, it shed new light that brought me comfort.

On May 7, the five month anniversary of William's passing, our group visited what was called the Cave of the Bats. I didn't realize it until I arrived, but the Balinese people visit this cave to pray for their deceased relatives and friends. They especially pray over any regrets, remorse, and pain for themselves or their loved ones who have passed over. How appropriate was the divine scheduling of this excursion!

With the information that I had now received through Stephan and my dream, the time had arrived for me to release with awareness (not forgiveness) what had happened at William's transition. He had indeed experienced sadness at leaving. He had longed to stay. However, somehow, he knew that it would be better to fulfill his destiny and move on. With all of the new insight that I had now received, being at the cave on that day felt symbolic and highly significant. The message I perceived was that I had to set William free. In so doing, I would set myself free as well.

Profound movement had occurred deep within me. Lest it not get too serious, a comical event soon followed. As our bus left the parking lot from the caves, I heard, *Stop the bus. Stop the bus.* Stunned at hearing this command from William, and not knowing what it meant, I repeated it

36

aloud to the person next to me. He then made it public knowledge. "William wants to stop the bus."

Being compassionate and accepting of William's antics, the group acknowledged him immediately. The driver stopped the bus. I rose from my seat and said sheepishly, "I'm not quite sure why." Then I heard, *The mask, the mask. Buy it for Jonathan.* I noticed that outside the bus windows a vendor was selling a mask of the monkey god. Our bus driver opened the door. I stepped out and purchased the mask. I returned to a round of applause. William had gone on a shopping spree for his son, and the entire group had supported him.

The land of Bali was incredible and the consciousness of its people quite evolved. Our journey neared its end when another climactic highlight unfolded. During our last temple stop, at a place referred to as the mother of all temples, something most intriguing occurred. Etched in the temple walls was a dancing figure, similar to what I had seen in Raymond Moody's psychomanteum as the dancing figure of light. What are the odds of seeing a vision from the U.S. now depicted on a wall in Bali?

I felt as if a great puzzle had begun to fit together. With William's message through Stephan, then through my dream, and now with the dancing figure from the psychomanteum, I had finally received the healing that William had promised. He had indeed been with me in a mystical way and had revealed the answers that I needed. My journey had been about compassion, acceptance, and truth.

ALASKA

Bali provided an unexpected and refreshing blessing. I returned home reinforced for my next step, which took the form of an invitation from my dear friend Dianne. She was organizing a spiritual cruise to Alaska. She made me an offer too good to refuse. Soon I was off on another journey.

Alaska is breathtakingly beautiful. I deemed it to be one of the best purchases America had ever made. In many ways Alaska also offered just what I needed, a journey filled with nature, beauty, and seminars at sea. All of these things became relevant in helping me to integrate the prior few months. William stayed rather quiet during the trip to Alaska.

Two of my most important gifts came from the glaciers and from metaphors that they provided. The first gift took the form of an excursion, a helicopter ride that landed on a glacier. Stepping onto this glacier, a seeming ocean of frozen ice, was an amazing adventure. I witnessed how sunlight hits the glacier, and I felt how this sunlight is reflected back. That brilliant light was the closest earthly manifestation of the Light that I had seen in my NDE, and it reminded me of that Light. It's not a bright, sun-colored light. Rather, it is a bright white light.

As I walked the glacier's surface, that white light reflected back and filled me with an awareness of the Light from my NDE, Light every bit as bright, as pure, and as radiant as the glacier light. For that brief moment I found myself reliving a sensory awareness of my NDE.

The glaciers also provided another insight about death. As our cruise ship passed between two glaciers, my friend Tricia and I searched for a quiet nook on the ship. We wanted to experience this passage meditatively. We went up to the deck and found a quiet spot. In the silence, I soon became absorbed with watching the massive glaciers and feeling the power of huge chunks of ice splitting off and crashing into the ocean.

My intuitive voice chimed in, *That's death.* Temporarily I felt puzzled. The voice continued, *The glacier symbolizes life in physical form, congealed energy. When the force inside becomes so great that it can no longer stay as part of that physical reality, then like the glacier it breaks off. It falls into the ocean of consciousness. There, it then becomes one with the whole. As it melts, its ripples are left behind as its legacy. Everything else moves on. You can't stop the flow, it moves on.*

I shared this realization with Tricia, and its wisdom touched both of us. Soon thereafter I had an appointment scheduled with another medium. However, the encounter would be a brief one. Hans took one look at me and queried, "What are you doing here? You can do what I do. In fact, just trust yourself and know that what you are experiencing is real. What I can offer you is that in ancient Egypt your gift was in helping souls cross over. That gift is still active today." Thus, I received yet another validation of my role. I thought, *No more need be said.*

The cruise soon ended and being so close to the North Pole we found ourselves with a strange desire to go there. Our small group spent one night in a hotel in Anchorage before our flight the next day. In the hotel lobby, intuitively I felt drawn into a magnificent art store.

There, before me, stood beautiful glass figurines that reflected the dancing figures that I had seen in Moody's psychomanteum. This included the flame of union. I bought them and proudly display them in my home today. They serve both as an inspiration and a crystallization of their message.

The following day, traveling with Dianne and two other friends, we set out to explore the cold and mysterious land known as the North Pole. Our jaunt was both exhilarating and exhausting. The culture of the Inuit natives, dog mushing, and the sun shining in its full glory at two in the morning, proved most memorable.

Following the Alaska trip, I planned to attend a mastery workshop with Anthony Robbins. Curiously the workshop was titled "Date with Destiny." En route from Alaska to California, however, I found myself enveloped by fevers and chills. Rapidly I became sick and disoriented. I missed my connecting flight to Palm Springs and collapsed at the airport. I protested that I was fine, but my words failed to make a difference to the airline agent.

To my embarrassment, this agent insisted that I sit in the wheelchair that she had summoned. I was to be transported to a car that would take me to a hotel for an overnight stay. I didn't want to be late for my workshop, yet I had no choice. I was forced to comply. My "date with destiny" was to be postponed. I mused, *What a way to start a course in mastery.*

Through sheer determination, somehow, I arrived at the Anthony Robbins workshop the following day. The gathering would be as magnificent as any Robbins production, even in my weakened state

I felt inspired to rise to the occasion. I played full out, as they encourage one to do. By doing this, I allowed awareness and wisdom to penetrate my veil of grieving and touch an aliveness within me.

I, who had been a teacher of these very topics, now had to turn to a mentor greater than myself to remind me of their truth. Two areas that had been my expertise were those of discovering our passions and living our purpose. I needed that awareness now more than ever.

To that end, Tony Robbins emphasized asking empowering questions for quality results. I was already clear not to linger on why things happen. Now I shifted to asking myself, *What is the bigger meaning in all that had transpired?* Reflecting on this, I further questioned, Could I use this awareness in some way to help others?

Further, his work proved beneficial in suggesting that we model someone whom we admired, someone who showed accomplishment in a field in which we wanted to be successful. In my case, I wanted to succeed in moving on after the loss of a deep love.

Two celebrities who had been my inspiration for their willingness to share their private pain were the former Beatle Paul McCartney and news correspondent Katie Couric. I held them both in mind as my models. I identified with them in how they had grieved the loss of their mates to cancer around the same time that I had lost William. I had been moved by their courage in facing their pain and expressing it creatively in ways that gifted others.

All in my group who were present at the Robbin's workshop whispered a hint of a possible purpose greater than my agony, although I did not yet feel ready to embrace this notion. Upon hearing my story, people shared that they felt inspired by the love and contact, and by the contribution that it could provide. They even began to refer to me as a mystic storyteller. I felt far from able to pursue anything along those lines, yet I filed this information away in my mind. I pressed on and completed the workshop, hardly realizing the toll that this effort had begun to take on my body.

INTERIM

By the time I returned home to New York, I had become extremely debilitated. Little did I realize that I faced my date with destiny in a fashion beyond anything for which the workshop had prepared me. I had a high fever, I couldn't breathe, and my chest grew heavy with congestion. I kept coughing, and each cough brought greater weakness. Since the symptoms were consistent with bronchial pneumonia, I wondered if I had come down with it. My confidant and William's former oncologist insisted on visiting me after hearing me on the phone. He confirmed my suspicion after a brief physical examination in my home. He wanted to admit me immediately to a hospital for observation and treatment.

Instead of attending to my illness medically, I allowed the thought of *This is perfect.* I knew that bronchial pneumonia, if left untreated, could lead to death. Here was my opportunity to allow nature to take its course. Since I had never regarded suicide as an option, could pneumonia provide the way?

I pleaded my case to him. "Just let me be. I'm willing to take my chances directly with God." His conflict was palpable. I could see how be grappled with my request before relenting. As much as his training would have wanted him to argue the point with me, his higher wisdom knew to surrender. I further reminded him of the wisdom he had imparted to me months earlier: after witnessing thousands of cases of people in various stages of illness. "No one dies before their time and no one dies after their time. All die when it's their time...and only God knows that time."

I would take no allopathic medicine and no naturopathic medicine. I sought no healing energy or prayers. I told no one, and I assumed that it would just be a matter of time before I reached my own date with eternity. My plan lasted about ten days.

One morning, I woke gasping for air and could feel my ability to breathe shutting down. This is a frightening experience under normal conditions. However, my first gut level response was one of excitement. This could be my moment to drop my physical form, perhaps to fulfill a destiny that secretly I still desired.

Willie Mae heard what was happening, rushed into the room and immediately began to call 911. I shook my head emphatically, *No,* and shot her a look that screamed, *Don't you dare.* Reluctantly, and in apparent torment, she complied, and came toward me to help. Shockingly, instead of moving into the Light, as I had longed for and expected to do, I found tumultuous emotional upheavals begin to rise from the core of my being.

Convulsions emerged from deep within me. Waves and waves of lower vibrations of emotions moved through me in unrelenting release. Curiously, the issues from my tissues focused in two areas. One was shame, guilt, and responsibility for not saving William, even though intellectually I knew that saving him had not been my job.

The other area was the incredible emptiness and loneliness of being in the world without my playmate in physical love and consciousness. These were the reasons I didn't want to continue living, reasons that had me craving my own death. After the emotions subsided, in a millisecond I was healed from bronchial pneumonia. I was enraged at God for robbing me of my exit. I was mystified as well.

I had been doomed to being healed. Having to accept my unfortunate aliveness, I went off to sulk in my hot tub. I had been healed, yet my body remained weak. Now I could identify even further with how debilitated William had felt.

In my despondent state, while immersed in hot water, I soon felt energy and a cool breeze. Recognizing the presence of William, I reiterated to him how upset I felt. His words were loving and comforting and meant to soothe me from my angst. *Beloved, we've had an incredible journey in physical life together. When we joined as spiritual partners, we made a promise that you would help me fulfill the destiny of my purpose and longing for ascension.1 would be there for you to live life fully, to laugh and to be loved. We fulfilled that promise to perfection. Every day together was blissful. I want you to be happy and to fulfill your purpose of passing on the living wisdom through your Initiation. And remember, Initiation in the 21st Century is through quantum consciousness and technology. I'll stand by you and help you however I can. Yours is to live. It's not your time.* Hearing his words, I cried even more. Inside of me I knew that I needed to surrender.

I had resisted embracing a life without William for long enough. Clearly, I was meant to be here. I trusted that a reason existed, although I had no clue of what that reason could be. Maybe God would reveal that I had more to offer than I had as yet become aware. I could fight life and cause more suffering for myself, or I could invite it in and embrace its experiences.

I implored God to show me how to live again and how to contribute again, in the arduous task of starting over. Those simple two words, starting over, felt immense when I had no idea of where to begin. Interestingly enough, this was July of 1998, time to renegotiate the agreement that I had made in this tub six months earlier. Obviously, the soul and staying alive had won out.

No sooner had I exited the tub than the phone rang and one of my dearest clients called. She told me of a back injury that she had just suffered.

I surprised myself as I heard words emerge from my mouth. "Come right over."

It was beyond startling. Something new had already begun. Despite my misgivings, the tide was turning toward life. Spontaneously, I found myself working again for the first time in six months, even though I couldn't fathom the possibility of doing it.

Upon concluding an intense four hour session and before leaving, this client turned to thank me for seeing her under such trying conditions. Now renewed and physically strengthened, she offered her perception. "I feel for what you've gone through, and your path doesn't surprise me. The first half of your life's work has been about helping to birth people's souls. It would be natural that the second half of your life's work would be about preparing people to face death. This is especially true now that baby boomers are facing that stage for their parents and possibly themselves." I was touched by her remarks and I mused over their truth.

Following that first session, my body increased in health and strength each day. Still, I longed for a way of working with energy that did not stress my body so fully. I began to believe that I had more that was worth giving, and that life had more in it that was worth living. Since it had become obvious that, despite my secret wishes to the contrary, I was going to live! I would live passionately, purposefully, and with pleasure.

When my father had died, and I had been devastated, I hadn't given up. I would not do so now. Also, just as I had vowed to pass along my father's wisdom and make him proud, I would do the same for my beloved husband.

I had already experienced the fulfillment of trusting God and embracing all of my father's training. This led me to become successful in a career in which mind-body concepts had been rather pioneer. Yet the depth of how people's lives had been touched and transformed by this work had exceeded my expectations.

Mind-body work moved beyond the accepted boundaries of traditional medicine. In the past I had found this work to be so exciting that I could not wait to get up each morning and start working. Maybe I could once again find that inner drive and empowerment.

However, in assessing my current state of mind-body condition and life, I knew that I had to focus on healing myself first. This step had to occur before I could have anything significant to share with anyone else. My healing would require a jumpstart. For that I needed what I lovingly refer to with my clients as a TLK, a tender loving kick. It was now my turn to receive one. I decided to challenge myself in a powerful quantum leap of faith that I recognized as the defining moment to which people refer.

My own moment would come in the form of not one but two self-mastery courses in Hawaii. One, with world-renowned motivational teacher Anthony Robbins, would be the culmination of a program in which I had already been enrolled. The other would be with inspirational author Alan Cohen. Content with my proposed plan, I made arrangements to travel in August.

Little did I realize that the Infinite had begun to make plans of its own for me, plans that moved beyond what I had so logically set into motion. The Infinite's plans would provide the tender loving kick that I had never expected or realized I needed. It came through my friend Michael.

I had met Michael years earlier at a Master's course for Avatar, a program that I considered to be one of the most advanced and enlightened courses in consciousness that I had become involved in delivering since my NDE.

Michael could not contain his excitement as he called me and announced, "I found a sequel to Avatar. It's taught by a man named Satyam Nadeen. I have his book, and he is doing a retreat in Costa Rica. We're going. It starts next week."

Half-heartedly I listened and replied, "There's no way I'm going to Costa Rica, because I'm leaving for Hawaii on August 11. There's no time for any more workshops."

Michael remained insistent and would not take *No* for an answer. "You can't miss this. I'm driving to New York to bring you the book because you're going."

"No way, it's impossible."

Determined to make this happen, Michael refused all of my protestations. That very day he drove from Massachusetts to my home and handed me the book. Without my even opening the cover, something mystical captured my attention. I began to feel waves and waves of bliss and freedom move through my body. Intuitively I heard the words, *Shift happens.* Shift happens, not "Shit happens." That was interesting. I couldn't deny what I had begun to experience. I urged Michael, "Tell me more."

Michael continued to explain Nadeen's work. As he did so, the waves of energy that moved through me showed no signs of letting up. Convinced that something here was worth exploring further, I asked Michael if he had any written literature about the course. He replied, "No, but we could receive a fax. "Imagine my amazement as I pulled a fax from my machine and read that the title of the workshop was "Shift Happens."

I could not believe my eyes, yet my resistance remained strong. I didn't know how I could do it. I had neither the time nor enough money. However, true to form, I'd send out a message to the Infinite. Airline tickets would provide either the clue to go, or my way out.

Everyone is aware that the cost of airline tickets purchased less than three days before departure is exorbitant. Yet I was able to book a round trip on my favorite airline, Continental, for under five hundred dollars. They even offered me an upgrade to first class. It was a done deal with travel plans now in place, in my right ear I heard laughter and the words, *and it's a go.* Could William have had a hand in this plan? I was soon off to Costa Rica with Michael.

Our adventure began in a rather ominous way. Torrential rainfall prevented our plane from landing in Costa Rica, so we were diverted temporarily to Nicaragua. As our plane touched ground and taxied to a stop, I found it impossible to ignore nearby vestiges of that country's military demise. It was in the form of skeletons of old war planes. It seemed like an eerie way to begin a spiritual journey.

To take our minds from the sight outside the windows, the airline crew humored us. We were prohibited from leaving our plane, which remained on the ground until weather in Costa Rica could clear. This delay lasted several hours, and since we were so late Michael and I assumed that the driver who awaited us in Costa Rica must have left.

To our relief, we found him waiting for us after all. He seemed like an angel, holding up a sign that read "Pura Vida." He helped us into his van and drove us through dirt streets that seemed endless. Both of us began to wonder what would come next.

We arrived at a huge black iron gate, like a fortress. In the darkness it looked foreboding. The driver unlocked this gate, drove through it, and locked the gate behind us! I turned to Michael and registered a shocked expression. *What the hell had we gotten ourselves into?*

It was now after midnight, and we were ushered through gardens to a lovely little cottage known as a tea house. There we collapsed until morning. I wanted so badly to be back in my bed in New York.

To my surprise, when I woke in the morning light, I noticed how beautiful and peaceful this space was. All seemed well. Michael and I found our way to the main house where people were having breakfast. The spiritual teacher came out, dressed in a Versace designer shirt. He was a blond-haired, blue-eyed American. Some ashram, *I mused*!

It turned out that he had a story of his own spiritual awakening that had occurred under unusual circumstances, to say the least. Without going into details, let's just say that it happened during his seven years in federal prison. *Okay, I'm in Costa Rica with a spiritual master whom the U.S. government identifies as an ex-con for manufacturing the drug ecstasy. He had also spent time in the seminary and had studied Zen and consciousness for more than two decades. What a dichotomy!*

All of us sat around his living room, from which we could see out over the countryside. This place looked like a drug lord's villa.

Telepathically I sent out the message, *William, it's just like you to lead me to a mountaintop to study with a spiritual rebel.* We were seven strangers, and we settled on designer furniture in a circle for *Satsang*. "Satsang" is an ancient Sanskrit word that means "sacred dialogue in speaking one's truth."

The energy in the room felt high, though no drugs of any kind were involved. The people who had gathered there were open and genuinely dedicated to expanding the awareness of their spiritual nature. I decided to stay silent and open in both mind and heart.

Nadeen began by asking us to sit quietly in a meditative state, following which we opened our eyes. Then he shocked us by stating, "There is no free will." He looked around the room at our stunned reactions and heard an almost unified gasp. Nearly everyone there, myself included, had come to believe that we create our own reality.

Sensitive to our collective confusion, Nadeen continued, "It's a challenge for the mind to hear such truth, so I'm going to illustrate this point with a story." He proceeded to use the metaphor of a limousine. "Imagine riding in a stretch limousine and you think you're the driver, but you're really in the back seat with a toy steering wheel. You have the freedom to play with that steering wheel any way you want. As you're playing and turn left, you think, *I created that.* However, the key fact is that the driver was going to turn left anyhow. It just seemed to you as if you did it."

My head went into a tailspin as my fingernails dug deeply into the couch. If ever any message were to command my attention, this was it! Only nine months earlier William had spoken nearly the same words. Now Nadeen underscored the same point.

I vividly recalled the day that I walked in on William as he lay helpless and bedridden. Despite his situation, he had been laughing and laughing. I asked, "Okay you...so what's the joke?"

He responded, "I got the ultimate cosmic joke, the big secret."

"Don't hold out. Let me in on it."

"Imagine a stretch limousine, and you think you're the driver. If you had awareness at all, you'd realize you're in the backseat. Why not put your feet up and let the driver drive? Enjoy the ride. What a way to go!"

Here was this same metaphor again, stereo for my ears to hear. Often, I would tell clients that if the Infinite wants you to hear something, you'll hear it once and it will resonate within you. If it really wants you to get it, you'll hear it twice. When you hear something in stereo, pay attention big

46

time. This was my stereo. Now at a deep level of knowing, a shift began to occur within me.

Nadeen began to share the experience of his awakening, and the truths of which he had become aware since then. He had spent time in federal prison, under the most arduous of physical restraints and with no freedom except within his mind. He recounted that he had been reading the book *Consciousness Speaks by* Ramesh Balsekar.

As he had read the statement, "Consciousness is all there is, and I am that," its words touched a core knowing. In that moment, for Nadeen the illusion of separation dissolved. So much so that even in prison he could enjoy the humor of knowing that his time there was "source experiencing itself." Later, I was to realize that Nadeen spoke primarily of the philosophy of non-dualism.

Nadeen then invited us to suspend our judgment for the week. Indeed, he prompted us not to just accept his truth, rather to trust our own experience. He encouraged us to allow whatever feelings and truths would emerge. The greatest benefit would result, he emphasized, if we would let our intuitive knowing express itself. Each person shared his or her own spiritual journey according to whatever they wanted the group to know.

In Satsang when someone speaks, others listen and offer no comment of any kind. One accepts what is said and reflects on what it touches in oneself. This process sets up a safe space for intimate sharing and synergy.

Group members would have "Aha!" experiences at different moments. As this happened, I watched each person's energy seem to pop, their truths having become illumined. Witnessing such an experience touched us all.

The words that most hit my intuitive core were, "Accept what is as is." *Wow, what a concept, especially after the year I'd had!* That was quite a challenge, to not want to analyze or change, just to accept. Indeed, Nadeen focused on saying *Yes* to whatever came up in life that caused the mind to want to say *No.* For me, William's death and my return from the Light had been a screaming *No.*

I shared my spiritual story with Nadeen and the group. I focused especially on the piece about William's leaving and my sense of brokenness. Nadeen offered an intuitive comment that just as prison had provided his own call to awaken, William's passing had provided mine. It alluded to the fact that my perception of his passing had been my prison.

When I heard this statement, my body trembled in recognition of its profound truth. In that moment a kinesthetic knowing, the same knowing that I had received in my NDE, flooded my body. I suddenly remembered that everything unfolds to its next moment, just as the puzzle pieces of our lives illuminate the wisdom behind seeming appearances.

Yes, William's dramatic exit had pulled into question everything that I had believed in, had been taught or had known. The rug had been pulled right out from under me. My whole world as I had known it lay shattered. The questions of free will, destiny, balance, the truth: all haunted me. I had begun to examine all from the inside out.

I had been led to this retreat in a kicking and screaming fashion. The experience soon became priceless. I experienced a great shift, as my consciousness began to expand. Even in its structure, this week in Costa Rica afforded me time for integration as these revelations unfolded.

Each morning we started with breakfast as a group, and then we did meditation and *Satsang* for about two hours. We had the rest of the day free and could go off on optional excursions, stay on the property to meditate, enjoy massage, sunbathe in the nude, do yoga, and so on. We were encouraged to do whatever would support our process of integration. It was entirely up to us to decide which options to choose.

Each evening we joined Nadeen for sumptuous dinners prepared by a chef. After dinner we continued with *Satsang,* in which we shared with the group whatever we deemed appropriate from our day's activities. In so doing, we nourished our bodies and our minds as we set ourselves free. As Nadeen exclaimed joyfully, "It isn't about seeking anymore. It is about finding."

During one memorable outing to a waterfall, I experienced a mystical awareness. In my expanded state I stood at the top of the waterfall and saw it as a metaphor for life. It seemed that where the water coursed over the land was an entry, or birth. As the water flowed down freely, that was the adventure called life. Surrendering to this flow would be easier than fighting it. When the water reached its end, just as with death, this water became part of the whole. Its individual flow merged with the other waters in a oneness. This metaphor left me in a state of awe that I later shared with the group.

Upon hearing my thoughts, other members of the group reported their own experience of a life metaphor represented by white water rafting. Anyone who has ridden a raft in rapid water knows that the river has a flow and a power of its own. If one relaxes and trusts the flow, the ride can be a high adventure. However, one quickly learns that if fear and tension and the need to control grow stronger, resistance to the flow can prove harrowing. The message simply seems to be that for the smoothest journey, one needs to trust the flow of life and go with it.

Nadeen's emphasis was, "You are not the doer, and neither is anyone else." This statement was another mind-blower. I realized that this truth meant that one needed to focus on being and accepting, and not on doing. Accepting becomes a freer experience. Life just happens through you.

Interestingly enough, William had been a master at simply being. He often advised. "Let the doing unfold from that." After spending so many years with him I had come to enjoy the liberation that this recommendation afforded.

That shift was what Nadeen called "witness consciousness." It suddenly became clear to me that I had been living the experience of witness consciousness since childhood. I had never realized this fact. As best I could explain, witness consciousness followed the metaphor that I have a body, but I'm not my body. I have a mind, but I'm not my mind. I have emotions, but I'm not my emotions. I am.

Now in acknowledging this truth, I felt intuitively that the time had come to change my name. After all, I had declared myself as Tina as my first act of defiance against my given name.

At 45 1 was not the same person I had been previously. Also, the name 'Tina" had been part of "Tina and William," soup and sandwich. William was gone physically, and in many ways so was Tina. What now emerged was the love name that William had called me. He had taken "Tina," which meant "little" in Italian, and laughingly transformed it by exclaiming, "You are far from little; you are about expansion. Your name sounds too limiting to me. I propose that your name reflect you as you are. You are my Tianna."

The retreat now ended, with appreciations given freely to Nadeen and the small group of strangers who had become friends. To think, how little the mind knows. This course that I had never heard about, that I had resisted when Michael went through such labors to invite me, turned out to be a major turning point to date in my journey through grief. It provided the first acceptance of what I had called the unthinkable, William's passing, and my destiny of witnessing and escorting his transition without joining him.

The realization then hit, *Oh no, I'm going now to two courses in self-mastery about doing, doing, involving intentional effort. What* is *Source doing to me? I'm going from "Just be, let it happen," to "You must make your choices and set goals."* The thought passed through my mind, *Just let it be. Let the experience be what it is. Be open and surrender to it all.* With this thought, no sooner had I arrived back home than it was time to leave for Hawaii.

HAWAII

I no longer pondered whether or not to take the two courses in Hawaii. I would just do it and play full out. However, after being with Nadeen I noticed a wonderful difference in that the "efforting" had gone. The "I" that had been doing all was now witnessed by a presence that enjoyed the show. I participated fully in both Hawaii workshops, and they proved to be effortless and rewarding. Since I recognized intuitively that I was not the doer, I no longer had to try so hard. I found the results amazing. It seemed that everything served, and everything worked with ease and grace.

In Maui, I attended the first workshop with Alan Cohen. It was there that I experienced my first most powerful, erotic dream encounter with William. We made love in that dream. This love felt so real and so passionate that my physical body exploded in orgasm.

Still in this dream, before William left me, he whispered, "Beloved, I'll love you forever and will be with you in spirit. It's time now for you to be with men in your physical world. I want you to know that I continue to watch over you and be your bodyguard. I will guide to you those men who can care for you and cherish you, as you deserve."

Upon awakening I felt devastated. This dream had been so real that I felt as if I had lost William all over again. I cried uncontrollably in my pain, until a knock on the door interrupted me. It was a man named Paul from the workshop. He had felt moved to check on me. His words chilled and yet comforted me. "I don't know if it's your late husband or my spirit," but as 1 was doing Tai Chi this morning I felt compelled to come here to take care of you and give you a hug."

I didn't know what to make of his statement, yet at that moment I knew that I could use a friend. I let Paul into my room with the understanding that all I needed was for him to hug me. He did just that, and we cried together. As I later reflected on this encounter, I couldn't help but wonder about the synchronicity of my dream, its message of William sending men to me, and Paul knocking on my door. Could

William have influenced him? Paul did say that he had been moved to come to me. The experience felt like another fulfillment of contact from William. The difference this time was that this contact actively included another person.

I shared this story with our group of about 25 in the workshop, and they honored my experience. I indicated that I had accepted that William remained with me. They agreed, and lovingly supported me in that acceptance. Indeed, some of these people were quite psychic and offered feedback to bring me even more validation. They also commented that I was stronger than I imagined. In many ways William resided within me, and not only as a memory.

At that point I shared with the group the conflict that I felt over my name change. The workshop leader invited me to stand in the middle of the circle. I was to look into each person's eyes and declare myself as Tianna. As I did so, I felt tremendously liberated.

During free time from the workshop, a few participants decided to take an excursion early the next morning to the volcano Haleakala to watch the sunrise. I joined them, thinking that this experience would simply be an enjoyable one. What transpired turned an enjoyable experience into a mystical one.

Innocently I watched the sun rise over the volcano's crater, only to find that it reflected a similarity to William's ascension. This sunrise transported me back to the moment when William had left his body through the top of his head. Once again I could see the emerging of a circle of light, and then the union that emanated from that circle as the radiance that had filled the room. In effect, this same union and radiance appeared at the volcano as the sun emblazoned the horizon. I felt visibly moved. As I related my experience, others in our group were deeply touched as well.

Once this weeklong program had ended, with appreciations duly noted, it was off to the Big Island. I had barely caught my breath, and now I headed for the grandest intensive yet to be. It was time for a life mastery seminar with Anthony Robbins.

My dear friend Mary joined me. From the moment we arrived, we could see that this seminar was to be an extravaganza. It would include brilliant presentations by Robbins and world-famous inspirational teachers, plus countless exercises and experiences with more than two thousand participants.

Opportunities for expansion and empowerment soon grew too numerous to mention. A peak experience for me was that of climbing a 50 foot utility pole that they called the "pamper pole." One dons a harness for safety while climbing, then stands on top of the pole and jumps off toward a trapeze twelve feet in front of it. The mere thought of this exercise terrified me.

I mused, *If I'm not the doer, let's see what* is *going to get done.* I could barely visualize such an activity, especially since I'm not athletically oriented. I hadn't even brought a pair of sneakers. Lucky for me I could borrow Mary's. Also, the thought of doing this exercise at seven in the morning went against my very nature. However, since I was there, and that was the program, I asked consciousness to do its thing through me. I remained curious to see what would happen.

To my amazement, I climbed effortlessly all the way up the pole and stood on the top. As everyone applauded, I found myself in an expanded state of mind. I even took bows on the top of the pole. I jumped toward the trapeze. Although I didn't grasp it, I touched it. Of course, the harness keeps one safe so fear is minimized.

Since I harbored no judgment about this exercise, none of my past conditioning or fears affected me. Just in leaping, never mind touching the rod, I experienced incredible liberation. I laughed and laughed as I swung my way down to the ground in the safety harness.

Robbins' closing touch to the workshop involved our walking on hot coals along a path 40 feet long. Considering that I had completed a ten foot fire walk during my first workshop with him, this longer walk felt like the perfect tribute to my new expansion. It also marked a triumphant affirmation of walking the path of life without fear.

Once again, all of us expressed tremendous appreciation for our experience, and we celebrated in true Robbins style. Mary and I then moved on to our next Hawaiian adventure, a colon cleansing program with body work. Specifically, this program included five days of fasting on a mixture that combined sea water with other nutrients, and a daily two hour massage session. In so many ways, having experienced both grieving and travel, I felt that this cleansing program rejuvenated my body from inside out.

During the process we also met with a female Kahuna who took Mary and me to what they called the caves of Pele, the goddess of fire of Hawaii. These caves, amazing lava formations, clearly reflected the female genitalia. Most especially, raised from the lava was an exact replica of the vulva with its lips fully spread and clitoris visible. We were able to be seated on this expression of the female form and feel its energy move through us.

We began our visit to the caves of Pele with this experience. The Kahuna guided us deeper into the darkness of the cave. It was literally a rebirthing into more of the empowered feminine. Having so recently taken on the name "Tianna," I felt purified and reborn, more ready to walk the earth alone and without my twin mate by my side in the physical.

This rebirth was strengthened even further by a nighttime excursion. In the darkness, with the Kahuna drumming, I entered an altered state in which my energy felt pulled into the lava flow. Spontaneously my menstrual flow, which I had not expected, bled onto the earth. The Kahuna commented that this phenomenon was, indeed, a form of blessing.

Looking at the flow of bright orange lava, I also experienced a mystical moment. I had a vision of a pair of eyes. The message was, *Yours is to see with eyes that go beyond the physical and burn away the veils of illusion that separate one from truth. There is no separation.*

INTERIM

With all that had transpired in Hawaii, I felt empowered as I returned home to New York. However, once I arrived, I faced the reality of all that I had left behind. Those memories hit me hard. I had to take everything that I had just experienced and use it to face the future that lay before me. The good news was that I had gained new inner and outer resources from which I could draw.

Back in my home I viewed life with a different twist. I had once longed to die. Now I knew that my death wish didn't matter. I would be here for the duration. One major question remained. *Without longing for death, what would life be like?*

The Infinite provided me with an initial answer to that question. A friend called and asked if I wanted to go skydiving. Earlier, such an activity would have been unheard of in my grieving condition. Now the prospect sounded like a wondrous adventure that I could view as a metaphor for my new beginning.

Quickly and enthusiastically I exclaimed, "Yes!" In skydiving, one has to let go into the unknown. This letting go reminded me of the dream in which William and I had leapt from a plane. Skydiving offered me a chance to act out this dream. I had no fear of death. If ever I was going to jump out of a plane, this was the time.

The day arrived with perfect autumn weather. The leaves were in full glory, and it seemed to me that the Infinite smiled on this adventure. My friend Mary would join me. She had agreed to come along in the car merely for the ride; however, when the Infinite has other plans, resistance is futile. She soon found herself preparing to jump right along with me.

We arrived, and the adventure began. I signed my life away on countless waivers and so did Mary. Even as we waited to begin our preparations, a 911 call came in to request the rescue of a parachuter stuck in a tree. Mary appeared terrified while I remained undaunted. We then underwent a brief training, suited up, and headed off toward the plane. I strode eagerly while Mary kept shaking her head as if to ask, *What am I doing?*

The time had come. At 14,000 feet over land, the airplane door sliding open took our breath away. The moment to jump was at hand. Taking a deep breath, I approached this exit into the unknown. To enjoy the ride as best I could I would need to let go with total abandon. *Baby, this is life,* I thought, and out I jumped.

I entered a free fall, one of the most enlightening experiences of my life! I almost forgot to pull the ripcord. My instructor pointed quickly to the altimeter, which registered 6,000 feet. I had to move on it immediately. To my credit I did pull the cord, and the brightly-colored parachute opened majestically.

Seeing the bigger picture of the land was a magnificent experience as I floated effortlessly in mid-air. I found the rush exhilarating. Witnessing my seeming bliss, the instructor signaled to me, asking if I wanted to participate in advanced techniques. Emphatically I nodded, *Yes.* He showed me which cords to pull, and soon I began to spiral as I wound my way down to the earth. I even touched ground on my feet in a perfect landing.

I had actively and grandly played out my question and received my answer. What life is about is letting go and trusting the free fall. In so doing, you can float creatively to your destination...destiny.

I planned no further journeys for now. The time had finally come for me to settle into life in New York. My body needed to regain its balance. I knew that massage could assist greatly in releasing the grief that remained in my body. I also realized that I longed for the nurturing touch of a man in a safe manner. Massage from a masseur would offer me that option.

In the past I had tried different masseurs. As with the experience of Goldilocks, I had found some to be too mechanical, some too rough, and others too stiff. Tired of trying to find one on my own I lamented to William, *Find me someone whose hands could give me as good a massage as you did.*

Telepathically I heard laughter. *Maybe not as good. I'll do the best I can.*

I did not expect that the next masseur would be the one. As soon as he entered the room I thought, *Oh no, not this guy.* He was young, and he looked like a super jock. I mused, *probably inexperienced.* So much for judgments, even trivial ones.

As soon as Ken placed his hands on me, I felt his healing touch penetrate into my cells. I began to sob deeply and profusely. He had the nurturing touch that I had sought. Ken also turned out to be a compassionate listener, sensitive in his responses.

He inquired gently, "Do you want me to stop?"

"No, you're just what I needed," I told him. I trusted him emotionally. I knew that I could share with him intimately about William's passing and my grieving pain. As the session progressed, our work together only grew better.

It turned out that Ken's parents had been incredible soul mates, and his father had died. Ken knew only too well the pain that I also. He was helping his mother through her own loss. Also, he perceived the guidance of his father from the beyond, so I could express freely both my emotions and my perception of William 's presence. At the end of that massage, I knew that I wanted us to work together on a regular basis. We did so and have since become lifelong friends and professional colleagues.

That night, in my hot tub, I thanked William for a job well done. I knew enough to attribute this connection to him. On my own
I had tried to find the right masseur and had failed miserably. It had taken only one plea to William, and someone I would never have selected became the perfect match.

William's response was one of laughter. I heard him whisper, *Time to go to India.*

Oh no, I thought. That *can't possibly be right. I'm not ready for another trip. I'm still recovering from the last year of travel...and of all places, India?*

For whatever reason, India was a land that I felt both drawn to and afraid. It was the same land that William and I had wanted to visit. We knew that such a journey would be challenging, so we had continued to postpone it. What could William possibly be thinking?

Quickly I put such a trip out of my mind and focused on preparing to honor the anniversary date of William's passing. December 7 approached rapidly. I now understood why people emphasized that the first year would be the hardest. Early in that year my memories had been so fresh and now they had grown starkly different.

All year long it had been firsts, firsts, firsts. Incessantly my mind had gone back, as if without reins. Haunted by the theme of *last year at this time...* I had found each holiday anguishing. I had now come a long way, yet my grief still lingered.

I started to imagine how to celebrate William. Never did I expect that he would take over. The morning before his anniversary date, tearfully I reached out to friends and family and asked to have a traditional gathering and perhaps a service. This was not to be. People's schedules did not permit it. Disillusioned, I thought, *All right, I'll just cry my way through it alone.*

Suddenly my tears turned fearful as I found myself moving in and out of consciousness in a trance-like state. Not wanting to be alone I called William's former wife, Rebecca, to tell her what was happening. "Do you want me to come down and be with you?" she offered quickly.

I was touched. "That would mean so much to me, and I don't want to impose."

"Get real," she admonished. "I'll be right there."

Rebecca arrived and immediately I began to feel better. I thought, *Maybe this was just a strange way of not wanting to be alone.* I never imagined that something might be going on behind the scenes. Even though Rebecca had arrived, she was tired and asked if she could lie down. Soon she had fallen fast asleep on my couch.

I noticed this and decided to go to bed and force myself to fall asleep as well. I waited and waited, and it didn't happen. Instead my trance-like state took deeper hold. Soon I became aware that while my body had fallen asleep in the bed, my inner being had moved elsewhere. Once again, I found myself having an out-of-body experience.

Suddenly, before me I saw several of my deceased relatives, my grandmothers, my aunts, and most notably my father. On a table in front of them sat a cake with a candle in the shape of a number one. Who do you think they were celebrating?

There was William, beaming and looking radiantly handsome. Extending his arms out to me, he exclaimed, *Welcome to my birthday party. You are my present.* As I moved to embrace him, the chorus started singing *Happy Birthday*... ending it with, *to your First birthday into eternity.* What do you say to such a party?" Thank you for inviting me?"

The next thing I remember, I was fully back in my body and in my bed. I feared that I had only been dreaming, and I started to cry. Laughter broke through my sobbing. I heard, *Happy Birthday to me.*

Since Rebecca had slept over, I ran to tell her what had happened. She was not surprised. In her usual witty style, she quipped, "Even without a body, he loves to celebrate a party. Happy Birthday, William." Together she and I agreed, *Okay, no more anniversary of death dates. It's birthday time.*

With that, Rebecca and I hurried out to purchase a birthday cake. We set a candle on it and re-enacted William's party. This ritual has since become our annual celebration. Rebecca and I get together on December 7, buy a cake, and celebrate William's birthday into eternity.

That first year had begun to come to an end. All that remained was a professional training program that I was taking. The program's subject, sound frequency energies, seemed easy enough and what I needed. A friend had told me that working with vibrational tapes from this training would accelerate healing. I was open to anything, especially something effortless that could help me to heal.

Curiously, during William's cancer journey I had picked up a book that addressed this same topic. Since sound had been William's passion and not mine I had passed the book along to him without a second notice. Now, several years later, I found myself studying sound frequency energies in depth. Indeed, in my own practice I had begun to recommend the use of sound frequency energies because of the results they produced. My clients often teased me by saying, "We know, take a tape and call you in the morning."

Intuitively I also wondered, since all of us are energy beings, what would happen if I could raise my vibration. After all, we know from quantum physics that energy can be transformed but can neither be created nor destroyed. Hazrat Inayat Khan, spiritual master and founder of the Sufi movement, seems to have expressed it best:

Now we get to the heart of the matter, for all matter is made up of vibrations. It is a scientific fact that, although we see solids when we look at an object, what we are really seeing is fluid vibrations organized in sufficiently gross frequencies to form solid matter.

Hazrat Inayat Khan's words confirmed my childhood knowing of seeing energy patterns. Could death of the body, I mused further, be a congealing of energy in physical form that drops off as the vibration rises? I vaguely remembered quantum physics alluding to our body being light trapped in gravity. If so, what could such a reality mean as I sought the truth behind the contacts I had been having, contacts confirmed by mediums? I found myself open to exploration. Not knowing what to expect, I worked with the vibrational tapes.

One immediate result was that I began to hear William with greater intensity. His repeated utterance, *Time for India,* became relentless. Had I been set up? Sound frequency healing and Sai Baba in India had been William's passion. Now I found myself in pursuit of these same things. Okay, I accepted William's challenge. There was nothing else to do but surrender and wonder, *which trip, with whom, and when?*

No sooner had I begun to ponder these questions than a flash intuition reminded me of an upcoming trip to India in January of 1999. It was to be led by Joan Borysenko. Thoughts of India had been the farthest thoughts from my reality. Now India beckoned to me. If ever I could consider the possibility of such a daunting journey, it would be with a trusted leader such as Joan Borysenko. Even this trip of hers was presented as a spiritual pilgrimage focusing on finding the beloved. I surmised that people drawn to such a journey would be exceptional companions for this kind of adventure.

I recalled my first meeting with Joan on the cruise to Alaska, and how touched I had been by her compassion. She had heard briefly of my love for and loss of William and touched her heart in acknowledgement. Further, I had long admired her work and respected her as a wise woman who had a great sense of humor. Her trip would be the perfect one, if she had a place available on notice of less than three weeks. I knew that the group would visit spiritual teachers and holistic centers, both of which are my passion. Without hesitation, I phoned and learned that space was indeed available. Guess who was off to India.

I invited Mary to join me, and soon we set off on another adventure. As usual I made arrangements for us to travel on our own and meet the group in New Delhi.

Our introduction to India included a crowded airport that was as chaotic as I had imagined it would be. We landed late in the evening and found the airport bustling with people who grabbed and pushed just to get to the exit. Mary and I needed to find a taxi to our hotel. This task sounded simple enough. However it wasn't. So many drivers wanted us that we found ourselves pulled from all sides.

The driver who ultimately took us didn't seem to know that a red light meant *Stop*. To our shock, cows also roamed the road freely. *Oh yes,* I thought, *what was your intention, William?*

I knew that the great saint of India, Sai Baba, had been William's guru. Yet William had never bothered to travel to see this holy man. William had tried for years to get me involved with Sai Baba. Although I greatly respected the man, I followed a different path. *Why was I here now?*

This question would be answered in time, only not quite yet. We would tour other cities before visiting Sai Baba's ashram in Puttaparthi. One of these cities was Agra, home of the Taj Mahal. Before us stood a magnificent structure that is actually a mausoleum erected by a grieving widower in tribute to his immortal love.

It was there that I found myself inspired to ponder how such a legacy to one's beloved could leave lasting beauty for others to enjoy. Could I ultimately do something to express my love for William so that others might benefit? It was a question worth considering.

India had already begun to touch me with her spiritual wisdom, and a spontaneous event soon occurred that would deepen this feeling. It happened in a tiny, remote village, an almost unknown town where we were scheduled to see some dancing. William had other plans.

As Mary and I strolled down the street, suddenly I felt William's nudging and heard, *Go inside, there's a present for you, a teardrop from heaven.* We stood outside a little jewelry store. I mentioned William's words to Mary, who knows me well. She replied, "Let's go in."

We stepped inside. To my surprise, just as I had been told, I beheld a large pendant, a teardrop lapis. *Oh my god,* I thought, *it's amazing.* I sought to buy, and I met the shopkeeper. He introduced himself in an intimate way.

"Hello, welcome to my store. I'm Mr. Jolley, and I'm here to help you." More than mere words seemed to pass between us.

Instead of concentrating on the pendant, I turned my focus to this man's name. I asked, "Is 'Mr. Jolley' your spiritual name or your family name? "He laughed and answered that it was his family name. I replied that I suspected "Jolley" was more than a family name. He had a presence and a way of speaking that extended beyond that of an average shopkeeper. "You seem to be a spiritual teacher in shopkeeper clothing," I added.

He glanced at me with a gaze that wondered, *Who is this American tourist?* He asked, "Why do you say that?"

I chuckled and replied, "From what you've said, from the energy in your store, and your bright eyes."

He looked at me as if he were assessing me. He then surprised me by remarking, "I suspect you are a master I've been waiting for. I've known that one day a master would come to my store and would be able to answer this question. I ask this of whomever I sense could be that person. So, if you are that person, here is my question."

"I'll try, what is it?"

He replied, "What is love?"

With no hesitation on my part, words flowed out of my mouth. "Love is who and what we are and why we're here. It's a frequency and not an emotion. It's you in me and me in you. There is no separation, that is the illusion. We are one."

He looked at me and with hands in prayer position of *Namaste,* exclaimed, "Yes, you are that being." Both of us stood transfixed and stared into each other's tear-filled eyes.

I flashed back to my NDE as well as my union with William. In my mind I asked, if *this is contact, give me a sign. I want a symbol, William, to know that it's you who led me here.* At that precise moment, Mr. Jolley turned around and pulled a candle from his shelf. As he lighted the candle, he looked me straight in the eye and began a deeply moving metaphor.

He began, "We are all candles," and each has its flame. If we enjoy our light and share it so others enjoy it also, then when it goes out," and he snuffed out the flame, "it's time, and it's the right time for it. The flame goes on inside the memory and lasts forever."

I broke into uncontrollable sobbing. The odds of his saying such words seemed beyond coincidence. Mary felt it, too.

It was William who had created our ritual of the communications candle to remind us of our divine flame within. Whenever one of us had a sensitive issue that needed the other's full and undivided attention, we lit the candle. The candle ritual signified, this *is important.* We both needed to clear our minds and let each other know when we were ready to receive this communication. It was about communicating truth. It was about communicating sometimes painful truth. When the message had been conveyed, the person who had lit the candle would blow it out as a signal, *it is done.*

Of all the things that Mr. Jolley could have done. He had used the candle as a communications instrument. He, then had blown it out. Who was this man, and what did he transmit? I gave thanks for this contact and this gift. Mr. Jolley and I had shared such a spiritual bond. What more could be said in this experience?

Next, two silver rings caught my attention; one had dangles of amethyst and the other had dangles of lapis. My favorite stone had always been lapis. William's favorite stone had been amethyst. I had received subtle pressure to remove my wedding band after the first year, and I had done so. Here, now, were its replacements for only me to know.

As I jingled the rings on my finger, I mused over the significance of the gems' meanings. Lapis is a stone to help gain courage in mastering life and easing into the present. This was relevant for me now more than ever. Amethyst improves focus and confidence and helps one to access inner wisdom and open to one's highest spiritual nature. It seemed to have worked for William.

After all of this spiritual connection, it became comical to recognize that Mr. Jolley and I were also human. We negotiated the prices of the lapis pendant and the two rings. We haggled a bit as we made a deal that worked for both of us. The two of us parted with heartfelt spiritual love, exchanging addresses.

As I left the shop, I recalled the mini tantrum I had thrown the night that William had announced he was going to die. I had argued, "You can't leave." "You always celebrate my birthday with me."

He had replied, "I'll be with you in spirit." I bought you a gift. It's coming in the mail."

The present that had arrived was a beautiful gold unisex necklace that William had purchased on a home shopping channel. I suspected that he had originally ordered it for himself. In my grief, when I received it, I rebuked it. If you want to get me a present, this isn't it. If you want to get me a necklace that is for me, get me one that is my style.

I now clutched the lapis teardrop next to my heart, knowing that it was a gift from William in spirit. I wear it to this day. Many who see it become mesmerized by it. To those who I feel are ready to hear the story, I tell it. To the others I merely say, "Thank you," and I smile.

When Mary and I returned to our group, and I shared this story with Joan and other group members, she touched her own heart in recognition. Her gesture moved me in a confirmation of its message and its power. William's present to me is really a present for all who behold it.

Then, at long last, it was off to Sai Baba's ashram. Many people believe that Sai Baba is the Divine Incarnate. We arrived at his ashram and were stunned to find a mini city. Indeed, we had to hand our passports to the authorities at the ashram. That was a most uncomfortable feeling.

The ashram followed a routine and recommended particular attire. Out of respect we dressed the part. Picture me draped in a traditional Indian garment, known as a Punjabi. As best I can describe, it is a long-sleeved gown that extends below the knees and is worn with matching and somewhat baggy pants. White was the preferred color at the ashram. This ensemble was covered by a head shawl that fell around the shoulders and hid one's breasts.

After dressing in this appropriate fashion, we were told to gather at five o'clock in the morning. We would not be forced to arrive at that hour. However, we felt great pressure to do so. Chanting and meditation would continue as everyone lined up, in sitting position on the ground, squeezed together. I called this "sardine fashion."

At the appointed hour we were ushered through security and into an open air temple, provided that we had first removed our sandals and left them outside the temple enclosure. Unfortunately for me, when herded into the crowd of people, I had forgotten to do this. I was admonished and directed to exit, after which the re-admittance process took another hour. Some 15,000 people from all parts of the world had gathered to await Sai Baba's appearance that morning. It was an amazing scene and being there felt humbling.

Our group had wanted a private interview and our request had been denied. However, on our final day they allowed all of us to sit in a row close to where Sai Baba walks. This was a special privilege that might allow us an opportunity to see the sage work some of his miracles. In particular, people sometimes saw *vibhuti,* an ash that manifests out of Sai Baba's hands.

Since we were sitting close to where he would walk, they told us to write a letter to him. He often took these letters and honored people's requests for healing or help with other spiritual needs.

At first, I resisted. Yet since we had to wait for so long, I kept hearing intuitively, *Write the letter.* I took a mini notebook from my pocket and scribbled a little letter. I did not expect anything to come of it, except for the nudging voice to stop. Soon thereafter, the moment arrived for Sai Baba to walk past our group.

We sat with letters in hand. Sure enough, he passed me right by. As I started to sit back into my kneeling position, I was startled by what happened next. From the energy wake that followed Sai Baba, almost into my face came a vision of William staring at me. I heard, *Beloved, be at peace. All was as it was meant to be and in divine order. All is well. Be at peace.* Then William's face disappeared. I felt as if a fireball of energy had been transmitted into my heart center. With this energy, my heart felt like a sponge being squeezed of every last pain of resistance to accepting destiny's call. The experience felt overwhelming.

I sobbed to the point where people who monitor the crowd almost asked me to leave. Apparently, I had become too loud and disruptive for them, yet mine was a spiritual release. I felt surprised at their reaction, as I thought that is exactly why people go to Sai Baba. He is a great spiritual master. Repeatedly I received the same message. In essence it was, "Accept, all is as it was meant to be."

After our visit to Sai Baba's ashram we moved on to Varanasi, the city where people who practice Hinduism want to go to die. Our group stopped at the sacred river, the Ganges, alongside which they burn bodies of the deceased on funeral pyres.

At dawn one morning, all of us made a pilgrimage to the river and boarded a small boat. As this boat moved down the river, we performed a holy ritual. We lit floating candles in memory of our deceased loved ones and released our candles to the river. As I watched the flickering lights of the candle flames that floated down the Ganges, symbolically I accepted William's ascension as the fulfillment of his destiny.

I recognized that the time had come for me to honor William's destiny in whatever way fulfilled mine. I hadn't brought any of William's ashes to cast into the river, so instead I collected some holy water to carry home in a small vial that I could place next to his urn. This water would be my gift to William from India.

Next, our group visited a holistic health center in India. Even though I had no need to consult a medical doctor, intuitively I felt drawn to see this one. He is a disciple of Sai Baba and a deeply spiritual man. His assistant conducted an extensive interview before the appointment.

When the doctor entered, he gazed into my eyes intently and spoke words that most doctors would never know. He expressed that what I had experienced in the loss of my husband was destiny fulfilling itself. Once again, this same message arrived through yet another person. His compassion and wisdom I found touching.

The doctor went on, "Many times for master teachers to be able to pass on the information, they have to live the experience, so others can accept their light and their teachings." He looked at me and continued, "You are one of those beings and it's your karma. You'll be fine." Some doctor he was!

The tour now ended. Members of our group expressed our love and appreciation to one another and bid tearful goodbyes. Mary and I did not leave India with the group. We departed to Mumbai (formerly Bombay) to visit one last spiritual master, Ramesh Balsekar.

During my time in Costa Rica, Nadeen had mentioned Balsekar, through whose writings Nadeen had awakened. Mary and I had not originally planned to seek out Balsekar, and we had no address for him. Yet intuitively it felt right to visit him.

With just his name, we approached a cab driver outside of our hotel and asked if he had heard of Ramesh Balsekar. Although that driver didn't know the man, he recognized the name. He called over his friend, who knew exactly where Baba Ramesh lived and where the teachings were held. What are the odds? His friend became our driver for the next three days. He drove us to Ramesh's home, where *Satsang* would be held by ten in the morning.

In order to sit in the presence of Ramesh, one had to arrive early. At the appointed hour, all who had gathered would rush up five flights of stairs in the dark. Ramesh conducted Satsang in a small room in his apartment, and the room held some thirty people. We found the other visitors to be mostly westerners from Europe and America. Ramesh himself had once been an Indian banker who had awakened and become a spiritual master. He is a simple man, with wonderfully articulate English.

On the day that we arrived, his topic was death. I would say, interesting timing. Since his teaching was basically that consciousness is all there is, and *I am that,* his question was, "Who dies?" This was quite an introduction for me to walk in on. I sat quietly, just receiving the information without asking questions.

In fact, in his affectionate way Ramesh seemed intimidating. A person would start by stating his or her name before asking a question. If Ramesh suspected that a person's name did not match the name on their passport, he would clap his hands together rapidly.

In a slightly raised voice he admonished, "Name on the passport!" Sheepishly the person would state his or her passport name. Ramesh would continue to listen. He didn't want to hear stories. He wanted questions. He responded to each in a sensitive manner unique to each person.

Ramesh's discourses illumined many aspects of consciousness. One question that I found especially fascinating was asked on the topic of enlightenment. The questioner wanted to know the difference in response between one who is, and one who is not, enlightened.

Ramesh answered that emotions are wired into the DNA and the brain just reacts. One who is enlightened experiences the emotions and they move right through. In one who is not enlightened. emotions arise, and the mind attaches meanings or questions to try to figure out the emotions. This process hinders the emotions from simply passing through.

He went on to demonstrate this truth with an example of a spiritual teacher. In one moment, the disciple may say something that engenders great anger. In the next moment, that anger has passed, and the teacher is laughing with the same disciple. All is well.

Ramesh continued that enlightenment is a concept that is often misunderstood. It does not mean that one does not have anger or other emotions. Enlightenment does not mean that the person is always in bliss. Life happens through each body-mind-organism. This life is merely witnessed, without any personal involvement or judging.

It wasn't until our final day there that my hand went up timidly. I stated my name, Tianna, with slight trepidation. I expected the usual admonishment. Instead, Ramesh graciously received my statement with, "Oh, my friend's wife's name is Tianna. How lovely." Feeling a bit guilty, I owned that it was not the name on my passport. He countered that it didn't matter, it was becoming to me.

Secretly, I regarded Ramesh's positive response as my own confirmation that the Infinite had accepted my new name. I then told Ramesh that I had a brief story before my question. I expected, "Question only!" Again, Ramesh surprised me. He welcomed my story. He listened attentively, intrigued by William.

He spoke words that were both compassionate and strong. "Tianna, you wouldn't be here unless you wanted truth. You were blessed with a spiritually awakened husband. Were you aware of that?" I nodded, *Yes*.

Ramesh continued, "He did complete his journey and fulfill his destiny. It seems that when Tianna likes the outcome, it's God's grace. When Tianna doesn't like the outcome, it's God's will. Tianna, all is God's grace. It's not about focusing on William's journey any longer. It was your destiny to witness and experience all that you did for your next step. Embrace it and go on."

I knew that with Ramesh's words I had received a powerful push and tender loving kick. This great sage had delivered a final piece of the puzzle in my grieving journey. His clear message was to let go and accept it all.

I found his words difficult to digest, and I now had to find the strength to do so. In my own way, I had to make peace with it all. I did so by defining our last kiss and my return from the Light as "fierce grace." Now I was ready. I realized that all of the memories that I had labeled good and bad were to be embraced with gratitude.

To show appreciation in the traditional Indian fashion, one would normally kneel and bow down at Ramesh's feet. When I had first entered and witnessed this custom, I had thought, *that'll be the day*. His compassion and wisdom had so touched me, however, that I found I had shifted inside. I, too, bowed at Ramesh's feet with deep respect.

Now the time had come to return home and officially start over.

CHAPTER FOUR

Starting Over

∞

With these journeys behind me, I realized that with each trip I had retrieved a different piece of the puzzle of grieving. The final piece had been given to me in India, or so I thought. As far as I was concerned my wholeness had finally been revealed. Back in New York, alone and exhausted, I now dreaded the arduous task of starting life over as a single woman in her mid-40's.

Midway through the second year without William, I saw myself as being at an awkward stage for widowhood. Again, I contemplated being too young to feel passionately fulfilled in life without a partner, and too old for the high degree of desirability that I'd been enjoying with the man of my dreams. As I grappled with awareness of my situation, my body began to reflect this conflict.

I had begun seeing clients again when something overwhelming happened. Near the end of one session I grew feverish and soon felt myself being pulled in and out of consciousness. Somehow, I managed to maintain enough awareness to complete the session.

As soon as my client had left, I lay down and collapsed, yet the fever escalated. Using a digital thermometer, I watched it climb to 104 degrees, at which point I passed out. I could sense leaving my body, and soon I found myself in a mystifying place. My body, lying on the bed, perspired and seemed at the point of melting. I hovered in a place where I could witness this phenomenon and not feel it. I had no fear because the place where I found myself was so peaceful. I knew that I existed as pure awareness, not a body and not a personality.

Whatever had happened to the "me" that I had known simply didn't matter anymore. I rested in a state where the decision whether to live or die would not be up to me. Call it God, call it consciousness, call it the Universe. This state had no name. It was infinite, compassionate, eternal love. I felt fine with whatever might happen, and in this space, I discovered an amazing sense of liberation. I had no attachment to living, and yet no longing to die.

If this were to be my time, life had been a great ride. With all of its ups and downs my life had been an incredible adventure. I felt ready to let it be. At the same time if destiny had more to unfold, I knew that I'd be back. So, I remained in an awareness of simply being in this place peacefully, just hanging out. Suddenly a force shot through me and I found myself back in my body. Physical life had won again.

As I returned to normal consciousness, I discovered that I had just received a tremendous gift. Abruptly gone was the life-and-death struggle that had raged inside of me for so long. I had experienced a major shift. In a subtle and dramatic way, from intense fever and expansive peace, that struggle had at last found resolution.

I also realized a truth that set me free in ways that I had never known I needed. I lived in a body that remained weak from fever and needed to rebuild. Yet this situation could not compare in any way, on any level, to the weakness and debilitation that William had suffered. This is to say nothing of the strength he would have had to mobilize if he had wanted to face the ordeal of rehabilitation. My experience with this sudden fever served to deepen my compassion for all that William had endured.

Also, from within that burning fever I realized that had I been in William's situation, I would not have wanted to be moved or disturbed while the fever raged. I had rested in a peaceful state outside of my body form. William, on December 7, had quietly dropped his body.

My former torment and guilt, that if I had called 911 sooner, even though everything happened so rapidly maybe the paddles would have brought him back. It had been an illusion, and that illusion now faded. After my experience with fever, I knew that William's path had already been determined. He had made his wishes clear, and he had left no time for me to make a phone call for help. Therefore, he had experienced a loving, sheltered passing, as an ascension. I finally realized the power of my last act of unconditional love. I had allowed William to leave me in a way that had honored his destiny rather than my own wishes.

I had once wanted William to remain with me in the physical no matter what. This was not to be. My remaining grief had now been burned out of my body, through the wisdom of the Divine within. Lovingly I named this experience my "millennium fever." For me it would become the beginning of a new age.

From now on, my grief would exist only in the moment. I still cried whenever memories surfaced. I no longer found myself pulled repeatedly into a whirlpool of the past. Instead I could allow emotion to move right through me. Rather than focusing on what I had lost, I was determined to focus on the good that I had in the present. I could then enjoy the next moment as life unfolded. My legacy was never going to be a lifetime of regrets.

Then a fortuitous thing happened. The doctor who had been so helpful to me in India arrived in New York. I noted the seeming coincidence of his presence soon after my fever, and immediately I made an appointment to see him. As he entered the examining room he smiled and observed, "You are more at peace than when I last saw you."

I described to him the fever that I had experienced. He assured me that this fever had been the gift of my spiritual nature burning the pain out of my body. His explanation confirmed my intuition. He continued, "Don't be concerned with illness or diagnosis. Once this has passed, you will be strengthened and be better than ever." Indeed, I was.

The cosmic joke now became that I had grown emotionally stronger and financially weaker. Since I hadn't expected to live, I had spent my savings freely. Now my hope to die had been foiled. As I continued to live, I had depleted my savings. The time had clearly come for me to return to work full time. I felt ready to do that, and fully functional. However, the fire inside of me, the passion that I had always brought to my work, had diminished. I didn't know if that passion would ever return. I pressed on to do the best I could.

I increased my workload and found that I grew stronger and my work became more fulfilling every day. Yet inside of me I knew that both I and my work had begun to change. At that time, I had no idea of what would unfold, and it didn't matter. Surprised at how, from the broken pieces of Humpty Dumpty, I was being put back together again. I would continue to trust the process and just do what came in front of me.

The forces of the Divine, the continued antics of William, and the compassion and wisdom of spiritual companions, some whom I knew, and others whom I had just met, soon bordered on the miraculous. I knew that I had been blessed, and I felt humbled by that fact. My attention now focused on living each day as fully as I could, loving people in my life as fully as I could and giving to my work everything that I had.

Life as I had known it with William had ended forever. A new life had begun to emerge, a life that I could enjoy. It's often said that when

God closes a door, a window opens. I now felt ready to embrace that knowing, and I looked forward to perceiving life differently.

To begin this new perception, I relied on one of my old favorite routines: to meet, do, experience, or discover something new each day. I began to socialize with friends on a more regular basis and to pursue creative projects and passions, such as theater.

I have always regarded theater as the invisible Divine that speaks to me through each performance. Mysteriously, each play would hold great meaning that reflected whatever I was experiencing. Thus, a play often revealed guidance for my life. Ready now to move forward, I felt open to receiving whatever messages would help me do so.

One thing missing, however, was my opening up the possibility of being with a new man. I viewed such a step as a daunting leap. I believe in honest communication for deeper intimacy. How could I have that communication, and also tell a man that my late husband hovered nearby? It's challenging enough when an ex-husband lingers after a divorce. Most people have come to accept such a reality, even though sometimes they resent it. I found myself in a quandary. I decided that since William now wanted me to move on, maybe he could help me do so. I addressed him directly.

Our conversation went something like this:

William, it's hard to imagine loving another man physically after being so fused with you, especially, you scoundrel, after the last time we made love. I don't mean in the dream, either. I'm a passionate woman, as you know. I desire to celebrate and enjoy the physical love that you can no longer provide.

Here is my proposition. I think you have a better overview of men than I do. I would like to experience the ultimate fantasy with which I indulged you when you wanted two women. I want two men, one on each side of the dimensional veil; you in spirit, and someone else in the physical who can embrace all of me and not feel threatened by you or by the love we share. I want someone who is spiritually evolved enough to recognize that our eternal love is part of me, part of my uniqueness. Our love would include him fully and would benefit all concerned. He would need to know that in the physical, he is my number one priority. He will get all of my love, attention, passion, and devotion with your blessing.

All I heard back was laughter, which I took to mean that William was now on the case.

One evening in November I found myself in Manhattan, having spent the day with a friend who had needed to leave early for a meeting. I thought I'd go to the theater. Unfortunately, as I arrived at TKTS, a discount ticket outlet, I found them closing up. I thought, I *guess the Divine wants me to have an early night.* I didn't feel like going home though.

I sent out a teasing challenge. If *anyone out there is listening, I'd like to have a fun and safe adventure.* I then began to walk toward Grand Central Station, a few blocks from the theater district. If an adventure occurred, I'd participate. If not, I'd take the train home. As I walked down 42nd Street, suddenly I felt a touch of energy on my shoulder. I looked around and saw no one. As I continued to walk, the tug of energy grew stronger. I heard, Okay*, you wanted adventure. Go into that building. There is a man you need to meet.*

The building in question held the Bryant Park Grill, a lovely restaurant and bar in the refurbished park behind the New York Public Library. It's one thing for me to send out a challenge like that. It's quite another thing, however, to receive a challenge back.

I had eaten at the Grill before and had enjoyed the place immensely. I wouldn't find it unnerving to go there. I thought I'd step inside, take a table, and order an appetizer. That would be simple enough, something I could handle.

I asked to be seated and learned that the tables were only for dinner. Appetizers could be ordered at the bar. Now, that was a whole other picture. I had never before walked up to a bar alone with the intention of meeting a stranger. What kind of adventure had I gotten myself into?

I made it into the room and intended to follow through. However, I didn't have the nerve to approach the bar itself. I saw no empty spaces there anyway. Noticing some tables nearby I figured, *These tables are okay, they're not for dinner. I 'll sit there and ponder my next step.*

This was New York City, where it's rare for anyone to sit at a table without eating, drinking or conversing with someone. I felt awkward and came up with an easy remedy! I pulled out my cell phone and spoke into it and looked as if I were waiting for someone. Who would know that I had no one on the other end?

I started talking and spoke aloud, "Okay, I'm here at the bar. What do I do now?"

The voice in the non-existent connection replied, *Be patient. In minutes, a few people will leave the bar. There will be an open seat. Sit there.*

Having received my instructions, I nodded and looked up. Just as foretold, people left, and one stool remained vacant. I hesitated, then telepathically I heard in my right ear, *Move, and do it now.* I did as I was told. I sat on the bar stool, hardly believing what I'd gotten myself into.

The bartender asked what I wanted to drink. I knew I'd better not drink at all. I mentioned that I'd rather see the appetizer list. I buried myself in it, whereupon my invisible partner admonished, *Stop hiding, turn to the man on your left and say hello.*

Attempting such a task took all of my courage. I turned to my left and noticed the man was smoking. Turning back to the right where my invisible partner stood, I beamed telepathically, *He's smoking.*

Without missing a beat, the voice urged sternly, *Get over it. Start there.*

I could resist the nudging no longer. I turned to my left and found an attractive man in his 50's. He had a beard and mustache and smoked a brown, rolled cigarette.

"I notice you're smoking," I commented.

He replied with annoyance, "This is a bar. You can smoke here."

I responded quickly, "I'm not making you wrong for smoking. I noticed it's a brown cigarette. What is it?"

Puzzled, he looked at me and answered, "It's a special, organic tobacco cigarette." To this he added in an almost guilty fashion, "I know, it's still tobacco, and will probably still kill me."

I surprised him by saying, "Well, personally, I believe that destiny takes care of that. In regard to the cigarette, I believe the pesticides do more damage than the tobacco."

That remark must have captured his attention. He eyed me inquisitively and asked, "Who are you?" I introduced myself as Tianna and let him know that I was into alternative healing. He told me his name was Alan. A surprising spiritual connection began to form at the bar.

Alan continued to look at me and he speculated, "The name Tianna is a bit unusual. Is it a spiritual name?"

I replied, "You could say that." I figured I had nothing to lose by telling the truth about how it came to be, and about my adventures with William in the afterlife. After all, this Alan was merely a man in a bar. I felt safe knowing that I would never have to see him again.

I told him about how Tina from three years old had now expanded to Tianna after my soul mate, William, had dropped his body. "We were kind of soup and sandwich," I confided. I even made the joke, "With the sandwich gone, the soup stands alone." I also risked telling this stranger how William had guided me to meet him at the bar.

Alan, humorously touched by this notion, began to share his own truth. At the moment when we met, he had been talking to God. His life had begun to fall apart, his wife had divorced him, and his business faced bankruptcy. Despondent, he asked for proof of God's existence. *Send me a soul mate or an angel,* he had pleaded mentally. Then he looked me straight in the eye and chuckled. "You found me." So much for being strangers.

Alan and I couldn't stop holding hands, looking into each other's eyes, and sharing from the depths of our being. We never even ordered a drink. At least for that moment, we seemed intoxicated with each other.

We needed to leave. Staff had begun to clean the bar around us in preparation for closing. Alan offered, "You know the George Harrison song that is appropriate here?" The Beatles had been one of my favorite musical groups and I had always found their words inspirational. However, I didn't know which of the many songs he referred to. Alan smiled and answered, "All things must pass." I knew it was time to go.

We left the bar together, strolled toward Grand Central Station, and stopped at Fifth Avenue and 42nd Street. There on the corner we embraced each other in a hug that wouldn't let go. We parted with tender words such as, "It's hard to leave you, and we must."

I had scribbled my phone number and name on the paper that Alan held in his hands. I exclaimed, "It's been a wonderful adventure meeting you. If I'm never to see you again in this lifetime, I wish you a great one."

He responded, "I'll call you."

I'm sophisticated enough as a woman to know not to count on it. I told him teasingly, "That would be lovely, and I would welcome a call. It needs to come from you."

I returned home that evening filled with wonder at what had transpired. What are the odds, in New York City, of walking into a bar and meeting a complete stranger who resonated with spiritual knowing, afterlife adventures, and soul mate love? In just one evening, our connection became a significant enough one that it has since blossomed into a mystical friendship.

In my hot tub communication back at home, I just relaxed and heard laughter, *All in good time.* I knew that my mischievous beloved had guided me to a very special man. Although Alan would not be my future mate, meeting him showed me that anything was possible.

I had even confided to Alan my intimate fantasy of having two men, one on each side of the veil. Alan's exact words were, "That works for me." *All in good time* would serve as a fine beginning.

The following month, as I faced a new century, I performed my usual New Year's Eve ritual. I was grateful for how life had begun to emerge again in its light. After having lamented for so long that with William's passing the light had gone out of my life, I could no longer claim that it had. I still found being without William in the physical world to be difficult, yet I had adjusted to enjoying him in the energy world. I would not have imagined that our future would take such a course. No one had ever said that "happily ever after" meant without a body, turning into "happily in the hereafter." However, William provided love and support in a most outrageous fashion.

While my inner life seemed to have entered its rebuilding phase, my body soon fell into a strange debilitating phase. Instead of feeling physical vitality I perceived the growth of a strange new discomfort. At first, I ignored this change, thinking it temporary. However, as the months passed, I also noticed unusual symptoms. Since my body had always served me well, even through all of my emotional pain, I found these symptoms alarming and even ironic. When I had wanted to die, I couldn't. Now that I felt ready to live, what was happening?

My abdomen began to blow up as if I was pregnant, and I experienced severe pains. I worked with alternative therapies, not wanting to face the medical route. Finally, the pain grew so intense that even if the worst were happening and I had become ill, I figured I would rather know. I went in for medical tests, and a curious realization that would climax my grieving journey began to unfold in symbolic form.

The doctors needed to check for an ovarian tumor. My beloved had had testicular cancer. This was an interesting turn of events. I was scheduled for all sorts of diagnostic tests to determine what might be going on. Only then did I realize that I was alone and frightened. I had given William a great gift of being there with him every step of the way, including through every test.

Much to my surprise, when I went for the tests alone, I sensed William's presence. He now began to do for me what I had done for him. In order to help me get through them he likened these tests to rides at Disney World. *Close your eyes. You're going on a ride,* I heard telepathically. As I lay there having a sonogram, I heard William laughing by my side. I felt reassured.

Within this new awareness, I suspected that my illness was a symbolic one and everything would be fine. It was as if my body, in its creativity, had expressed birthing of a new me through symptoms that resembled an illness.

Unconsciously I had tortured myself for falling short in my compassion, and for not understanding what William had gone through. I had done the best I knew how. Truly, unless one is going through it, the experience is impossible to grasp. I had wanted to do it all; save William, heal him, and be his ultimate lover and spiritual partner.

The truth is that I was human and could not possibly fulfill all of these expectations. However, I now realized the gift that I did provide, and I focused on that. If someone who loves you is by your side as you face the challenges that life presents, especially the cancer journey, you are indeed blessed. In that aspect I had been a star. I needed to give myself credit and honor the role I had played. This realization would set me free.

I underwent the tests. Whenever I face a difficult task, I try to balance it with a reward at the end. My reward at the end of all of these tests was to go to the theater. As I stood in line to purchase a ticket I heard, No, *no, not that ticket. Go to the street corner.* Normally I would ignore a request like that, street corner for tickets? I recognized that voice, and I moved to the corner as instructed.

A well-dressed woman approached me and commented casually that she had been given two complimentary tickets to *Aida,* tickets that she couldn't use. She wanted to sell them. How did forty dollars sound? My rational mind reminded me of the last time I had done that. Naively I had lost my money to a scalper.

The laughter in my ear remained incessant. It urged, *Take them they're a gift.* If purchased at the box office each ticket would have cost eighty dollars, and this was two for half that price. How could I go wrong?

In situations that require a risk I ask myself, *What's the worst that can happen? If I can live with its consequences, go for it.* I decided, *Why not?* In this case the worst that could happen would be the loss of 40 dollars. The best was that for half price I would get to take in a sold-out Broadway play that I longed to see. Even as I pondered what to do, William's laughter continued. I held the 40 dollars in my hand. The woman assured me that I would be sitting next to her. I bought the tickets. Even though one was all I needed, I figured I'd call friends to see if anyone was available at the last minute. If not, I would pass the remaining ticket on to a stranger as my gift.

I went to the play knowing that *Aida* was the story of forbidden and timeless love, set in Egypt. I arrived late. As I slipped into my seat quietly, a spectacular scene unfolded on stage. At that exact moment a replica of the mystical, all-knowing eye of the Egyptian god Horus began to open its lid.

Telepathically I heard, *Beloved, physical eyes cannot see through the veils of illusion known as separation. Death is the greatest illusion of them all. Open your spiritual eye of knowing. Only it can see, and the heart knows the truth that there is no separation. You are not alone, and no one is alone. Trust it.*

I cried as I watched the play. Some of the words that the lovers spoke were identical to words that William and I had shared before he passed. These words were of our love, of our truth, and of how painful we found it not to be able to express our love to the world, as fully as it was. The play, and my experience with William, held so many similarities that each one took my breath away.

What moved me most were the lovers' vows that if they were to be separated physically, they'd reunite and find each other as soon as possible. I remembered the time when William and I first united and he had brought home a movie called *Made in Heaven.* In it the lovers had been separated, the man in heaven and the woman on earth. By a certain period of time the one in heaven was to come down and find the one on earth.

William had played this movie for me, with the message that we had found each other in time. That was also when he proclaimed that we had been married in heaven. We enjoyed that union in the physical during this lifetime. Was that physical union merely Part One? Now had he joined me again, from heaven, in this lifetime? Was this Part Two?

In the opera *Aida,* two lovers from Egypt come together in a future century. Was William, by leading me to this production, letting me know that he and I had also reunited? We lacked only his physical body? I continued to cry through the entire story, which reflected these messages to me right through to the closing scene.

At the end, before curtain call, the stage revealed a background of stars twinkling in the evening sky, with one star shining brightest. It reminded me of the shooting star that I had seen in St. Lucia. William's laughter then broke in and I heard the words, *I'm your guiding star now.*

When the opera ended, I turned and thanked the woman, who indeed sat next to me. She had given me an incredible gift, one that extended beyond what she could have imagined. All the way home, I cried and cried. The next morning, I understood deep in my soul that William and I remained together. Our relationship continued-only the forms had changed. This truth was just as he had promised in the mystical love letters I had received after his passing. For the first time since 1997 I celebrated what my heart and soul already knew. It was time to stop longing for death and start embracing life totally.

I had yearned for death, so I could be reunited with my beloved. The truth is that he had never left me. His words of, "We can never be separated, there is no end to our love," proved wise beyond my knowing.

We had always believed that the power of our love could get us through anything, and that nothing could keep us apart. Despite the many obstacles we faced, from our controversial beginning, to cancer, we always proclaimed our love was true and timeless. Could that love possibly be defying the mysteries of death?

With all that had transpired, I had been disillusioned. Two years had now passed since William had left. It had taken me two years to realize that he remained by my side.

That morning, I found myself able to do something that previously I had found impossible. For the first time I took out William's picture, which I had hidden in my drawer. I gazed into his face once again. The eyes that looked back at me were burning through the illusion and filled with love. I felt happy for the first time in two years. A new journey had dawned.

CHAPTER FIVE

Step by Step

∞

The first symbolic act by which I embraced my new life, and my transformed relationship with William, was to find a place for his picture. This place needed to allow William's image to serve as an inspiration, not an interruption. What manifested was the idea of an altar to honor his memory.

On a shopping trip that weekend I found a perfect table in the form of a camel, in tribute to our Egyptian connection. On it I placed our picture in a frame that depicted twin flames and a small love bear that held meaning for us. Even now this altar changes dynamically as I continue to add pieces that capture our legacy.

With this altar now in place, the time had come for a new legacy of my own. It began with two phone calls.

One call, to my medical doctor, Salvatore, gave me assurance that despite the appearance of a distended abdomen and pains, my health was fine. Upon hearing this, I realized that any symptoms had been symbolic of pregnancy and of birthing myself. Indeed, soon after this awareness my physical manifestations cleared as mysteriously as they had begun. I could now enjoy a new beginning from the inside out.

I waited and wondered what would come next. I didn't have long to wait. No sooner had I hung up the phone with the doctor than it rang with a call that would change the course of my life. In fact, it was an opportunity that would set me in a new direction. It was my friend Dianne, of Dreamtime Journeys. She was busy organizing two cruises for the coming fall season, she wanted me to know about them. I assumed that she hoped I would take one of the voyages, but I didn't think it was the right time for me to travel. I had just started my new life and thought I needed to stay home for a while.

Her message surprised me. "No, Tianna, I don't want you to come along as a passenger. I want you to be a speaker."

I couldn't believe what I was hearing, me, a speaker? She was inviting me, not on one, but on two cruises? I hadn't done public presentations in more than five years. I felt ill equipped, rusty, and unready! I had endless excuses. Despite my protests, Dianne pressed on and adamantly refused to take "No" for an answer.

Exasperated, I questioned her. "What do you want me to talk about?"

She answered spontaneously, "What you've been through. This cruise is about life and death. You're perfect."

I told her that I had barely assimilated my experiences. The thought of speaking in front of a group felt like a stretch. October lay right around the corner. Dianne assured me that I would be fine, and she even teased me back. "Say yes, because we may not even get enough participants, and would have to cancel the trip. Let the Universe be your guide."

With this assurance, I surrendered and worked closely with Dianne to make up a bio and a workshop description. I titled one workshop "Circle of Life." In an ironic twist, Dianne thought that would be a great title for the entire cruise. It soon became the voyage's theme. My workshop title changed to "Life as an Infinite Journey." The second workshop would be called "Spiritual Hedonism." The die was cast.

I put both cruises out of my mind, attended to living in the present, and became fully engaged in my private practice. I associated once again with colleagues in my field. During this third year after William's passing, life had become dynamic, both professionally and personally.

One intriguing meeting occurred through my friend Sally, whose connections had always seemed magical. This experience was no exception. Sally had faced some health challenges and she enlisted my aid in consulting with her new holistic physician, a man named Neil. What began as a simple call to a colleague over a healing issue soon expanded into an awesome encounter. Yes, we spoke about Sally, and then so much more.

In moments our talk turned more intimate as we recognized that we could safely share with each other our innermost thoughts and feelings about love and soul mate connection. Neil became the first man with whom I could speak who comprehended fully the love that William and I had savored. Neil was living that same depth of love with his own wife. His ability to listen with compassion and wisdom was immense. After several hours of speaking together on the phone we felt compelled to meet.

In a matter of days Neil came to my house. I welcomed him in and soon discovered a deep feeling of familiarity with him. He appeared to be in his late thirties, handsome and portly, with dark hair pulled back into a small ponytail. Immediately our connection became obvious, and meeting in physical form solidified our friendship.

Out the door we went, to a spiritual healing center that Neil wanted to show me. This center was located at a nearby estate on the water and was run by a medical colleague. Neil and I walked the grounds of the estate and I thanked him for the tour. Yes, I would be interested in participating in the center and would go to the next advisory board meeting.

Neil and I returned to my house expecting a simple goodbye. This was neither to be simple nor a mere goodbye. Neil wanted to share with me something special that he had created, an album that depicted the journey of soul mates. In it, two souls had been separated and longed to find each other. Disillusioned at first by false possibilities, after many attempts they finally came together and made their union permanent.

This book had been Neil's engagement album. He had assembled it for his wife when he had asked her to marry him. I was moved to tears that Neil trusted me with something so intimate. I also identified with its essence.

Our next period of time together occurred after the planned board meeting. Neil accompanied me home and we settled together on my sapphire blue Cleopatra couch in the living room. As we did so, an amazing energy force seemed to be present. We both felt it, yet neither of us verbalized or acted upon it in any way. We found ourselves mesmerized by a power of attraction of love and lust.

We resisted this energy with everything in us. As a matter of fact, we both pressed on as if nothing was happening. Each of us hoped secretly that the other wouldn't notice. We brought our evening to an abrupt end. Each in our own fashion, to dilute this energy of attraction. We did not have further contact for months.

Only after a long hiatus, after which Sally needed another consultation, did Neil and I speak again. At that time both of us knew that we had to address what had happened earlier. We were intrigued to discover that our attraction had been a mutual experience.

Neil began, "I have something to confess that I thought I'd never tell you, and I need to. That night when we were together on your couch, it wasn't me alone with you."

Not understanding him clearly, I prompted, "Say more."

Neil replied that he had been having thoughts and feelings about me that were foreign to his commitment to his wife. These feelings had tormented him so much so that he had consulted with his own healer to work them out. In that process he discovered something that stunned, relieved, and annoyed him.

He went on to say that he had felt William's energy to be present around his own body, urging him to reach out and embrace me. Neil had admonished William that he, too, wanted to be here to support me. Still, he had his limits that needed to be respected. Quite easily William released his influence.

I laughed and confessed that now I understood my own impulses, too. With William having hovered so close to Neil, I had felt a magnetic draw. Now all was well between Neil and me. Neil even shared this experience with his wife, who enjoyed it with a teasing comment.

It was confirmed to me now to be more than a suspicion that William was up to delightful support with my male companions. After all, as a gifted healer Neil was sensitive to energies. Also, it had been Neil, and not I, who first intimated that William had had a hand in our impulses. Neil had come to me with that knowing. This disclosure freed me to trust the process.

So, in my usual fashion, while soaking in my hot tub I thanked my invisible beloved. I encouraged him to keep up the good work. I assured him that I would do my part in staying open to him and to the possibility of a new mate. William's laughter then came through clearly. His message remained the same, *All in good time.*

Somehow, I sensed that William didn't think I was ready for a mate. The men who had begun to come into my life were extremely high caliber, spiritually evolved, and good looking. Each relationship became unique and extraordinary. I felt blessed and grateful.

William knew my tastes well and he was doing a great job. His awareness of my state of readiness, or lack thereof, remained quite sensitive. He demonstrated this awareness in a lighthearted way one evening when I felt a prompting to go to the Internet and scroll down through the personals. I had never done such a thing, and the joke of this is that I'm not even computer literate. Yet the urgings had been strong and my curiosity intense, so off to the Internet I went.

I found it fascinating to read name upon name of tempting men who sought contact. I had no idea where to begin. Who do you think broke through my trepidation? It was his laughter! The familiar sound of

William's trademark chuckle. Some things never change. I continued to scroll down until I heard, *Stop.* I did so, and then I read the entry.

It turned out that the man in the next listing was in his fifties and he sought a spiritually evolved and metaphysical woman who would be open to friendship and possibly more. I believed I qualified. I replied with a brief e-mail. Not knowing the etiquette of online dating, I actually included my first name and my phone number. To my delight, the man called the next morning and we arranged to meet that day.

This man's name was Bill, he lived in the same state as William's former home, and he was himself a healer. What are the odds? To me, these facts alone offered proof of intervention. My belief intensified, however, when Bill handed me his card. It actually included the words "divine healing." The only other person I knew who had used the word "divine" in relation not only to healing but as a signature for the touch of the mystical had been . . . you guessed it. William's ministry had been known as The Church of Divine Intervention. Need more be said?

Thanks to William I had safely been navigated through the world of the personals. As an added treat, I had even met a wonderful man who awakened me in a personalized way to the healing powers of chocolate. His compassionate understanding of the challenges I had been through motivated him to whip up a batch of chocolate truffles. His unique recipe, which blended exotic spices with the chocolate, tinged them with a flavor that hit the mark. I had long heard that contained within chocolate is a chemical, phenylethylalanine that raises endorphins inducing subtle pleasure. His concoction surpassed expectation. My motto became, *A chocolate a day keeps depression at bay.* Never did I realize that his gift of chocolate would so help to ease my pain. To this day we are friends and colleagues.

Time now drew closer to the cruise that my friend Dianne had organized, and it seemed as though the voyage would take place after all. I needed to prepare, or so I thought. I began to jot down notes to share about the experiences I had lived through during the previous three years. Chronologically it seemed like a short time, yet the immensity of all that had occurred felt overwhelming.

Then a dream provided me with an amazing breakthrough. It featured William who embraced me, kissed me gently on the lips and placed in my hand a circular object of light. I woke with no idea of the significance of this orb. The dream occurred on a Thursday. My first thought was that Thursday had always been our special day. Pleased that William had visited me on that day, I soon became aware that a shift had taken place within me. Because of the dream, this was the first Thursday that I felt comforted, without the usual pangs of pain. At first, I assumed that the ball of light had brought this comfort. It had served as a magic pill to take away the pain. Grateful, I thought nothing more about it, at least until that weekend.

On Sunday I experienced a memorable and powerful session with a client named Natalie, regarding communication with the dead. Natalie, a psychically sensitive bereavement specialist, had begun to suffer an emotional upheaval over the death of a man who had sexually molested her when she was a child. We opened our session seeking emotional release and closure. However, it soon turned into something far deeper.

Both of us had trained in Gestalt therapy. We agreed to call in the Spirit of this man so that Natalie could address her issues of unfinished business. As I encouraged her, she verbalized the pain of what she had gone through. What soon transpired was an intervention of mediumistic nature.

Both of us felt a presence enter the room. We had the sense that someone else was listening. Neither of us wanted to admit this fact at first. The energy soon became so strong that the gifts I possess, mediumistic gifts that the Brazilian healers had warned me to use with caution, activated spontaneously. I recognized this opening when Natalie uttered the words of her anguish, that by dying, this man had gotten away with what he had done.

Both of us paled at what we heard next. *I didn't get away with anything.* In that moment a most unusual healing process began to unfold. Natalie and her perpetrator entered a dialogue, which I facilitated. This exchange continued until she had fully expressed her truth, and the presence had fully received it. They worked it out with each other and reached a mutual resolution.

When they had completed their exchange, Natalie expressed her willingness to forgive him. This forgiveness set both of them free, whereupon the presence departed. Natalie and I were left in awe and gratitude at the immensity of what we had just participated in and witnessed. The session over, I walked her to the door and assumed that I would now rest and integrate the experience. It was not to be so. I heard, *You're ready. Write, write, write.*

Exhausted, I protested, *Not now.* The energy persisted. Quickly I grabbed a pad and pen. As fast as my hands could write, I took down the dictation I heard. It began, *The body does die. The emotional pain of the physical loss is real. We never die and love never dies.*

In those first pages of transmission, the words that I heard focused on the seeming extinguishing of William's light and the loss of our union. Lingering questions remained, questions such as, *How could all that love die? Is there more?* This transmission brought up intense emotions within me. After an hour of listening and writing, I felt as though I had blown a fuse.

I knew that I was being compelled to write, yet I also knew that I could not do it alone. The amount of emotional intensity involved, combined with the fact that I don't type, made writing seem impossible.

I turned to the heavens, to the Divine, to William, to whoever wanted me to do this writing. I pleaded, *If this was meant to be and I am interpreting the message correctly that I need to write, send me a partner. Let it be a person who can facilitate the process and provide the support needed to hold the space for such intimacy to be shared.*

Previously I had tried to write with others, but to no avail. I felt like Goldilocks. One writer changed my words too much, another writer didn't add enough, and a third writer became all emotionally distraught. In a quandary as to what to do, I surrendered without another thought. It was time for the cruise.

As I prepared for the voyage, a slight twist occurred that could have waylaid the trip entirely. Above my lip I noticed a strange looking mark that had a dark aura around it. On the surface this mark appeared negligible, as if it were a whitehead that needed to be popped. Something inside kept gnawing at me to get it checked.

I relented and visited a dermatologist, and at first, he dismissed the mark as sun damage. Upon reconsidering with respect for my intuition, he decided to be on the safe side and do a biopsy. The result was a diagnosis of basal cell skin cancer. He recommended immediate surgery to remove it, stating that possibly it would require plastic surgery because of its sensitive location.

Interestingly enough, I sensed another eerie reliving of William's journey. I had been the one to pass my hand over William's testicles and discover his tumor. Now I had passed my hand over my lip, only to discover a mini version of the same. William's cancer had been diagnosed in October.

Here was mine, also in October. He, too, had had a cruise looming on the horizon. His had been the mildest of the malignant cancers; mine was the mildest of the skin cancers. Both cancers were rare, his for a man in his 40's, mine for someone with olive skin. Both cancers had appeared in sensitive sexual regions, his testicle and mine the lips. Each of us respectively regarded these areas as our greatest assets. What to do?

Although most people in my situation would opt for surgery, intuitively I didn't see that option as right for me. Even with the emotional progress that I had made, my pain of the previous few years had been overwhelming. The stress had taken a great toll. I wasn't surprised that a mild cancer had surfaced. I knew that ninety-five percent of the underlying cause of all disease is based on stress.

In pondering my situation, I recognized three key factors in my decision. Integral to my way of living I acknowledged that we're spiritual beings who experience physical challenges. The mind- body dynamic was an important one for me to explore. After all, since childhood I had perceived the body as a living organism. I often referred to cells as having the ability to listen to our thoughts. How could I ignore that now? To me healing has always been an inside job, the body being a partner with its inner wisdom and innate ability. In many ways, I considered symptoms as messages from the soul and the body as its living metaphor. Lastly, I referenced the wisdom of Louise Hay, a teacher whom I respected. Her book validated that grief and emotions can eat away at the body and contribute to cancer.

These realizations were all I needed to go forward with confidence. Being a speaker on the upcoming cruise offered deeper purpose and meaning for my life. I didn't want to jeopardize that opportunity.

The cruise won out. I knew that destiny's plan was already in motion. I had the beginnings of a new life that would expand to a larger audience. I felt willing to risk it. My fear was tinged with excitement over the infinite possibilities that lay before me. There was no way I could turn back now.

CHAPTER SIX

Living Bridge

∞

The much anticipated and somewhat daunting day had finally arrived. It was October 21, 2000 and I set off for the airport to fly to Genoa, where I would meet the first of two cruises. En route I made a slight detour. It happened that the Indian doctor whom I had seen twice earlier had arrived in town. I could consult with him on how to handle the skin cancer.

The doctor assured me that the spot above my lip represented an inner pattern that I needed to shift. He alluded to this pattern as having to do with the long ordeal I had experienced with losing William. After giving me some homeopathic remedies, the good doctor wished me well on this journey that would truly serve as my professional "coming out." He sent me off with a hug and a "bon voyage."

After a smooth flight, albeit a long one, to Italy, I arrived at Genoa's crowded airport. I joined other passengers on a shuttle bus that would take us to the bus terminal. Every passenger wore an appropriate label that indicated which cruise ship to board. I was going to meet a bus for the ship *Costa Victoria.* As I waited in line for this bus, fate played its first hand.

Next to me stood an attractive woman in her late 50's whose striking nail polish caught my attention. However, what beckoned to me was something other than her nails. I followed an intuitive hunch. Who was she? I didn't recognize her. My curiosity tugged at me to learn her name, although in a subtle fashion. I didn't want to seem too forward.

I struck up a rather casual conversation about her fingernails. As we began to talk, she mentioned that she was from Maryland and planned to take the cruise to the western Mediterranean. In an instant I flashed on my memory of the other speakers on the "Circle of Life" cruise. That was all I needed to trust my intuition.

"Janet Cunningham?" I asked boldly.

With a startled look the woman replied, "Yes, how did you know? I didn't expect anyone in Italy to know who I am."

I laughed and introduced myself as Tianna, a fellow speaker. Our immediate camaraderie would continue throughout the cruise.

This camaraderie became especially evident on the evening of Janet's presentation. After a day of touring in Tunisia our small seminar group gathered for her workshop on the interlife. This is the period of time that the soul spends in spirit. During her introduction Janet brought out a picture of the Egyptian image known as "The Weighing of the Heart." This image captivated me. Janet spoke of it passionately, with a depth of understanding that extended beyond intellectual knowledge.

When she began to speak, my heart fluttered in recognition of a wisdom and a connection that reached beyond the present moment. I knew from my NDE that for me a heart flutter signals something important. Affectionately I refer to such a response as a "calling card." It always means, *Stay open, its meaning has deeper roots to destiny.* I focused on this signal and realized that it hinted a collaboration in regard to writing. However, since the full meaning of my inner signal had not yet become clear to me, I filed it away in my memory.

The next day was to be my own presentation, titled "Life as an Infinite Journey." The evening before, as I prepared for my talk, I became aware of William joining me on this adventure. Mine was to be the last of the scheduled workshops. With each presentation having built upon the others, expectations for the final workshop ran high.

A bit nervous, I soon felt a peaceful reassurance in the guise of an embrace from William. His message was, *Go to sleep and trust that, in the morning when you wake up, the right words will be there, and so will I.* Following the whisperings of my invisible beloved had the usual effect of lulling me into a peaceful night's rest.

In the morning, just as predicted, I knew exactly what I needed to do. It wasn't at all what I had planned. Instead it felt intuitively right that I share the intimate story of my NDE. This decision surprised me, as I had not even considered doing so. I had never shared this story with any but close friends. In addition to relating the experience, I was to structure partner exercises to give participants an experiential awareness of the messages that I shared. I had no idea how I would accomplish such a task. Then I heard laughter and I knew that all would be well.

I needn't have worried. The workshop was well received, after which I felt well relieved. Indeed, for presenters and participants alike, all that remained was a closing discussion to mark the end of our series of highly successful seminars. With applause and appreciation given generously, everyone felt free to explore our scheduled shore excursions with abandon.

Our first port of call was Palma De Mallorca, Spain, with its pearl factory. I expected only to enjoy watching the process of crafting pearls into fine jewelry. This experience proved fascinating in and of itself. It paled with what came next. We entered the showroom and soon found ourselves overwhelmed with dozens of counters, each of which displayed a myriad of jewels. Where does one begin to look at them, much less make a purchase?

Before long, I discovered a counter of cultured pearls and had begun to investigate its offerings. I heard laughter and the words, *Over here-not that counter, this one.* Distracted, I followed the voice to a counter across the room.

Soon I beheld a most amazing single strand necklace, one side of which held pearls of shiny white, and the other side translucent gray. A teardrop pearl hung at its center. I found myself mesmerized by the beauty and one-of-a-kind features of this necklace.

When a saleswoman came over to ask if I were interested in it, I hesitated. I wanted to know the price first, for fear that I would find its cost intimidating. William's laughter sounded in my ear as the woman said $99. I couldn't believe it. It felt to me as if they had dropped a zero from the price that I had expected. Thinking they were cultured pearls, I was stunned at having been fooled by costume jewelry.

As I turned away, I heard, *Get over it. They're perfect.* Stunned by this reproach, I examined the necklace more closely and without judgment. William's voice continued, *Your seminar was on the Circle of Life and the Agony and Ecstasy. The pearls are a celebratory symbol, capturing the essence of the dark and light as a never-ending circle. Wearing them around your neck is a reminder and a gift for speaking your truth. Congratulations. You did great.*

As in life, William knew my tastes well He never ceased to amaze me with his purchases, as usual with my credit card. As I continued around the store, I realized that not another single piece of jewelry contained light and dark pearls together in that split fashion. Humbled at how perfect these costume pearls were, I purchased the necklace with gratitude. It remains one of my most treasured pieces.

Our next port of call was Barcelona, Spain. The delightful thing about cruises is how one wakes in the morning in yet another location. This time

I selected a shore excursion to the vineyards and monastery of Montserrat. The journey would be an arduous all day event. My intuitive promptings had urged me to go. I could not have known that this visit would transform my life.

I soon realized that only one other member of our group, a man named Ricardo, had chosen this journey. All of the others had opted for the Picasso museum. Ricardo and I laughed as we discovered this fact, and promptly we sat together on the long bus ride that took us to the Codorniu vineyards, far from the Barcelona city limits.

We found both the scenery and the buildings breathtaking. One enters a building whose archways are surrounded by stained glass windows and huge monuments to bottles of sparkling wine. Soon I jokingly called this place "The church of the divine grape."

The highlight of our tour was a trolley ride into the deep basement of the vineyard, then along miles and miles past thousands of bottles. This magical ride was hypnotic.

After what seemed like a joy ride through "champagne heaven" we arrived in a room where they had prepared an array of bottles for us to experience. They popped open the corks and poured bubbly into our glasses freely, filling them as often as we wished. Ricardo and I each enjoyed a glass and chuckled that we were drinking first thing in the morning. What would people at home think?

After an obligatory stop at the vineyard gift shop, we were off by bus to the monastery. It seemed like an interesting combination of the sensual and the spiritual in one tour, from the underground caverns of the vineyard to the pinnacle of the mountain. As our bus climbed higher and higher toward the top, our journey began to feel like a pilgrimage.

Ricardo slept in a seat beside me as I conversed with fellow passengers. Our talk centered around the purpose of our cruise. The others were intrigued that I was a speaker on the topic of life and death.

As I shared with them, I mused on possible workshop titles: "The Passion of Life and The Passion of Death," or "Near-Death, Dear Life." They were fascinated. As we neared the top of the mountain our conversations expanded into spiritual mysteries. Unbeknownst to me, all this was leading to a mystical experience that would soon unfold.

I nudged the sleeping Ricardo to announce our arrival. We stepped off the bus to an immediate chill. We marveled at the dramatic difference in temperature between the cold of the mountaintop and the heat of the countryside below.

Our next awareness was of a monastery with huge rock formations behind it. We found the scene breathtaking. Tourists milled about the courtyard, their cameras clicking. Out of the comer of my eye I spotted a long line of people who waited to enter a building to see something. Upon inquiring, we learned that they were paying homage to the statue of something called the "Black Madonna." I commented to Ricardo, "Who is the Black Madonna?" Even though I had been raised Catholic I had no clue. "That will be the day that I'll stand in such a line for a statue."

We decided to explore the cathedral in the monastery itself. Entering, we encountered a standing room only crowd of people. We soon learned that a wedding was in progress and that we could watch it on the TV monitors at the periphery of the room. Content at first to witness the nuptials this way, we soon discovered that this was not to be.

Immediately I heard telepathically, *Stop looking at the TV monitors. Go to the front of the cathedral and stand behind the bride and groom.*

Recognizing this voice as that of William, telepathically I argued vehemently, *I have no right to push myself through a crowd like this and I won't do it.*

William remained insistent. *You need to be there.*

I surrendered. , I replied, *Okay, if you want me to go behind the bride and groom, make it happen.*

On cue, as if by magic, one person and then another began to move out of the way. In front of me a person stepped to the right and I moved forward. Then ahead of me someone moved left. I stepped forward again. Someone else exited, and I moved one more time. Gradually the path in front of me cleared. Before long I stood directly behind the front section of pews where the bride and groom continued to exchange vows.

I was now front and center and musing, *What's the deal?* After all, I had attended hundreds of weddings as well as performed many. I wondered, *What is it about this union of man and woman in marriage that is so important for me to see?* Trusting that William had a higher purpose for situating me so strategically, I challenged him. *So, I'm here. Now what?*

I heard, *Look up.*

I looked up and noticed nothing unusual in this Catholic cathedral. There was a cross with a crucified Christ upon it. I gave blessings. *Is that it?*

I heard again, *Look up.*

Amazed, I noticed something that I had never seen in any church. Diagonally vertical to the crucifix, a magnificent depiction of the ascended Christ overshadowed it. Now was the moment that began to reveal the deeper mysteries that had called me to that spot.

Simultaneously I heard, *The agony and the ecstasy. As you fully embrace the agony, the ecstasy emerges.* As I heard this statement in my head, something began to happen that involved energy. Suddenly I felt waves of love pass through the ascended image, down through the crucifixion, and straight into my heart. I started crying and shaking. The energy of love felt so intense that it reminded me of what I had felt in my NDE.

Again, I heard, *Look up.*

This time the ultimate force of the Divine began to hit me. I saw a little archway window from which this energy seemed to emanate. Behind that portal lay the sanctuary of the Black Madonna.

Waves of love intensified as they passed through my body. Expanded awareness began to flood through me. A quivering that shook me to the core made my knees weaken. Sensing that I might collapse, I spotted Ricardo off to my right. I called him over to catch my near fainting body.

Quickly he came to my side and held me as I shook with the energy. Tears streamed down my face. I could see Ricardo's bewilderment at what was happening. I wanted to reassure him that I was okay, and to share with him what was going on. All I could mumble was, "Let's go to the line."

With Ricardo's arms around me, helping to support my weakened body, slowly we left the cathedral. I never would have believed we would be joining the long line to honor the Black Madonna. Suddenly gone was my ego's earlier attitude. All I wanted to do was give to the Black Madonna my gratitude for the waves of love that extend beyond the pain of appearances.

I was realizing that the agony that Christ had suffered symbolized the ultimate brokenness of a human being. The ecstasy of ascension symbolized resurrection into the miraculous. Intuitively, I felt that for me, the message of the Black Madonna was one of accepting the darkness within ourselves and embracing its pain. In doing so, keeping the heart open allows for the possibility of transformation.

As best I could mutter, I blabbed nonstop to Ricardo about what was transpiring. I could see by the puzzled look on his face that he didn't totally follow me. To his credit, despite his confusion he provided the support and acceptance that I needed. I could express freely the thoughts and feelings of this experience. His ability to listen to me, without the need to understand, created a safe space. I then moved through my vulnerability into a balanced state, more aware of the here and now.

As soon as this shift occurred inside of me, a man in front of me turned and admonished me sternly. With rage in his eyes, he spoke cutting words that the situation didn't seem to warrant. "You! Can't you read the signs?" He pointed to a sign I had not seen that indicated, "Silencio." In that moment, with my heart so open and my feelings vulnerable, I would normally expect to shut down with the impact of his anger. Instead, my spontaneous response surprised even me.

Rather than shut down, I stayed open and simply received the man's anger. I addressed him with appreciation, "Thank you. I didn't notice, and I will honor it." He appeared perplexed at my calm countenance and quietly he turned away. Inside of myself I mused that I must have been under the influence of the Black Madonna.

As all of us continued to walk in silence, I could feel the rapture of love increase. Unknowingly, this man had done me a great favor. The energy that I had been dissipating by trying to verbalize soon became contained. As it did so, its effect expanded within me.

By this point I had reached a set of steps, poised to enter the sanctuary of the Black Madonna. Filled with love and deep gratitude, I longed to linger there. However, I was sensitive to the line of people behind me who patiently waited their turn. All I could do was clasp my hands in prayer position and bow as a sign of deep affection.

I found it hard to move on, with the energy connection so strong. I realized that I could capture a few more moments by waiting for Ricardo to pay his own respects. As I stood there, I focused on the wooden statue and noticed that she had a darkened face. She held the baby Jesus in one hand and a globe of the world in the other. Her hands appeared to be much lighter than her darkened face. Even then, I still didn't have a clue as to why they called her the Black Madonna.

With Ricardo now ready, slowly we descended the stairs thinking the experience over. Not so, as I heard the inner voice command, *Turn here.* To our right stood a doorway that led to a small room with chairs that had benches in front of them for kneeling. There was also a large altar with flowers. I entered, unaware that Ricardo followed. This would be my opportunity to let the intensity of feelings continue to move viscerally through me. I also took time to pray to the Black Madonna. I wanted to begin in the traditional fashion of reciting the Hail Mary and was embarrassed to realize that I no longer remembered the words. It didn't seem to matter. Energy waves of love began to flow through me. Again, I heard, *Look up,* and there she was. The irony was that I had wanted to spend more time with the Madonna. I found that this sanctuary had a portal to the back of the statue. I had received what I wanted, without even knowing how I had arrived there.

As I continued to immerse myself in spontaneous words of prayer and gratitude, a most astounding vision began to form. Physical reality faded as the vastness of a oneness, so grand and beautiful, emerged beyond the illusion of any sense of separation. As a vortex, this vastness began to funnel into an energy form. That energy form solidified and grew denser, into the physical forms of male and female. The image simulated the divine union, perhaps as a marriage.

With my eyes closed, I watched this vision as, in the form of energy, it moved like a funnel into and then down through the top of my head. It passed through my third eye, through my lips, into my throat, into my heart, all the way down the front of my body and right into my vagina. The energy jolted me with an impact that passed through me. It was as if I was giving birth. It emerged as a ball of light that resembled a globe of the world.

As I watched this ball of energy, in my mind's eye it swirled and mystically re-entered me with a force. There it produced an immense, sacred orgasmic release. I had to cover my mouth to keep from screaming in ecstasy at its vibration. My entire body quaked in its aftermath. The energy directed itself upward in the same pathway and out the top of my head, leaving me trembling.

Stunned and bewildered, inside myself, I begged for an understanding of what had just occurred. I heard only William's familiar laughter, which relaxed and assured me that all was well. The words of the Beatles, whose music I most admired as reflecting spiritual knowing, started to play in my head the lyrics of their song "Let it Be."

Silently I chuckled, in both awe and appreciation of the blessing and the gift that I believed the Black Madonna had facilitated for me. I felt humbled, aware that I had undergone a massive cleansing from the inside out. It was as if the Divine Feminine had entered my body to transform any remnant of unhealed wounds from the sexual violation of my past and the sexual void of the present. I felt cleansed not only of the grief that I had carried inside of my body. I felt it was also as a metaphor for the pain of the wounding of the feminine still alive in society today.

Once this message had settled into my awareness, the energy that continued to move through me began to lessen and release me. Again, I felt capable of standing on my own, both physically and symbolically. It was time for me to move back out of the sanctuary. Only then did I realize that Ricardo had witnessed my mystical encounter.

With him by my side I returned to the courtyard. I so wanted to express what had happened. In a comical twist, Ricardo told me that he had seen my hands cover my face, and he had watched me trembling. He thought I had merely been crying.

I now believed that these mystical events had concluded. Ricardo and I soon had to board our bus, and I assumed we would be leaving. Not so. Telepathically I heard, *Light the candles.* Displayed before us in a shrinelike area were devotional votive candles that people could light if they made a donation in Spanish currency. Curiously, I had borrowed a token amount from a friend that morning for what I thought I would need as a tip for our bus driver.

Instead, I found that I had enough to purchase two candles, one a tall reddish-pink taper and the other a shorter blue one. In my innocence I viewed the reddish candle as a symbol of the feminine, and the bluish one for the masculine. I turned and handed the blue candle to Ricardo.

A Spanish woman in front of me had just finished lighting her own candles from the main altar candle. She turned to light mine. Telepathically I heard, *No! You have to light your own flame.* Startled, I thanked the woman by uttering the words, "No, gracias." She understood and moved away.

I lit my candle from the main one. Then I intuitively heard, *Take your candle and light Ricardo's.* It was interesting to note the symbolism of the feminine candle lighting the masculine one. I then set my feminine candle into one holder, and Ricardo anchored his masculine candle in another. We gave thanks with our hands in prayer position, and we bowed.

I thought we were now leaving. Yet soon I heard one last message. As we exited through the portal doors, intuitively I heard, *Pass this experience and energy to Janet. Also bring home a little replica of the Black Madonna for your altar.*

The force then lifted. Ricardo and I realized that our bus would depart very soon. However, I couldn't leave without a replica and didn't know where to purchase it. Ricardo noted that he was hungry. I accompanied him to the cafeteria, where telepathically I heard, *Over here.*

On the far side, in a little boutique, I found the perfect little image in a stand up icon that showed clearly the black face of the Madonna. Only then did I realize that I had no Spanish currency left. I heard more laughter. *Use the credit card.*

Finally, we could hurry and board our bus. On the ride back down the mountain, Ricardo and I discussed in detail our adventure to the monastery and to the Black Madonna.

"Leave it to you, Tianna, to have a theophany," he observed with affection.

Having never heard such a word, I exclaimed, "What are you talking about?"

He explained that people in ancient days would make a pilgrimage to a mountaintop so that they could have an encounter with the Divine and receive a vision for the purpose of their life. I had done so without even knowing what had happened.

How do I integrate all of this? I pondered that question as we returned to our cruise ship. What do you say to someone who asks casually, "How was your day?" *Oh, I just had a major mystical experience that transformed my life. How was yours?* I laughed as I played with these ideas.

For the first time in many years, I sensed a lightness within my being. I chuckled at my ego's earlier trepidation over this trip. Simultaneously I marveled at all that had unfolded. The trip had surpassed my greatest expectations. It had truly become the cruise of a lifetime, as promoters love to declare. I felt that it had brought me a miraculous healing and initiation as well.

I couldn't wait to share with Janet all that had just transpired. The voice had instructed me to do so. I hesitated. Yes, Janet and I had made a strong connection, however, we barely knew each other. How could I confide in an esteemed colleague such an intimate experience and not feel uneasy? There was no turning back.

At dinner, quietly I went up to Janet and whispered, "Something happened today involving the Black Madonna and the divine feminine. I was told to pass it on to you. Let me know if you're interested and have a private moment to hear a story."

Janet was open and invited, "Tell me more." Right then, the person who had been sitting next to her left the table. Voila! A seat.

I began to relate my story, with all of its unforgettable details, leaving nothing out. I bared my soul to her. To maintain some semblance of professionalism, I prefaced it to a dinner conversation of a few evenings earlier when we had spoken about the divine feminine and evolution of consciousness. This day's experience seemed to be a direct correlation to that evolution.

Janet listened empathically and attentively, responding that it seemed to be a powerful experience of feminine energy, reflecting its healing potential. Although stunned at her brevity of comment and sense of peace over my incredulous escapade, I accepted her wisdom. In so many ways, it was typical of Janet to crystalize with grace the essence of my spiritual epiphany. We went on to enjoy a wonderful conversation, after which we agreed to just let the message marinate within us.

The Universe had a slightly different design in mind for us. That evening, without our requesting a psychic reading, one was offered to us by a participant on the cruise. She laid out the Tarot cards, looked us straight in the eyes, and affirmed enthusiastically, "You will be writing a book together." Upon hearing this, Janet and I just looked at each other as if to say, *We'll see.* We would both stay open to the possibility, yet neither of us took steps in that moment to formalize it.

The cruise now over, everyone embraced with warm affection and goodbyes. Each in his or her own way had been touched by this journey. I returned home filled with the afterglow of this first cruise, and excited over the next.

Intuitively I found myself pulled to thoughts of the Black Madonna. After such a powerful experience I needed to learn more about her. Questions came into my mind. *Who was she? What did she symbolize?*

I phoned a friend who specialized in workshops related to the Black Madonna. She did not return my call. I mentioned the matter to my friend Loria. She told me she had a catalog that listed these workshops. She mailed me the description.

Upon receiving the material, I was inspired to read that the Black Madonna is the embodiment of the divine feminine that embraces the shadow side of our nature through compassion. In many cultures she is known by different names, Isis being one of them. Other names include Virgin Mary, Quan Yin, Pele, and many others.

Moved by this realization I phoned Janet, who then discovered voluminous additional information from the Internet. As she pieced the various descriptions together, the mystery of the Black Madonna began to reveal itself.

Imagine our surprise on reading that to the mythical traveler, which I indeed embodied, she is the compassionate one who shows the way through the darkness into the light. Various descriptions mentioned her deep eyes and mysterious smile as catching a glimpse of the troubadours' ancient songs of courtly love and soul-making. Others expressed the goddess in ecstatic embrace with her God, our shadow nature and light blending in a cosmic dance of Creation. Ultimately she is the healer extraordinaire of the eternal feminine.

Again, I felt humbled at the scope of my mystical experience on the mountaintop. Indeed, I recognized how intimately perfect it was that the Black Madonna had served as my guiding presence after the darkness and travels of my grieving. To think, I had never even heard of the Black Madonna before. Now I would never forget her. I had at first dismissed the line of pilgrims who had waited to pay homage. I had rebuked them, "No way." How little we know.

Janet and I both fell silent at this knowing. I gave thanks, and now I have deeper reverence for the Black Madonna. How appropriate it is that her small icon sits on my altar to William.

With the experiences of the first cruise integrated within me, it was on to the second one. This time I traveled to Mexico and Honduras to launch my ideas on spiritual hedonism. Unlike the intimate Mediterranean cruise, this one included about fifty participants. The flavor of each of its ports of call, and the seminars themselves, were of a more casual nature. Highlights of this journey were both playful dolphins and the antics of William. Dolphins embody the essence of spiritual hedonism. Their nature of joy, sensuality, and telepathic oneness soon made them the mystical mascot of my workshop.

In addition, it was during my workshop that William made his presence known to those participants who were psychically gifted. As had the dolphins, William teased me joyfully in loving support. I enjoyed my camaraderie with him as I continued to present the workshop.

It was only later, when some of the participants enthusiastically shared with me their ability to see him clearly, that I fully realized his impact. He had been a bit of a distraction, yet all proved successful and all was well. We were still a dream team. Another great cruise had come to an end.

Returning home from this cruise meant going from a carefree tropical environment to a daunting winter re-entry. It was early December, nearly the third anniversary of William's passing, and I had a full client schedule.

This combination meant that I was consumed with the heaviness brought by holiday depression as well as my own lingering memories.

Even though my healing and new beginning had by now been anchored within me, painful emotions continued to well up from within. Their hold was not as great as it had been earlier. William even nudged me further with his next loving admonition, *Make new memories.*

I pressed on. I focused on helping clients through their difficult holiday memories as I put my own feelings on hold. This was the first holiday season in which I worked full time. Interestingly, I completed my work by December 23, pleased that I'd been able to do it. I planned to take a few days off and enjoy some leisure. This was not to be the case.

Little did I expect that on the morning of Christmas Eve I would wake to find myself plagued by an overwhelming depression. Surrounded and enveloped by waves of darkness, I felt unable to get out of bed. Instead I fell deeper and deeper into depression.

Suddenly I recognized this experience as reminiscent of my painful episode of three years earlier when I had phoned my therapist in California for emergency intervention. He had reminded me then that I should not resist it. Here I was again. Dramatically, a power inside of me erupted through the darkness with a message. *No more. I am not going to accept this grief and depression any longer. It's time for new memories.*

I heard laughter and William's words, *So, stop with the old memories already.* In our usual playful one upmanship I went one better. It's easy for you to say. You're not the one who has emotions welling up inside. I'm ready to make a new tradition.

A new tradition for new memories, that became my vow. This new tradition would include my major loves: a dear friend, spa treatments, theater, and a holiday dinner.

I called Mary, who also had Christmas Eve free. I knew that to make new memories I needed to get out of the house. I wanted to go to the city, and I asked Mary if she was game.

"Whatever you want," she assured me.

I had mused about visiting a spa for a body wrap, and I proposed that we find a place in the city for an overnight stay. As I waited for Mary to arrive, I made some inquiries and found the perfect hotel and spa. It even had an opening for the two of us around half past six that evening.

By the time Mary arrived, my plan for a new tradition had already begun in motion. I announced to her that first we would go to the theater by stopping at TKTS to see what was available that the Universe wanted us to see. Then it would be off to the spa, where she could enjoy a massage and I could have the body wrap I wanted. We would both indulge in an aromatherapy bath, followed by Christmas Eve dinner. Impressed with my planning, Mary chuckled, "Fine." She added that she also wanted to attend a church service. I was okay with that.

In no time we stood in the TKTS line and perused our options, wanting good seats with clear viewing. The play that spoke to us was Copenhagen. It was a Tony award winning play that was an incredible production, and rather serious. Its theme centered around the relationship between Heisenberg and Bohr, in reference to the atom bomb. We purchased our tickets and found our way to the theater.

The play's amazing stage setting, shaped like a big atom, was structured brilliantly to convey that energy matrix. Three actors moved freely about the stage, much as an electron, proton, and neutron would move.

The first half of the play focused on dialogue about quantum physics, dialogue that drew one into a contemplative state of mind. The words I remember most were about how energy is invisible, yet it exists. It can neither be created nor destroyed, only simply transformed.

During the second half of the play I heard how energy is so powerful that it can create a bomb. Then I heard intuitively, *What would happen if that energy were harnessed in consciousness of love to create an Initiation?* I thought nothing more of that notion. The play ended, leaving us barely enough time to reach the spa for our appointment. So off we went.

When Mary and I arrived at the spa we found the place silent, like a temple setting, with hardly anyone there. A lovely receptionist greeted us and reviewed our options. Of the many body wraps, I selected one called chocolate and honey. It sounded delicious and felt like a Christmas treat.

The woman ushered me to a treatment room and asked me to disrobe and lie on the massage table. She applied the gooey mixture all over my body, then foil wrapped me in a nurturing manner and tucked me in blankets.

This woman was from Ecuador and very much a *curandera,* or native healer. As we began to converse, she asked my birth sign. I replied that I was Sagittarian, and she returned that she was a Leo. Hearing this, I laughed. "I love Leos, my late husband was a Leo."

She grew quiet and looked at me intently. Then she remarked casually, "He is here, isn't he?"

Surprised, I responded, "You can feel him?"

"I sense spirit."

We both smiled at each other with that knowing. She asked if I needed anything before she left. I shook my head *No*. She exited and left me alone, in the stillness, in the chocolate body wrap.

With body wraps, as heat penetrates the skin the relaxation and detoxification unfold their magic. In this case, as apropos for chocolate, I felt that I was divinely melting. In the first *Aha!* awareness that popped into my mind I saw the word "stressed" spelled backward, to read "desserts." I chuckled at that. All month I had felt stressed. Now I had become "desserts." This thought alone felt liberating.

I continued to bake in the warmth of the chocolate when the next *Aha!* Experience popped up, this one more profound. In it, I reflected back to my NDE and my realization that agony and ecstasy were like bittersweet chocolate. The agony is at first bitter, and as you let it melt into you without resistance, ecstasy emerges, and sweetness lingers.

In truth, life contains both the bitter and the sweet. Experiencing the bitter facilitates an appreciation of the sweet. This thought moved me into a new perception that, although a bit of a stretch, seemed metaphorically accurate.

I could have melted in that body wrap all night. However, as they say, all good things must end. The attendant returned, signaling the end of my blissful melting. It was time for her to unwrap me. As she did so, I felt as if I were my own Christmas gift being unwrapped. Being a consummate chocoholic, I looked at myself as I would a piece of chocolate. Spontaneously, without a thought in mind, I took a long lick. Starting at the crease of one elbow, this lick moved down my arm and into my hands, climaxing with sucking my fingers.

The woman appeared horrified when she found me licking myself. To assure her that I had not lost my mind I commented, "Finger-licking good is one thing; I'm enjoying being body-licking good as well. It's Christmas, and I feel that the greatest gift we can give ourselves is to love ourselves unconditionally, as best we can. We're delicious from the inside out." My message relieved her.

She agreed. "That's very good. I'll remember that."

Later in the shower, cleansing the remains of my chocolate and honey experience, a song played in my head. Sung by Whitney Houston, it was

'The Greatest Love of All." While hearing this song served as confirmation of my perception, another memory came up. This time it was a quote by Oscar Wilde, "To love oneself is the beginning of a lifelong romance."

How appropriate, I mused that on this Christmas Eve of a new tradition, this line was for me. This was especially in regard to overcoming the grief. The message of being the one person who would never leave me, never abandon me, that I could count on was me!

I emerged from the shower brimming with holiday spirit and the gift of myself and a new sacred rule: Love yourself first. How wondrous it felt that the hydrotherapy bath would come next. The attendant wasn't quite ready, so she asked me to wait patiently. I remained in such ecstasy that waiting was not a problem.

Quietly I entered the room that held the hydrotherapy tub. The room was small and dark, with one lighted candle. A mirror behind that candle expanded the room. In my melted condition, the hydrotherapy tub appeared as a sarcophagus. Next to it I sat on a tiny seat shaped like a little throne. I sensed Egypt.

While waiting for the attendant I used my time to ask inwardly for an even greater Christmas gift. I had already received the gift of myself. My ultimate request was for William to manifest so that I could see him physically. I knew that my request was a farfetched one. I'd heard him, and I'd felt him, yet my gift of sight had failed me when it came to seeing him. I longed for that experience.

The ability to actually see William would confirm our union beyond the illusion of our separation. We would celebrate that we were still together as each other's reflection. His inner fire had been so bright. I imagined the mirror he could provide would reflect the light of the divinity within me. In that way I could enjoy the bliss that is my essence. This was Christmas, and I felt that I deserved this visual presence as his gift to me.

Relaxing with my request, and in the meditative state that this room engendered, I awaited the attendant's return. She arrived and helped me remove my robe, almost as she would help a princess prepare for a great ritual. I stepped up on the footstool and into the tub.

The water was both warm and soothing with aromatherapy herbs, and I slipped into it. My senses began to enjoy a feast. I prepared for a wondrous journey, as the attendant planned to turn on the jets that would massage my body. I anticipated that this hydromassage would raise my energy vibrations so that my wish could be fulfilled. The fantasy that I had created in my mind grew so large that I savored its possibilities.

Nothing happened. The jets, which had been working moments earlier, would not turn on. I felt let down and saddened. I whispered, "No problem, just leave me here in the nice warm water. I'll be fine."

The attendant would not have this. Concerned that the malfunction might electrocute me, she insisted that I get out of the water immediately. She needed to call the engineer. This abrupt jolt rattled me. However, I respected her command and grudgingly stepped out of the tub. The relaxing moment that I had anticipated was quickly becoming its opposite.

I donned my robe and moved to the treatment room that had the massage table in it. The attendant apologized profusely that the tub would not work.

"Just lie down on the table and I will soothe you with a moisturizing treatment," she urged. I acquiesced, thinking that a nurturing touch would be beneficial.

Again, it was not to be. Suddenly, and without any obvious reason, the overhead sprinklers turned themselves on and dowsed both of us with cold water! We were soaked to the skin.

At this point the attendant began to shriek "Spirits are here. Spirits are here." She pushed the table, with me on it, out of the way to keep me from getting further drenched with water.

Composing herself, she then urged me to get up and don my robe and move to yet another room. "No way." By this time, I had grown agitated. I proclaimed that I was not moving one more time. "Just cover me in blankets and leave me alone. I'll be fine. Do what you have to do. I'm not moving."

I spoke so adamantly that the attendant complied. She continued to apologize as she left the room. I felt myself shift from a blissful state into an ornery, cantankerous one. Heaven had been replaced by the stress of the human condition.

I mumbled to myself about how I hate cold water. Even with towels and blankets now covering me I could feel myself contracting. My earlier expanded state now dissolving, I felt as if I had crash landed on earth. It was then that I heard familiar laughter. *Oh no, William. Could this be you? Would you do this to me?*

I felt only the warmth of his love surround me in almost an etheric massage. The frustration and tension that had begun to build now let go. I had arrived in bliss again. William had delivered his version of my Christmas gift. He had manifested in dramatic style, just not in the way that I had desired. Talk about throwing cold water on my fantasy! This was just like his sense of humor. Some things never change.

The attendant returned to say that the spa was now closing. I didn't comprehend fully what had happened. I knew that it was significant. In less than an hour I had moved from ecstasy with the body wrap, to irritation with the cold water drizzle, and then back to a state of peace, albeit with a chilled body. I dressed quickly and waited for Mary. She had enjoyed an incredible massage, and greeted me with a melted countenance.

I welcomed her with, "Some new tradition. Wait till I tell you what happened." She nodded in an acceptance that bore witness to my perplexed state. We thanked the attendant. I, especially, let her know that she had no fault in what had occurred. She appreciated the acknowledgment. We wished her a merry Christmas and left the spa.

As we walked down fifth Avenue, we spotted The Plaza hotel. I knew I could always count on one of their restaurants to serve a great meal. I wanted no more surprises. We entered and were delighted by its wondrous Christmas tree, fully decorated to reflect holiday cheer. As we had hoped, our meal was delicious. I shared with Mary all of William's antics in the spa, and we laughed until tears rolled down our cheeks. We had indeed experienced a new tradition, one that I would not soon forget.

Mary reminded me that she still wanted to go to a church service. We weren't far from St. Patrick's Cathedral. With Mary being Episcopalian I asked, "How do you feel about going to a Catholic service?" She was open. It was onward to church.

On the way I became confused as to the location of St. Patrick's and noticed a church with an aura of light surrounding it. This church beckoned to me. I intuitively heard, *Go there.* We crossed the street and entered, surprised to find that it was Presbyterian. An inner feeling reassured me that we should stay, so I honored that prompting. Mary and I participated fully in the service. This was a new experience for both of us.

There was much singing of Christmas carols, and the highlight of this service was the incredibly enlightening sermon that the pastor delivered. It was titled something like, "Have you done the night shift?" By the night shift, he didn't mean midnight to 7:00A.M. work hours. He referred to the darkness in one's soul, when one feels unbearably alone.

His words reminded me of the darkness of Christmas Eve of three years earlier. That night had marked the beginning of my descent into what is known as the *dark night of the soul.* As I heard the pastor speak, memories of that dark time came back to me in encapsulated form. The pastor urged us to remember that even in the night shift, the light is still there, no matter how dim it may appear.

Hearing his words, I paused to reflect on how far I had come and the immense gratitude I felt toward God and life. Now I understood why I had found that church. I needed to hear that particular message on that night, so as to affirm its power.

Three years earlier, that darkness had almost killed me. I had seen no way out. If anyone had told me that I would emerge with such lightness and strength and renewed love for myself and others, I would have had a hard time believing them. My probable response would have been, "From your mouth to God's ears." This meant that I would be open to such a thing. I wouldn't count on it.

What I realized during this Christmas Eve service was that despite myself and my earlier helplessness, a powerful set of circumstances, people, and experiences had been drawn to me. This phenomenon had unfolded a healing and empowerment that went beyond my limited human comprehension. It had brought me to this moment.

The end of the service further expanded the Christmas message.

From the altar's main candle, each of the ministers lighted a candle. A few members of the congregation, selected as representatives of the people, lighted candles as well. The electric lights dimmed, leaving only the flickering of individual flames. I watched as people moved through the darkness with their lighted candles.

In that moment I recalled vividly the dream I had had as a nine year old child. Now I witnessed its metaphor being played out before my eyes. I remembered how one light had touched another and another, and the dark spots had all disappeared as the world filled with light. No sooner had this thought entered my mind than the pastor confirmed it.

He proclaimed, "With your lighted candle, know that you dispel the darkness. Take your light into the world and pass it on."

CHAPTER SEVEN

Empowered Woman

∞

My three year journey through grief had just culminated in a Christmas miracle! It marked my emergence from the dark night of the soul. The immensity of this realization rendered me speechless and in awe.

William's passing had plunged me into darkness, extinguishing the fire inside of me, or so it had seemed. William had been the love of my life and the light of my world. With William no longer present for me physically, my own death had seemed the desired option.

Unbeknownst to me, that Christmas Eve morning the stage had been set for me to experience a miracle. My inner fire welled up alchemically to burn away the remaining dregs of depression with the words, *No more. I am not going to accept this grief and depression any longer.* The old year had begun to come to an end. So had my old paradigm. The time had come for the light within me to burst forth through that darkness and claim its own power.

I realized that my ultimate gift had come in a most unexpected way at the conclusion of the Christmas Eve church service. Its gift could not have been more perfect. That one service reflected the whole of my grief journey. Its message of the night shift reminded me, in loving gratitude, of how far I had come with support that had been extraordinary and multidimensional.

This reminder joined in turn with the service's ending ritual. As the church lights had dimmed, I could feel the energy waves of blackness that had been my pain release as they wash over my body. Then as candles were lighted, I could feel the sacred fire within me ignite and erupt. It felt as powerful as my experience with the Black Madonna. This time I was in a fully packed church, so my experience remained contained. I found its impact unmistakable.

That moment had revealed a deeper truth. The memory of my dream as a nine year old child had manifested before me, both metaphorically and physically. I could feel embodied in the message of the Black Madonna the same wisdom that had been given to me in that dream so many decades ago, by the woman from the stars. She had shown me how to work with energy and to heal my own wounds first. Only then could I pass on the Light so that others could dispel their own inner darkness. Then the world could be filled with Light.

With my inner fire lighted, I remembered the greatness within. I became the embodiment of that flame. Then as if on cue, individual members of the congregation had carried their lighted candles through the darkness. I had witnessed and resonated with the spreading of that light one person at a time. This visual reenactment of my dream would leave a lasting imprint with me forever.

Mary and I had left the church knowing that something special had occurred. I felt as if I had been touched by the Divine, that a new aliveness inside of me had been birthed. The mirror that had once appeared shattered had now been restored. In it, my face looked back at me as the beloved. I reflected the Divine within myself. This reflection is the truth within us all.

How significant that this moment had come at Christmas. This is the time when the consciousness of humanity is aware of the birth of Jesus, whom Christians call the *Light of the World.* For me, Christmas had brought the birth of a new consciousness within myself.

Despite my earlier sense of disillusionment, I had not been abandoned. I had not been left alone, either by the Divine or in an eye opening way by William. He had fulfilled his own destiny, and now through the veils he had begun to help me fulfill mine. This was the message revealed to me at Christmas. It set me free. Now the fire within me, ablaze with a creative force, demanded expression.

As the year 2001 approached, my sense of emptiness of the past few years turned to excitement. 1 felt pregnant with my story and a need to share it. Prior attempts to record its messages had all proved frustrating. Would it be any different now? That problem no longer appeared to matter. The process seemed to have a force all its own. It was around that time that Janet felt an intuitive prompting to call me and did so. She suggested we get together to see if a collaboration might be possible. Always open to opportunities that God unfolds through people, emphatically I agreed.

Back on the Mediterranean cruise, Janet and I had found an intriguing connection worthy of pursuit. She lived in Maryland, and Amtrak made it convenient for me to journey to her home. I did so that December. After Janet picked me up at the train station, we learned that we both harbored similar thoughts: *Why am I doing this? What is this about? I don't really know what I have in common with this person.* An intuitive inner knowing kept moving both of us forward toward something inevitable.

From the moment I walked through Janet's doorway, William's laughter became contagious. Not only did I hear my invisible beloved's familiar signature chuckle that all was well, I noticed my own amusement at what 1 was seeing. Before me in Janet's home were holiday decorations that captured the best of both Egypt and Christmas. After all, how many people have only Egyptian ornaments on their Christmas tree? To me, this was a setup that revealed the cosmic humor of the Divine.

While on the cruise Janet and I had discussed the dance of my love story and her wisdom of Egyptian mysteries. At Christmas I made peace with my destiny. I knew that for greater good to come from these experiences, they had to be communicated. Janet and I had come together to discuss the possibility of writing this story. Here was what I comically refer to as a cosmic clue.

True to that clue, the writing between us unfolded spontaneously. The safety that Janet and her home provided allowed for my surrender. Words poured from my mouth, to be captured by Janet's rapid fingers at the keyboard just as quickly as I could deliver them.

At the time, neither of us knew that the story would become a trilogy. I just knew that I had a burning desire to express all that I had experienced, and to do so without holding back. At the very least I needed to find meaning through the trauma of the prior few years. Finding meaning would bring emotional closure to this chapter of my life so that I could move on. At the very most, I found a miracle unfolding itself.

Our writing seemed to take the form of a spiral. My initial expression was of the story in stream of consciousness fashion. The second level involved moving deep into cellular memory and emotional expression. The third level brought a depth of spiritual wisdom, as pearls sprinkled throughout the story. That was the beginning. It flowed and flowed, with both our human endeavor and William's mystical intervention.

By Valentine's Day, most of the energy behind the story had been expressed. Its culmination became a special gift to me from my invisible beloved. Valentine's Day marked the anniversary of my engagement to

William four years earlier. That day had made our previously hidden love visible to the world. However, painful memories had been anchored to Valentine's Day ever since. With the birth of our love story through its telling, its legacy lives on for others to enjoy. No longer is Valentine's Day a painful one. New memories have replaced the old ones in my paradigm shift.

In addition, for Valentine's Day 2001 I acquired the most wondrous magenta stuffed bear, named Bradley. It was a humorous token of William's and my love. Due to its color and softness, I refer to him laughingly as a symbol of the ideal combination of masculine warmth with a welldeveloped feminine side. He came to me in a most unusual way.

After brunch with a friend near Valentine's Day, we headed toward the car when I heard telepathically, *Cross the street, and do it now.* I didn't know how to tell my friend what was going on, so I proposed casually that we take a walk and do some shopping. The inner voice continued, *Go to the toy store.* This sounded like a strange request to make of a woman my age. The place also appeared to be closed. I listened and crossed the street as the voice had instructed.

In the store window I found a human sized bear with a big white heart on its chest. Then I heard deep inner laughter and, *Happy Valentine's Day, beloved. It's the best I can do to keep you warm at night.* I felt touched with a mixture of joy and tears. William's spirit animal and our mascot had always been the bear. The store was closed, and I eagerly returned the next morning to retrieve this one. Bradley now sits proudly on my bed, and I snuggle with him sometimes during the night.

The playful and supportive presence of William through the years has proved invaluable. In ways beyond human comprehension, he has honored his promise of being by my side until I regained my strength. The truth is that I have finally reached that point, for which I remain grateful to my invisible beloved.

Now what is awakening within me is love's fire to be enjoyed with a man who can appreciate its mystery. In my darkest hours I had doubted that this fire would ever ignite again. Now I know that it has. It is as a sacred flame that empowers me from within as a woman, and it calls to be united with a man whose fire mirrors mine. I had found such a union once with William and I wondered whether it could be possible again. No sooner had I mused on these thoughts than I received a phone call that provided my answer.

It was early on a Saturday morning. As I was waking up I heard the voice of a dear friend of mine named Joshua on the answering machine. Since the first time I had heard that voice many months earlier, it had sparked a fluttering in my heart. Anytime this happens I respond spontaneously to its calling card. My response to Joshua was no exception.

Indeed, our friendship, although primarily by phone, has become a sacred one. He is a man who honors the feminine, and he has supported me with his wisdom and his love. His support had been evident from our first phone encounter. This time I picked up the phone quickly. Soon we found ourselves engaged in a deeply intimate conversation.

Curiously enough, both of us had begun to go through changes in our lives, changes that resulted in our individual expansion. My expansion came from being a speaker on the cruises, and from my experience with the Black Madonna. His came from transformations in his personal life and work, which specializes in relationships.

Joshua also acknowledged that I was a reflection of an empowered woman, balanced in her feminine and masculine natures. Coming from him, I regarded this statement as a compliment and a confirmation. He continued that he admired me for this trait. He affirmed that I was his teacher as well.

In the course of such closeness, even though Joshua and I had not entered a romantic relationship, spontaneously he spoke words that I longed to hear. I had wondered if a man existed who was secure enough in himself that he would not be threatened by my love for William. In my heart I knew it had to be so because this love remained an enduring part of me. Joshua represented that answer.

At first Joshua felt uncomfortable with the thought of living in William's shadow. He didn't want that. However, as he has come to know me and feel the love that I embody, he acknowledges that this love within me is a product of the love that William and I shared. It is also an inclusive love that does not threaten to withhold itself in any way. Joshua loved William for it. Hearing him say so, I realized that all things are possible, all in good time. I treasure Joshua as a friend, a colleague, and a teacher who seems to light my way.

Joshua's influence in my life has been significant ever since our first conversation. I spoke with him about my swollen abdomen that could have signaled an ovarian tumor. I had by then grown tired of life, and I longed to join my beloved. This call occurred after all of my medical tests, and after I had seen the play Aida. Joshua, who has his own deep connections with ancient Egypt, had listened attentively. He would not accept that it was my time to die. Instead, he likened me to the goddess Isis.

Joshua's observations planted seeds that would bring to my grieving journey an awareness that I was experiencing a 21st century version of the myth of Isis. In that myth, Isis is inconsolable in her grief over the death of her beloved Osiris, whose brother had murdered him and strewn pieces of his body throughout Egypt. Isis searched for and retrieved the pieces of Osiris and brought him to wholeness. They made love one last time. From this union Horus, the sun god, was born.

In this ancient myth I saw my own metaphor but with a significant twist. Instead of bringing William to wholeness, I had brought myself to wholeness with William's support, through my magnificent spiritual odyssey. I had traveled around the world in search of my pieces, and this search inspired the writing that would become my story, born of our love.

As I continued to grow stronger, each day I felt a gradual lessening of the presence of my invisible beloved. This lessening process concerned me at first. However, in my heart I knew that it was to be so. Our destinies would still be fulfilled through the telling of our story. I recalled William's mystical love letters that I had received in December of 1997. My pain of loss at the time had been so great that I had rebuked those letters. Now, years later, the wisdom that the letters expressed appeared staggering, and offered a blueprint to our truth.

Especially in the first letter, William's words now took on new meaning: *My mission is with and now through you. Know I'm with you and surround you with divine love, and continue to protect you and your incredible light, into the full empowerment of your mission.* The innocent promise that we had made to each other so many years earlier continued to unfold its magic.

I realized that William was not, and had never been, attached to me out of any obligation or need. His mission had been to fulfill his journey in full mastery, and then to oversee the telling of our story. Intuitively I felt that once that story had been told, he would embark on another adventure. Whenever he had finished a project his words had always been, ''I'm outta here.'' I needed to know if he intended to leave this time. So I asked him. He laughed, and I heard, *Soon truth will be revealed.* As had always been our way, no sooner is a question asked than a response is given. This time I found my answer at the theater.

Mary and I decided to take in a play, so we set off for TKTS to see what the Divine had planned. When we arrived there, I looked at the board and was stunned to find tickets to *Beauty and the Beast* available. That particular show is rarely on TKTS. I hesitated.

William and I had often joked with titles of various movies and plays in relation to our life. *Beauty and the Beast* had been one of our favorite take offs. I would tease him that I was the beauty, and that whenever he acted out in anger, he was playing the beast. He would reply, "Mirror, mirror on the wall." We also valued that story's deeper messages about love.

This combination of history made Mary's and my choice a challenging one. I don't know if I would have had the courage to select that play myself. Mary suggested it. When she did, I knew that I was ready, and it was time. Little did I expect that this magnificent stage production would be rivaled by interaction with my invisible beloved at intermission.

I usually sit through intermission. Not this time. I felt promptings to get up and visit the souvenir counter, something I rarely do. I went there not knowing why, then heard inner laughter and was pointed toward my left. There I found a CD for the Egyptian opera *Aida*. I had been wanting one and never imagined I would find it at the counter of another play. I thanked William for his help.

Not thinking any more of it, I then heard, *Buy a rose, buy a rose*. I didn't have the cash and borrowed some from Mary. Intermission over, artificial rose and CD in hand, I returned to my seat.

In Beauty and the Beast, a rose symbolizes the beast finally being able to break the spell of the enchantress, by learning to give and receive love. I heard, *let the rose be our symbol that death is like a spell. There is no end to love. As in Aida, we found each other once and will do it again. It's soon time to say goodbye. It's a brief interlude. It's time to move on.*

This message from William coincided with a transformation taking place on stage, as the beast turned into a handsome prince through the love that he and the beauty shared. Between the play and William's message, I sobbed profusely. I recalled the words, "an ocean of endless tears." As I did so I felt a warm embrace, laughter, and the words, *ocean of endless love and infinite possibilities.*

CHAPTER EIGHT

Kiss from Heaven

∞

I knew it was time to let William go. His words to me as I watched *Beauty and the Beast* spoke of a parting soon to be at hand. Would this parting be a permanent one or merely a temporary one in this lifetime? He referred to a *brief interlude,* but I didn't know what he meant by that, since in spirit there is no time or space. He could have meant days, months, years, even lifetimes. I would witness, however, that he did not plan to leave just yet. He continued to find reasons to nag me.

I had already noticed that his presence was no longer constant, as it had been through the early days of my grieving. He now seemed to show up under any of three different circumstances. First, his antics abounded whenever I worked on writing our story. Second, if he wanted to bring an important message or support for loved ones, he would do so. Third, whenever I mentioned him lovingly in a fun way, he would suddenly arrive.

The timing of William's visits mattered less to me now than it once had. I knew that William was going to do whatever William wanted to do. This message was even captured in our wedding vows. They were carefully crafted by us: "With this ring, I set you free to be all that you are meant to be." Since I had never kept a hold on William in physical life, I surely would not keep one on him in the afterlife. He had already broken through the spell of death. I mused, *What will my invisible beloved do next?* No sooner had the thought entered my mind than its answer appeared in a fascinating way.

Months after William's transition I had heard of a man named Mark Macy and an organization that he had founded called International Network for Instrumental Transcommunication (INIT). Macy had formed this company to research interdimensional communication. Apparently, the organization had achieved some success in communicating, through

115

technological means, with those who had died. Tape recordings, computer messages and photographs appeared to make such communication possible.

This information had come to me during Raymond Moody's workshop back in April of 1998. Too brokenhearted to pursue it at that time, I had filed it in my memory bank for future reference.

Then during the tail end of my grieving journey, I received a catalog indicating that Macy would soon speak at Wainwright House, only a few miles from my home. *Hmm...*Wainwright House had been the location of William's memorial service, the place where my hair had caught on fire.

As I considered attending the Mark Macy program, I marked the date in my mind as February 22. Suddenly I heard laughter and the words, *Be there.* Merely considering would not be good enough for William, who insisted that I needed to attend. He emphasized the point more emphatically, as I spoke by telephone with my friend Joyce. I wondered aloud if the reason William wanted me to attend the workshop was that communication had been his thing.

Joyce laughed and agreed. "Sounds right to me."

I replied jokingly, "Well, if he wants me to get involved with technology, he is going to have to really support me. He was the one who always teased that I was a techno-peasant."

At that moment the line went dead. I tried to call Joyce back, and I couldn't get through. She has more than one line and I dialed each of them and none of them worked. Of all the friends to be talking to, Joyce is the one who is the most technologically proficient. This was strange. Finally, she called me back and we had a good laugh.

"Okay," I conceded, "I surrender. I'll be there."

As if to further insure that technology must be my next step, another strange event occurred. Everyone is familiar with both Call Waiting and Caller ID, which flash out a number and allow one to transfer to the incoming call.

Well, I have what I laughingly refer to as *callus interruptus.* By that I mean that a selective awareness seems to be at work, and this awareness knows when I need to shift to another conversation. The shift happens most often when the incoming call is from one of William's loved ones. I need do no switching of lines myself. The phone transfers me automatically.

At first, I had assumed this phenomenon to be a phone company problem, so I reported it. The phone company concluded that my unit must be defective. They replaced it. The same thing happened with the new unit. I called the company once again. When the agent heard my story she replied, "That's not a service we provide. You must be working with a higher power."

I hung up the phone and chuckled. I finally realized what, or shall I say who, was at work. Familiar inner laughter followed my conclusion. I now surrender to this phenomenon's humorous wisdom. My only caution is that when I'm switched spontaneously, I need to get my bearings. Before I say anything, I need to find out who is on the other end. This problem has proved to be somewhat challenging.

How amusing that my invisible beloved now pointed me in the direction of technology. Somehow his antics, although comical, also seemed quite profound. They awakened in me a deeper calling to research afterlife communication.

In my own mind I now reviewed the progression of my communication with William. I had started out by feeling and hearing his contact in disbelief. Wanting to be sure that I wasn't losing my mind as a grieving widow suffering a psychotic episode, I had turned to the experts, in this case mediums. They listened to their own guidance and acknowledged my gifts. After their assurances, I began to trust and enjoy this communication from William. My next step seemed to be research, as the scientist in me had been stirred.

Through the recommendation of my friend Mary I had heard of another workshop in afterlife communication sponsored by the Association for Research and Enlightenment (A.R.E.). This is an organization that promotes the work of Edgar Cayce, often referred to as the "sleeping prophet." During his lifetime Cayce gave thousands of readings, helping people by using his own psychic abilities.

Mary and I attended the A.R.E. Workshop. Robert Grant, a leading authority on Cayce's research into the afterlife, made a most illuminating presentation. Almost all of the experiences I had had during the years since William's transition appeared to be validated through Cayce's knowledge. I found this new clarification especially evident in regard to Cayce's view on dreams about the deceased.

I knew that whenever I experienced lucid dreams, they felt so real that I found it difficult to dismiss them as mere dreams. Cayce had affirmed that dreams of the deceased are not dreams as we know them; they are contact. According to Cayce, during the sleep state our spirit travels to other dimensions. We can reunite with our loved ones there because no one dies.

This confirmation was all I needed to hear. I realized that it was the reason I had come. Understanding this phenomenon especially validated the power of what had transpired the night that a dream had transported me to William's first birthday into eternity. I thanked Mary for her recommendation and thanked the speaker for his excellent presentation.

At long last February 22 arrived. The night of Mark Macy's program was also the night that a blizzard began to blanket New York. As much as I had looked forward to attending Macy's talk, the comfort of a warm home began to win out. This was not to be. My invisible beloved remained insistent. I could feel a demanding quality to his words, *Get going.* I asked him for a sign to prove that I was meant to venture out in this storm. William quipped telepathically, *Fine, bring Macy's book.*

I don't even have a clue where it's hidden in *the messy storage room,* I replied mentally. Then William laughed and simply told me which box to search. As I opened its lid, I found the book right on top. I didn't even remember putting it there.

As I held Macy's book in my hands, suddenly the phone rang. A friend who was going to the seminar asked if I wanted a ride. How much easier can it get? I headed out the door when telepathically from William I heard, *Bring my picture.* I did so.

I found Macy's lecture to be informative, intriguing and enlightening. He started by likening his own research to that of Galileo. When Galileo first introduced the telescope to show how infinite the galaxy was, people ridiculed him. Their limited perception would not accept such a concept. Even the scientists and religious leaders of his time refused to peer through his telescope. Today we take for granted how vast the universe is. This is where Macy believes that afterlife communication is now at the cutting edge of pioneering research. Most likely, in years to come, such communication will be taken for granted.

Macy continued to cite instances of communication with the deceased. He offered proof in the form of a slide presentation of photographs and tape recordings. I was especially moved when I saw the photo of his own father.

I felt thrilled to hear all this. If Macy's workshop had ended there, I would have found it more than fulfilling. However, the best was yet to come. Macy asked if anyone in the audience wanted to have their picture taken. He used a special instrument that, together with a camera, illumined the energy field around a person. This included both the subject and non-physical energy of any presences around him or her.

I volunteered readily. In fact, telepathically I implored William, *This is your moment. If this is what you've been waiting for, show up. You got me here against the odds. Please show up. I know your presence is real. The mediums have confirmed it. Yet you know that one picture* is *worth a thousand words. This can be that picture for those who rely on eyes to see in order to believe.* All I heard back was familiar laughter, which validated William's presence.

I stood in line with everyone else from the audience. The room was filled with committed seekers, each with an energy of eager anticipation and openness for discovery. My photo taken, I waited with curious expectancy for the image to appear on paper. I knew that I felt William's presence. Would he show up on film? At long last, the moment of truth arrived.

As my Polaroid picture began to grow visible, chills ran through my entire body. The photo went beyond what I could have imagined. There was my beloved reflected clearly through my face. As I looked carefully, I couldn't believe my eyes. At the same time, I felt ecstatic.

William's face somehow showed through the right side of my own face. I found it humorous in that the photo showed me with a little mustache and beard. Even more dramatic, the shape of my skull appeared to be masculine, and the eye and eyebrow on that side of my face were William's, not mine.

Not wanting to trust my senses alone, I turned quickly to my friend and handed him the picture. He had known William well, and he laughed. "Leave it to William to be in your face."

Many of the other participants soon came up to see it. I felt pleased that I had heeded William's message to bring along his picture. Each person, in his or her own way, acknowledged what I perceived. Even total strangers saw William in the image of my face.

Macy then asked if anyone wanted a second photo taken. By that point I no longer felt William around me, and I wanted to check out what a second picture might show. Predictably, no image of William appeared in the second photo. This one was clearly of me, standing alone. Comparing the two pictures revealed a striking difference between them.

Macy himself examined both images and honored their value. He even asked if he could use them in his research. I agreed, hesitantly. I especially didn't want to let the picture that included William leave my hands. That photo served as my proof, in visible form, for those who might question the expanded truth that I have lived.

I had already tucked the photo away safely in my copy of Macy's book. I was prepared to abscond with it. However, higher principles won out. I turned over both photos. Macy promised to mail them to me as soon as he had scanned them into his computer. He did so, and to this day they are a significant part of his presentations. I appreciate that he kept his word. These photos are a treasure in my album of memories. [For those who wish to view these astonishing photos, please see the back pages.]

Excited about my exposure to Macy's research, I let it be known among acquaintances that I was open to workshops that could deepen my understanding of the afterlife. In response, a former client soon sent me a flyer about a workshop that included a spiritual ceremony that would illumine death. This workshop piqued my interest and I went.

What I found to be of greatest interest in this program was its information about rigor mortis. The presenters stated that when a person has no fear of death, that person "knows their way home." In the absence of anxiety, the body doesn't stiffen. Its muscles stay relaxed because there is no fear. Most often, at death a person experiences tremendous fear. In such cases the spirit does not know its way home, so the physical body contracts.

I realized that William had experienced no fear of death. The evening before his transition he had actually announced, "It's time now for me to go home. It's time to die." I now had undeniable understanding of how deep his preparation and his knowing had been. It accounted for why his body had remained relaxed and warm at the end of the evening of his transition.

Another special part of this workshop was a ceremony in which the leader used a lighted candle to light the flame of a symbolic eternal candle. In that exact moment, when the already lighted candle touched the new wick and ignited a flame, I had a vision; it was of William's essence leaving his body in a great blaze of light, as a flame. That flame then became part of a larger flame that radiated outward. One memory, the memory of how my energy had been drawn into that experience with him, now filled my body. As I witnessed the eternal candle being lit, I merged into oneness with its flame.

This felt sense of myself as the torch being lighted transported me next to a memory of the visions that I had received in Raymond Moody's psychomanteum. These visions now grew astonishingly clear. It had taken years for that understanding to permeate me.

In the psychomanteum I had seen a jeweled bridge across which two figures of light danced. Now I finally understood that William and I had bridged the dimensions. He had gone to spirit while I remained in the physical. In my vision the two figures had danced and shared their light. William and I had been doing that very thing for the last few years. In the dance that I had seen, only when it was time did, they merge as one single flame.

Here in this ceremony I felt the oneness of that flame, as if I was fire from within. I felt like a human torch. In my psychomanteum vision, the flame had then separated into individual figures of light. As one continued on, the torch passed to the one left behind.

I had felt devastated, being the one left behind. Now I held the torch of the knowing and the light. I had become the torch bearer, and I had been entrusted with it. That was my destiny. By sharing this knowledge, I pass love's fire to others. The dance continues for all to join.

After relating to Janet my experience of the candle lighting ceremony, I assumed that Book Two of our story was complete. I titled that chapter "The Grand Finale." Not so. No sooner had I rested on my laurels than William showed up in a dream to make major changes. Our "ghost writer" did not yet feel satisfied.

William objected vehemently to my choice of title. He argued, *The whole point of our story was that no finale existed, grand or otherwise.* He continued at length about how love extends beyond known boundaries and forms, on into the unknown. This truth formed the essence of our journey, both in the physical and now in spirit. *Love never ends, only its forms change.*

Playfully William further charmed me to remind his former wife, Rebecca, that he was sensitive to her discomfort over revealing the secret of our trio. However, our experience remained integral to the message of love extending beyond boundaries. Our sacred trio was what had begun our exploration. We had trusted our hearts to be guided by our spirits, to risk traditional form. That trust had been the essence of our love.

I acknowledged that I would convey William's words to Rebecca, as I believed he had now finished what he needed to say. Little did I realize that William would soon devote his full attention to admonishing me over the cancer that continued to take its silent toll on my upper lip.

Just days prior, I had begun to apply an herbal salve to the cancer. It was an eerie reliving of the same compound that I had applied to William years earlier. Its effects on my lip began to be significant. Even though the salve was a topical compound, I could see it extend down into the roots of the lesion, outlining it like a map. The result felt like a volcano erupting, spewing out emotions of guilt and shame.

Stunned, I recognized how I continued to bad mouth myself for not having spoken up with my full and complete truth during William's cancer journey. Even though I believed that I had released these toxic emotions long ago, there they were. Thoughts of not pushing William into chemotherapy, not confronting him with the fact that his tumor had grown worse, and most tormenting of all, that final week of questioning our love continued to eat at me. All of these thoughts continued to haunt me.

Somehow, my emotions seem to have embedded themselves in the cells of my upper lip. In addition, how many times had I proclaimed, "I'm ready to die?" Could all of these utterances be a metaphor for my body's wisdom with this cancer?

I knew that this basal cell skin cancer probably would never kill me. However, I didn't fear death until recently I had even longed to die. What I faced instead was a cancer that, if not treated, would be pervasive. It could invade the tissues of my entire face and body and possibly predispose me to other cancers. The only treatment that medicine offered was surgery, with its possibility of disfigurement. I found such an option frightening.

Doctors had informed me that in surgery they would excise tissue until clear boundaries indicated that no more cancer remained. Regardless of how extensive this surgery needed to be, only microscopic examination of the removed tissue could identify its limits. I had no frame of reference, and without surgery the doctors wouldn't know how far the cancer might already have spread.

Indeed, I found the prospect of cutting into my lips, lips that I held so dear and that gave me so much pleasure, to be unthinkable. Nor did I feel strong enough emotionally to face the ordeal.

As if on cue, memories began to well up from within, memories that ignited my passion of a vow made long ago. As a young teenager who had experienced the death of her dearly beloved father, I innocently vowed to explore all that I could about cancer. I never again wanted to lose to that dreaded disease another person I loved.

This time I was no longer a naive child, I was a successful doctor in the healing arts, specializing in mind-body dynamics. This challenge would be my opportunity to make good that promise. I mused over whether choosing not to have surgery was a risk worth taking. In my favor, I had a cancer that is rarely life threatening and I had the wisdom to delve into alternative methods of treatment. I would do my own research prompted by my own body. Rather than cut out the cancer and be done with it, I committed myself to call on my inner and outer resources to explore other possibilities.

Unknown to me, however, William had been listening. His perception was amazing, as if he had witnessed all of my innermost thoughts and feelings. He comforted me with his knowledge that the power of our love remained pure and that intuitively I was on the right track. He also added an intriguing twist, blessing this healing journey as holy. He reminded me of our secret code word, "Kiss, "our shorthand for, *Love you more than words can say.* My lips were treasures that needed to be cherished and forgiven, not condemned and mutilated. The best that I could muster through this ordeal would be to forgive the words that I had spoken through my lips.

From our history, William and I knew that where words could and often did fail us, kisses never did. Kisses always spoke truth, revealing love. Whatever we couldn't say with words, we expressed with kisses.

In many ways William and I had also played with the word itself. Many have heard the translation of k-i-s-s as, "Keep it simple, stupid." We changed it originally to, "Keep it simple, Sweetheart." One day we took it further, with "Keep it spiritually succulent."

William reminded me of all this. Adding the spiritual to the sexual is a simple way to access the spiritual through a kiss. William continued that kisses remain an easy and intimate way of transmitting love's fire when the heart is opened fully. Kisses offer an alchemy that burns off the impurities so that a higher order is established.

William and I had delighted in our daily way of passing on this fire through our kisses. His message now was that I stop beating up on myself for words I had and had not spoken. He reminded me *Cherish and celebrate the memories,. We made the best of an enormously challenging situation.*

William also pressed to force a confession out of me. My unspoken words hadn't been all of it. He confronted me to delve deeper into myself, to connect with both my buried secrets of the past and my fears of the future. He urged me to remember my own teaching that healing is an inside job. Now it would be up to me.

123

Then in playfulness William presented me with a clue from an oldies song that I didn't fully recognize. It was strong enough to have me wake from sleep to capture its words on paper. What lingered of the fleeting lyrics sounded like, *We have to say goodbye . . . and I send you all my love, every day, sealed with a kiss.*

What to this day stuns me is that as I scribbled these words, I knew that he was still present. I was awake, and his energy was by my side, laughing. He offered new chapter titles such as "Kiss from Heaven "or "Sealed with a Kiss." Before leaving he teased, *Now, you pick.* I got to choose.

Excited and still disoriented, I mused over what had just transpired. It was Easter morning. I paused to reflect on the deeper meaning of receiving William's message on this day. From my Catholic roots I remembered that Easter celebrates a rising from the dead. It was in this way that Christ had proved death to be an illusion.

The ongoing saga with William also showed me that death is not as it appears to be. I began to move on with my life in a way that seemed, on the surface, to be successful. However, if I were to be true to myself, I had to admit that the fire of my spirit had not yet risen from the dead. I had focused on death more than on life. I needed to change that focus.

It seemed to me that this was the real message that both my invisible beloved and my body tried to send to me on that appropriate day. I also heard clearly from William that I had to shift my view away from relying on his being by my side constantly. He suggested that I had more strength than I realized, strength to rise from the ashes, like the phoenix.

For several more days I treated the cancer with the herbal salve. I watched as this salve seemed to pull toxins from the depths and draw them to the surface above my upper lip. Anyone who viewed such a demonstration of this salve eating away at the cancerous tissue would have been appalled. The amount of puss and burning that it produced felt overwhelming.

Concurrent with this treatment, my emotions released energy explosively, uprooting memories right along with the cancerous tissue. I felt as if layers of past pain began to leave me as the salve burned through layers of my skin. As this process continued, I gave thanks for what I assumed would be a total healing. Not so.

Once the effects of the treatment subsided, I noted that the cancerous lesion remained. So many powerful memories and emotions had erupted that the lesion's continued presence confused me. However, there it was. The cancer remained on my face with no visible change.

By that point I just wanted to forget both the treatment and the cancer. I had planned an exciting sacred journey to the Himalayas in June. I had longed for and waited three years for this journey, which would be led by Gregg Braden. Ever since my body's cellular response during Braden's earlier workshop two months after William's passing, I had known that I wanted to go on one of his journeys.

Indeed, it had been upon hearing the words "Initiation in the 21st century" that I had felt a connection to this particular trip. I knew that the journey would take me to one of the highest spiritual places in the world, one that had beckoned to me for years. I would also be going with a leader who understood magnetics and frequencies of high altitude. The combination proved too much to resist.

The very way I heard of this trip seemed itself a good omen. Imagine finding an answering machine message from a tour company, saying that they were returning my call about my inquiry. I had placed no such call and almost dismissed their message. Telepathically I heard, *Call and do it now.* Following up on William's insistence, I phoned them back.

To my amazement, one "Tina Conte" had placed the original call. Not surprising, I had also been listed in their records under that name. However, I knew that I hadn't called them, and I urged that they double check. What are the odds that a "Tina Conte" from another state who was also in their records had phoned them? I took the opportunity, however, to ask them if Gregg Braden planned to lead a future trip to Tibet. They answered that such a trip was even then in the pre-planning stage. It was so popular that it was already half filled. I asked them to add my name and that of my friend Mary as participants in this future trip that had no date set. Not long afterward, they confirmed a June departure date.

Eagerly I devoted all of my attention preparing for this journey. However, my lip would not leave me alone. Each day as I faced the mirror to apply makeup, there it was. I could not hide from it. Oh yes, I could use cover-up to mask it on an appearance level. Still, cosmetics couldn't change whatever continued behind the scenes. Disappointed, yet not disillusioned, I decided to give the herbal salve one more try.

I summoned my courage to face the process once again. My first experience had been explosive, and I knew its performance could be repeated. I saw no turning back. Surgery did not seem an option in my mind at this time. Bravely, I applied the salve to the same region and waited in trepidation for its results. My fears proved well founded. The first experience had been explosive, and it paled in comparison to what happened the second time around.

This time my emotions roared up with memories from my childhood abuse. Most particularly, I remembered secrets about having protected the man who had sexually violated and abused me. For his family's sake, I have been protecting him to this day. As these memories erupted, the burning in my skin intensified. I felt as if someone held a lighted match and passed it back and forth across my upper lip. The area burned and burned. With each searing, the cancer's outline became even more apparent. To my honor I saw that it had spread to include more tissue, and that now it bordered on the lip line.

It was early morning. As I examined my face in the mirror, I grew faint with the realization that despite all of my efforts, the cancer continued to grow. I cried. I knew that I faced a defining moment. Most rational people would heed such warning signs and schedule surgery immediately. I prayed for guidance.

It seemed that for now, my spirit was calling me instead to make the journey to Tibet. I knew instinctively that I had to follow my spirit's wisdom. I knew that such a decision meant either a miracle encounter or healing in the Himalayas, or a return from this journey with enough strength to face the spread of the cancer. Either way, I had to trust my decision to go forward. If I were ever to live fully, I knew that fear could not become the dominating factor in my life.

In a dream in which I saw William, I found validation for my decision. In this dream he held out a little stuffed bear that had been our mascot. The bear had a heart that read, "I love you." This animal had been with us on every step of his cancer journey and had been our constant companion. It had always mirrored our truth as a source of love and laughter, particularly helpful during those stretches of silence that illness creates.

In a symbolic act of letting go, William now urged me to give this stuffed toy to an Asian child who would approach me. He showed me this child as being a little boy of nine or ten with big beautiful brown eyes and a warm smile. The child would recognize me, and I would recognize him. This boy would be a worthy custodian of our love bear. Upon awakening, I took my dream to mean that William supported my decision to travel to Tibet. I wondered who this child would be. I readied our mascot for his new home.

Speaking of homes, the phone soon rang with a call about my villa in St. Martin. This home had always been our love nest get away. The co-owners wanted to know if I had made a decision about selling it. Overwhelmed by all that was already going on, I informed them that I needed more time. They said firmly that they had waited long enough and needed to know my decision before I left for Asia.

In a quandary as to what to do, I sensed the immediate presence of William. He reminded me, *You lovingly called it your spiritual home before it was our love nest. After all, we affectionately referred to it as our private corner of paradise. Think future and long term. It was you who taught me to look at the question, "If money were not an issue, what would your answer be?"*

I took William's remarks to mean that he recommended keeping the villa. Still, I didn't know if I should do so. I wondered whether the memories of our honeymoon times spent there would taint my enjoyment of it. Could I handle going back?

At that point the co-owners mentioned that they had installed a sliding door on one of the walls, facing in a new direction. Intuitively I realized that my future visits there would result in new perceptions. I assured the co-owners that when I reached a decision, I would let them know. I ended the call.

I now realized that during the grieving process, my memories of cherished places had remained too painful for me to contemplate returning there without my deceased partner. In my healing studies I learned that a sign of grief's completion is the ability to return and take back everything that one had given up. I had once vowed never to return to St. Martin in this lifetime because of its memories. Had I finally become ready to take that leap and be willing to risk its pain? I didn't yet know.

I turned my full attention to Tibet. Preparing for such an extended trip seemed a daunting challenge. My friend Mary would travel with me and joyfully we tackled the task at hand. We needed to outfit ourselves for temperatures that would range from the eighties to as low as the twenties in high altitude. We would also be traveling during the monsoon season. My existing wardrobe did not include rugged clothing. Mary and I set out to buy the recommended attire, along with food, health aids, and miscellaneous items on our suggested travel list.

We did not know where to begin. A comical adventure soon unfolded as we found ourselves driving away from New York toward Connecticut. At first our travel direction didn't seem unusual, except that we ended up

127

in William's favorite stores. I even purchased clothing that had been his style, not necessarily mine. All of it was quite appropriate for this trip. Mary and I chuckled and wondered if we had been *under the influence,* so to speak. With that remark I heard familiar laughter and knew that all was well.

Suitcases packed, Mary and I felt that our journey was already underway. Our flight to Tibet would originate in Nepal. We decided to fly there a week earlier than the rest of the group, so as to enjoy the beauty of Nepal as well. Little did I realize, as I booked our flights, the macabre event that would soon unfold in Nepal. I did not even hear about it in the news. A client brought it to my attention. The entire royal family of Nepal had just been massacred. Mary and I and the world were stunned.

We felt both pain for the people of that country, and confusion over what we should do next. Was this tragedy a sign that we should cancel our trip? For me, what would it mean to visit a grieving country in the midst of rioting? Intuitively I knew that I was meant to be there. The timing appeared unmistakable. The call of the Himalayas seemed to be a call to embark on a sacred journey to climax my own grieving and provide comfort to those grieving in Nepal.

I received an inner message to re-route and not cancel the trip. There was no doubt, and no cancellation. Contact with the airlines informed me of their penalty policy, which further confirmed our decision. We needed to leave New York on the appointed date and time or we would lose the tickets altogether. Agents who handled our connecting flight with an Austrian partner airline understood graciously. They gave us a week's delay with no penalty. It seemed that we were being re-routed to spend a week in Austria rather than in Nepal. I wondered what surprises our new itinerary would bring.

CHAPTER NINE

Ultimate Pilgrimage

∞

Once Mary and I had waded through the chaos of last-minute itinerary changes we took off for Austria. Weary and eager to get there, we arrived with no hotel reservations. Nevertheless, the wondrously beautiful city of Vienna provided us with a welcome respite. Even our hotel gave us an upgrade to a duplex room. In Austria we found a refreshing pause for the journey ahead. For that we were very grateful.

On our first night in Vienna, Mary slept soundly in the bed on the opposite side of the room. I, on the other hand, tossed and turned. I kept going over in my mind the wisdom of my decision not to sell my home in St. Martin. I wondered if I should call New York while I still had the chance to change my mind.

In the midst of my restlessness, William showed up on cue. He soon made it clear that I had done the right thing. Since I remained unsure, he and I engaged in a telepathic *tete-a-tete*. I was absorbed in this passionate mental conversation that, Mary admitted, woke her up. She looked at me and asked innocently, "What's going on? I feel an energy change in the room. Everything is of a lighter vibration."

William and I had been caught! Sheepishly I confessed that he and I were engaged in a hot debate. Mary just gazed at me with a look that implied, *Leave it to you both. I'm not surprised.* I acknowledged Mary's sensitivity. I also wondered if William had grown stronger.

During our week in Austria, Mary and I spent our time sightseeing. William stayed out of hearing and out of mind as if he had gone elsewhere on vacation. At one location, however, William's participation became evident. Mary continued to tour a museum while William lured me into a shop outside. His voice grew insistent. By this point I had learned to surrender more graciously.

I entered the shop, amused at what I perceived as an endearing gesture on William's part. Before me I found the work of Klimt, whose art I have long valued for its portrayal of lovers in embrace. Indeed, Klimt's famous piece "The Kiss" continues to grace my bedroom. I assumed that this work in Vienna was what William wanted me to see; I was wrong.

I had begun to immerse myself in the vast array of Klimt merchandise when abruptly William tugged me elsewhere. He led me to an open box that held wooden frames shaped as puzzle pieces. His laughter grew infectious. I soon laughed out loud as well.

Here were pieces that I could use for upcoming workshops to frame photos of people's lives a la cosmic jigsaw puzzles. I had found the beginning of my future endeavors. I thanked William for being on the case.

This stay in Austria provided Mary and me with an unexpected gift and a blessed detour on our journey to Nepal. We hadn't even realized how much we had needed this respite.

Now we had to face the grieving country of Nepal. From the moment we boarded our plane for Kathmandu, we could see that the upheaval of Nepal's royal assassinations had resulted in major turmoil for that country's tourist flow. Our plane flew practically empty, a fact that led us to wonder what state of affairs would greet us. When we landed in Nepal we found the airport nearly desolate.

The Hyatt Hotel, which is normally my haven in travel, also appeared nearly empty. This was hardly a surprising fact, given what was going on in the country. On the other hand, it felt strange to be one of very few guests. Staff members were so pleased to welcome us, that they honored us for our courage in coming. As it turned out, many tourists had canceled their reservations.

As our Nepalese hosts explained these things to us, Mary and I realized that our visit to Nepal served a greater purpose. We needed to offer comfort in any way we knew. We traveled throughout the region and soon recognized that our mere presence, and our ability to listen compassionately, touched many people and seemed to make a difference in their suffering. They opened up to us about their pain, and we witnessed how deep had been their love for the royal family. Most especially Nepal's slain king had been more than just a ruler to them. They had looked up to him as a father, almost a deity.

For me, having grieved through the last few years I recognized how my own experience could contribute. In some way the Nepalese looked to

Mary and me as ambassadors of goodwill from the U.S. Our presence made them feel supported, and not judged for such a tragedy having occurred in their country.

Intuitively I felt that the message being revealed through our journey thus far was one of compassion. This message could not have been more highlighted than by an experience I had in the spa treatment for which Mary and I registered.

When we arrived, we found a scene that was perfect for invoking an altered state. I entered a small, windowless, candle lit room that held a large mirror. My experience began with an incredible massage that anointed every part of me with warm oils.

This massage was followed by an ancient Ayurvedic treatment known as *shirodhara*. As I lay quietly on the table, the attendant stood behind. She monitored a vase like container filled with warm sesame oil, from which a thin stream fell onto the third eye at the center of my forehead. This oil flowed backward, over the crown of my head and into a waiting bowl. The process was intended to remove veils from the spiritual eye of knowing.

I began to sob quietly. As the oil touched my third eye I cried for myself, for the people of Nepal, and for all others who suffered. The message I received was that the highest form of compassion is the union of the third eye and the heart. The spiritual eye knows that there is a greater truth beyond physical appearances. As one remains in awareness and without judgment, while simultaneously feeling the human condition in the heart, one's response is true compassion.

This realization moved me deeply as I began to see how impossible it is to walk in another's shoes. However, we can attempt to do so as best as we know how. In that way, we can be most helpful to others through the challenges that life presents.

As my treatment ended, the attendant helped me to a sitting position and I faced the mirror. Still in a trance like state, I watched as my reflection changed into William's face, then into Mary's face, followed by a multitude of other faces, as spiritual sight continued to unfold its mystery.

We are all many faces that mirror one another in the oneness. All of us are *Re-membered Beloved,* as each person finds the love within his/herself as their own beloved and allows this love to radiate out. I felt blessed in this experience. I left with humble appreciation of what had transpired. This memorable event marked my readiness to enter Tibet.

Our tour group soon welcomed Mary and me as wayward family members. Prior to our flight to Tibet, we heard cautions that we had to be mindful of our bodies in high altitude. Acclimating would be essential to a successful experience. We would need rest, plenty of water, and no alcohol. After our plane landed in Tibet we recognized that the weight of the air seemed different. Any kind of strong exertion could exhaust us.

An unexpected benefit of this need for caution was that we had to stay more present to the moment and the richness that each moment brought. Our trip included visits to many monasteries, and our caution became invaluable in focusing our senses to the sights and sounds around us. Buddhist statues were plentiful and awesome to behold, their beauty matched only by the wisdom of this land. Within Tibetan temples, sacred texts abound.

Gregg Braden had titled this journey, "Search for Original Wisdom." Tibet's monks and nuns appeared to be the keepers of this wisdom. Their studies and traditions include a mode of prayer that is relatively unknown to the West.

We were soon privileged to witness and participate in chanting rituals. Buddhist monks and nuns would chant for hours, praying mainly for all sentient beings to be free from suffering. All of us were moved by such displays of devotion and compassion.

On a previous journey to Tibet, Braden had inquired as to the nature of the prayers of these monks and nuns. He shared with us an interesting awareness. The chanting itself is not the prayer, he explained. Chanting is vocalized to create a feeling in the body, as if the prayer has already been answered. Braden continued that this feeling in the body becomes a singular force that speaks to creation through the heart. He referred to this practice as the lost mode of prayer.

I further learned from him that Western tradition includes four modes of prayer. The first is colloquial or informal prayer. The second is ritualistic prayer, with a predetermined sequence of words. The third is petitionary. The fourth is meditative prayer in which no words are used. The lost mode is the fifth mode. This is the prayer that the Tibetan monks and nuns embody.

It's one thing to hear about Tibetan spiritual practice; it's quite another to be immersed in the sacred spiritual traditions that remain alive in Tibet. Although the outer life of Tibet seems simplistic and devoid of technology, the inner life of its people is rich beyond measure in spiritual technology.

The inspiration I received was imprinted within me and will be forever lasting.

Another powerful spiritual practice that Braden shared with us was the "gift of the blessing." We were instructed on the power of blessing as a first step in compassion. Words of blessing seem to be the lubricant that can release the emotional charge that holds us to events and people that hurt us. In particular, Braden encouraged us to bless both the people who hurt us the most, and events that we cannot reconcile. Blessing them would not mean that we have condoned or agreed with the hurts, rather that we have seen and acknowledged them as part of the oneness of all that is. In doing so, we become agents for change. We become part of the solution instead of the problem.

This blessing is threefold. First, one blesses people who have been harmed in any way, either directly or indirectly. Then one blesses the people who did the harming. Finally, one blesses oneself as the witness.

This message transported me back in time to childhood dialogues with my father about love and spirituality. His words continued to resonate within me as timeless and applicable. He would ask, "Can you love someone if they are attacking you? Remember, that's the test of love; if you can love somebody even if they are hurting you."

As once again I registered these words upon my heart and mind, I could feel the truth of their knowing. I found myself especially moved by one of the Buddhas of compassion that seemed to depict this truth. It was Avalokiteshvara, who is represented as having thousands of arms and hands, and an eye on each fingertip. Avalokiteshvara's message is to have the eyes and ability to touch and release suffering whenever possible. This message reminded me of my earliest training with a blind physical therapist who taught me to use my innermost senses. I now took home a tapestry of Avalokitesvara, as a symbol of this ancient wisdom.

Indeed, the Buddha served me in a multitude of ways. At the Jokhang temple I experienced a mystical encounter in one of the shrine chambers. In a temple filled with pilgrims and tourists, I found myself drawn to a small room that was devoid of people. As I entered, I became mesmerized by the massive, colorfully decorated statues of the Buddhas before me. I looked up at the title plaque that read, "The Eight Medicine Buddhas."

I sought wisdom from these Buddhas in reference to the cancer that had invaded my lip. The telepathic message that I received touched me deeply. It came in two parts, one that I understood readily, and another that needed to be deciphered. I heard, *Bless yourself and life instead of cursing both.* Then I heard a question, *In relation to healing, what is the legacy you want to leave behind?* Baffled by this question, I quickly put it out of my mind.

I rejoined our group just as Braden began his first lecture permitted in the temple itself. Synchronistically enough, his topic was the science of compassion. It included the above-mentioned gift of the blessing. Here again, wisdom was right in my face. It was all I needed for confirmation. Despite my pain and great loss, life and my living it remained a blessing. Perhaps I needed to trust that a greater purpose was unfolding, a purpose that I could not yet see. I shed a tear and silently thanked the Medicine Buddhas.

Our journey soon included a visit to a Tibetan hospital that does not use medicine. We witnessed the treatment of disease through application of herbs, acupuncture, and various alternatives to drugs and surgery. I was fascinated with such an approach. Imagine an entire hospital system devoted to treatment that used no allopathic medicine. I wondered if I could also receive treatment there for the skin cancer on my face. Unfortunately, they didn't offer much in this regard.

A great fulfillment for me, however, was a visit to an orphanage. As soon as I stepped off the bus, a young boy approached us. He was the very image of the child from my dream. He looked into my eyes and took me by the hand. Immediately we recognized a familiarity with each other. He even spoke a bit of English, so our communication ran even deeper than expected.

I found myself moved by how closely the encounter resembled the dream that I had had prior to leaving the U.S. This young boy led me into his classrooms and then to his sleeping quarters. He acted as a perfect gentleman in showing me his world. I had no doubt that he must become the custodian of William's and my love bear.

As I gave it to him, his eyes lit up and for a brief moment I even felt the energy presence of William. A slight tear came into my eye as I sensed what it would have been like to have a child with William.

The little boy picked right up on my thoughts and inquired, "Your husband?"

Stunned at his perception I responded, "I believe so."

The boy and I hugged and exchanged names on paper. Together we read the inscription on the bear's little heart, *I love you.* Ours became a meeting so special that I looked into adopting him, if it were at all possible.

The remainder of this Tibetan journey took our group to some of the most sacred sites and most remote areas of the world. The people and the places of Tibet embody a joy of spirituality that I will long treasure. As I walked this land, that of the exiled Dalai Lama, I reflected on his many messages that I had heard over the years. They now filled my being. Most especially I remembered that we are all the same, and that we just wear different costumes.

Our time in Tibet became unique to my life's journey. Our group of travelers departed from that land with a sense of awe and gratitude beyond measure. It was now time to fly back to Nepal. I felt grateful for all that I had experienced in Tibet. I believed the journey was done. I was not prepared for what would soon happen on our flight over the Himalayas.

As our plane flew over Mt. Everest, sunlight reflected off its ice in a magnificent light. Immediately I found myself transported to a vision that I had seen in my NDE. The love and the perfection of this vision touched me deeply. Filled with tears, I sensed an acceptance beyond words that the agony and ecstasy are part of the oneness. In embracing all of it, one is set free.

I realized that my grief had been the agony that had masked the ecstasy of my emerging destiny, in a picture far bigger than I could yet see. The power of my NDE of more than five years earlier now became illumined as a cellular blueprint. Its wisdom had unfolded slowly through my grief journey, as I had released illusion, as well. For me, it meant the revelation of a secret desire of seeing William. I hadn't even known until that moment that I continued to harbor this desire.

I had heard Braden say that the veils between the worlds are thinnest at high altitude. Unconsciously I took Braden's words to mean that physical manifestation of William could be possible. I had had hopes that during this journey I would encounter him in a more visible from. Not only had I not seen him, I had not even heard him. I had walked the land of Tibet with my own inner strength and guidance. I had emerged from that experience with deeper compassion for myself and for others. The time had come for me to celebrate the climax of my Initiation. Mt. Everest offered my mirror.

Our group's stay together in Nepal would be of short duration, since the main group planned to leave the following morning. All of us celebrated with a recounting of our most memorable moments. We feasted until exhaustion set in. Our tearful goodbyes were mixed with love and laughter as each in our family hugged, "until we meet again."

Mary and I planned to savor a few more days in Nepal. We visited one of the cities in the region, only to discover that reports of a possible bomb had drawn police there hours earlier. The reports turned out to be a false alarm. In many ways all of Nepal continued to move through its grieving process, with grace permeating its challenges.

Our shopping had been minimal, so we decided to give it a try. My invisible beloved, who had remained so quiet in Tibet, now made his energy presence known. As Mary and I peered through a closed jewelry shop window, I heard distant laughter and the words, *Over here.* Behind us stood an open jewelry store. What a curious metaphor for life. We had salivated in front of a closed door, even as an open door beckoned. I signaled Mary to follow. In we went.

This time, William's primary purchase with my credit card was a jeweled serpent bracelet that bore a remarkable resemblance to the logo of our company. He also directed me to a lapis pendant. To my surprise, both items were incredibly underpriced. Mary and I made our purchases and returned to our hotel room for final packing.

The Kathmandu airport had grown more active than when we had first arrived in the country. On one delightful banner I read, "Celebrate Nepal: Festival of Life." This slogan seemed appropriate in oh so many ways.

Mary and I returned to Austria for a weekend stopover prior to our flight back to New York. I had heard of a spa in Baden, which was located near mineral hot springs. After our long hiatus in Asia I scheduled a visit to this spa as a welcome re-entry. The spa exceeded our expectations. It brought us immense relaxation as well as a rejuvenation of our bodies and minds.

One treatment in particular carried a sense of ancient Egyptian wisdom. In a chariot like chamber with Venetian blinds drawn down around it, I lay on a magnet mattress spread with sand. Long tubular lights surrounded me, in the colors of my choice. Blue and white appealed to me the most. Aromatherapy fragrances filled the chamber and an attendant placed stereo phones on my head to pipe music according to my needs. It was a feast for awakening all of the senses.

In a meditative state that seemed timeless, I began to integrate the sacred journey that we had just made to Nepal and Tibet. This integration began in a most intriguing way. The image of my new lapis pendant appeared in my mind, along with an awareness that I hadn't previously had.

During the earlier trip to India, William had gifted me with a lapis pendant in the shape of a teardrop. In Nepal he had gifted me with a lapis pendant in the shape of a dewdrop. The words that I now heard intuitively were, *mourning turns to morning as the Initiation is completed and a new life is dawning.* How well this jewelry symbolized that truth. My treatment in the spa chamber felt like a magic ride from which a new me emerged. Then I heard laughter, and *A job well done.*

I chuckled that the spa had scheduled a Cleopatra bath of milk and honey to follow my multisensory experience. If this sacred bath wasn't confirmation of Egypt, I don't know what was. Indeed, at the end of the bath an attendant helped me on with my robe and handed me a glass of champagne. The spa, its magnificent service, and most especially the caring of its owners, gave me memories for a lifetime.

Conversations with the spa 's owner soon established a special bond. His father had died recently, and our closeness allowed me to reveal my perceptions of death and my ongoing connection with William. This man resonated with my words, since they spoke a truth that he recognized. We knew that ours had become a friendship that would last and perhaps evolve into a business liaison. This would be the perfect spa from which to launch workshops that could delve into transformation from the inside out, on the theme of Initiation.

With warm embraces and fond farewells, Mary and I bid goodbye to our new friends in Austria. All that now remained was to witness how the assimilation of our journey would show itself in our lives. Mary and I were ready to go home. We wondered what would await us.

CHAPTER TEN

Remembered Beloved

∞

When I arrived home from the journey to Tibet, I recognized an awakening of a new perception of the beloved within. This perception made me realize that I now had to deal with the skin cancer that had already taken its toll. In the past I had subscribed to a paradigm of, "After you, I come last." Now I embraced a new paradigm, "After me, you come next."

As soon as I returned, however, I became immersed in a pile of phone messages, emails, and letters that needed attention. Clients expressed their eagerness for appointments. Forgetting my original priority, I jumped right in. The lesion on my face soon became less important than other people's needs until William clamored.

My invisible beloved appeared in a dream that, on an emotional level, shook me to the core. He was nononsense, his brown eyes fierce as he gazed at me. His words sounded loving and stern.

You need to really hear this. It's time to put yourself first. Your lip challenge is not going to hasten our reunion. It's not your time to die and this won't kill you. We won't be together that way. It won't have me manifest more visibly for you either. Your kisses were ecstatic. They are not for me anymore. It's time you let another man in your world enjoy the pleasure and sensuality of your lips and savor your kisses. Get on with it!

With that admonition, William placed his left hand over his own heart and stretched out his right hand to me, over my heart. He did this in the Tantric fashion that he and I had used in the physical whenever we had needed to communicate sensitive issues. He now emphasized:

It's time to move on. Know that I'll watch over you, but I can't be the one there for you. You can't count on me anymore. You are stronger than you realize. If needed, turn to others. There are many who love you and will be there for you. It can't be me.

Having delivered his message, William let his countenance relax as he sang the words that we had often sung to each other when we had needed tender loving care.

How could anyone ever tell you, you were anything less than beautiful? How could anyone ever tell you, you were less than whole? How could anyone fail to notice that your loving is a miracle? How deeply you're connected to my soul.

With these parting words, William placed his right hand over the left hand on his heart and bowed to me. He turned his back and walked into the Light. There were no more kisses. There were no more hugs. William had made his intention absolutely clear. There had been no touch of any kind. All that remained was my memory of his loving gesture to my heart. I stood alone in the wake of William's departure.

I woke with tears streaming endlessly from my eyes onto my shocked body. Had this been a dream, or had I entered a space between the worlds to be admonished? This encounter had been intense. For the remainder of that day I found myself unable to shrug off William's words. I even pondered if this meeting had been our last.

I recalled my mother once telling me of my deceased father having come to her often in dreams. She remarked that one night she had dreamed that he said goodbye. After that dream, he visited her only when something urgent arose that needed attention. Had my own dream been William's version of that goodbye? For all of that week William remained silent. I missed him. However, I realized that I was indeed fine.

July 28 approached. That would have been William's birthday, and a date that would serve as my gauge of how I could celebrate living without even his invisible presence. That day I lay in bed with just a few tears welling up in my eyes. Immediately I heard telepathically, through what felt like a veiled distance, *No more tears! Birthdays celebrate having a physical body. When you don't have one, it doesn't make a difference. It's no big deal. Get over it.*

140

I couldn't stop laughing. William was still around. Even though I felt more distance between us, his humor continued to amuse me. I could have spent that day reviewing memories. Instead I called my friend Mary. I announced, "It's party time. Let's drive to the city and see what unknown awaits us."

In the city we landed once again at TKTS and faced an outrageously long ticket line. Being a consummate theater goer, I was prepared to wait. Mary vacillated. Intuitively I heard, *Go to Lincoln Center.*

Anyone who knows New York City knows that finding parking space at Lincoln Center on a Saturday evening is nearly impossible. I answered telepathically, *Okay, you want us to go there. Have a parking space waiting for our arrival.*

Don't ask me how it's done, and there it was. Just as we drove up, someone pulled out. We even found enough time left on the meter to explore whether or not an opportunity awaited us. Mary knows me well. She agreed to risk the adventure.

Outside Lincoln Center we found the gathering of people, music, and dance intoxicating. We milled around and just enjoyed the electricity that is New York. Telepathically William's voice piped in, *Go to that building.* There we found a theater that had performances scheduled for that evening. I heard, *Buy a ticket.* Astonishingly, the ticket booths had no lines. We asked what was playing.

The ticket clerk replied, *"Chaucer in Rome."*

Neither Mary nor I had heard of this play. We looked at each other and at him and inquired, "What is it about?"

He responded "It's a comedy. That's all I know. It's closing soon."

I intuitively heard laughter and, *that's the one.* I turned to Mary and asked if she wanted to do it. She nodded. We purchased our tickets and returned to the car to move it. In a funny synchronicity, the parking meter expired just as we arrived.

The play itself brought even more surprise. Its opening scene in Italy involved, of all things, *skin cancer!* The main character's surgery had been completely successful. I could not believe my eyes and ears. Who would ever have guessed that's where we would land? Of all the shows in New York City, this was the one that dealt with my most immediate issue. Soon I heard familiar laughter, and *Gotcha.*

This play also spoofed pilgrimages. Mary and I glanced at each other in disbelief. We had just returned from our pilgrimage to Tibet, which could be considered the mother of all pilgrimages. Another aside that made my ears perk up was that the play also included reference to lead in paint, alluding to its contribution to skin cancer as well as effects on the testes.

William had worked with paints, both in art and in house painting. Could this message also carry meaning? All I knew was that the play began to push me toward action. As if I had not heard enough, as we exited the theater I heard telepathically, *Call a friend.* I assumed that such a call would constitute a baby step in dealing with the cancer.

To my credit I started the following week by placing a phone call to William's former oncologist for a recommendation. This man had been my colleague and trusted friend. He had seen me through bronchial pneumonia. Unfortunately, I soon learned that I had waited too long to request his assistance. He had suffered a heart attack and passed away during my stay in Nepal. How precious time is! Gone was a treasured friend, colleague, and member of my support team. The news flooded me with shock and sadness.

The following day I had an inner vision of a second friend, a fellow shaman who neared her transition. She had tried to phone me several days earlier, and I had been unable to reach her. Finally, I got through. Even though I had witnessed death intimately, this was the first time I had spoken with someone dear to me and known consciously that it could be our last conversation. Tearfully we expressed our goodbyes with awareness. We thanked each other deeply for an awesome lifetime journey. Our love would last beyond the borders of the physical world, and we knew it.

I shared with her William's words that love never dies. In life, surrounded by those she loves, and also in transition, there is only love. We honored the truth that love is all that matters. It is the only force that is lasting. We hung up with kisses and hugs. I set down the receiver and paused in silence. I realized, at the deepest level of my being, the importance of this everlasting message.

Now two of my soul companions had left the physical tapestry of my life. My awareness of this fact proved sobering. I had been gifted with their love and their wisdom. Since I still wore a physical body, I needed to treasure it. I had much wisdom to share with others. This realization was the last kick that I needed, to mobilize myself through any fear and procrastination. In addition, my inner vision flashed a picture of a ticking time bomb with a clock. That evening I called a dermatologist colleague. I made an appointment for the following day.

Bravely I faced the expert. It had been almost ten months since a trained physician had examined the lesion on my lip. I must admit to feeling both fearful and sheepish. I found it comforting that this man was also a friend.

He examined my skin thoroughly, took copious notes, and made sketches. With each scratch of his pen my heart took another blip. When he had finished his reporting, he showed me a medical textbook that illustrated the possible progression of such a lesion. It seemed to me the ghost of Christmas future if I didn't make a change now.

I shut the book and responded that I'd had enough of the negative pictures. I wanted to deal in the present with what is. Ready to combine this man's medical expertise with my training and intuitive wisdom, I had come there to be proactive. I had not ruled out surgery as an option.

His recommended route was surgery, and he was qualified and prepared to do it. However, after we discussed the highly sensitive nature of the lesion's location, we both decided that a physician who was also trained in Mohs surgery would be best. This special procedure would excise the cancerous tissue. Layer by layer, with a pathologist available. Thus, the smallest amount of tissue would be cut out. The option sounded good on the surface, with my illusion that I would receive a general anesthetic until the procedure was complete. With the name of a surgeon in hand, I left the office with seeming composure.

Upon further research, and much to my shock, I learned that Mohs surgery sounded torturous. This procedure would be an all day event. I would receive only local anesthesia and be fully conscious during the entire ordeal. After the surgeon had excised the first layer, hours could pass before he received the pathologist's report.

The time that I would have to wait for the results would feel endless. If more cancerous tissue were discovered, another layer would be taken. The surgery would continue deeper and deeper into my lip until microscopic examination confirmed that all the cancer had been removed.

Later, when I consulted with the Mobs surgeon, I learned that the extent of the surgery into my face and lips would be predicated solely upon the pathologist's findings. I wouldn't have a clue in advance and would have only the knowing of what was going on. As if this would not be hard enough to hear, the surgeon warned me that I might lose more of my lip than I had imagined. It could be reconstructed, he assured me.

In a clinical fashion he told me that I have "full lips, so perhaps enough tissue could be salvaged" from the lips on my face. If reconstruction required further tissue, the lips of the vulva are the most similar. To me, this option sounded as if my vagina could be the next site for grafting. These were the surgeon's closing comments as I left his office. In my mind's eye, I cupped my hands over my vagina. My mental image was one of strip mining my treasures.

All I could hear from my body was a shrieking, *No!* Memories then flooded me, memories of childhood sexual violation and abuse of that tender area of my body. Now as I thought of surgery without boundaries, performed by a clinical doctor who had minimal awareness of my sensitive past issues, this was more than I could bear. I had spent a lifetime of work, training women to use the lips on their face to speak their truth so that the lips surrounding their vaginas would not be violated. How could I submit to such a procedure? The possible violation of myself by myself was unthinkable.

Recognizing that with God anything is possible, I prayed to find another way. In that moment the memory flashed of my near fatal bout with bronchial pneumonia. In a millisecond I was healed. Both the illness and the healing had redirected the course of my life and served a higher purpose greater than I could have imagined. I felt confident in trusting God and the innate healing powers of my body. I would now stay open to possibilities outside of the traditional route, unless it became painfully evident that no other way existed.

Once out the door I realized the seriousness of my situation and it hit me with full force. I burst into tears as soon as I arrived home. My tears provided an excellent release, as I had needed to face the truth. However, I didn't have much time to indulge my emotions. I had only half an hour to prepare for a full day of clients. It still stuns me how the consciousness can shift in so short a time, from having an emotional breakdown to being a centered professional.

Once I had completed my work day, I turned my attention to sifting through the many options of various surgeons, all of whom my physician colleagues and friends had offered. I felt overwhelmed. Not knowing where to begin, intuitively I did something that surprised me. I turned to the pages of my own written story for guidance and support. Most especially, I read in the chapter in Book One titled "Agony and Ecstasy," where I had detailed William's cancer journey. Whether it was because I read my own wisdom, or because I found the content instructional, reading it left me inspired and strengthened.

I began to move within my own psyche to explore its mysteries. *Why had my body left clues such as this cancer that had invaded my lip?* I had already dedicated a lifetime to working with the body as a mirror of consciousness, with symptoms as its messengers. This background had prepared me to journey inward. I already knew that the location and the etiology of a presenting illness can offer significant clues to uncovering its deeper meaning. The time had come for me to walk my talk. Awareness began to flood me. I grabbed my notebook and began to jot down the insights that came. One's mind-body wisdom is a reservoir of truths not faced.

As is my style, I began with the metaphor of my body's reflection. In this case it was my lips. Lips are the seat of both pleasure and communication. Immediately I recognized that my loss of pleasure had been my loss of William. With this realization I began to craft exercises that would take me deeper into the secrets that I knew were locked in my cellular intelligence.

What emerged was a focus on undelivered communications, appreciations, and especially withholds. I wrote down names and messages. I prepared myself to deliver these messages to the appropriate receivers. I vowed that I would do so from my heart as best I could, with full truth. What a revelation that was! In its innocent simplicity this process opened a lifetime of stored emotions.

As I sat with the voluminous amount of information that my inner intelligence produced, I felt moved to review the Initiation chapter of Book Three. This was the teaching volume that Janet and I had drafted and not yet published. We had defined Initiation as any challenge in life that can lead to a spiritual awakening.

Here I was again, in another Initiation. With no time to rest on the laurels of the Initiation I had completed through William's passing. This time the Initiation was literally in my face.

I assessed where this cancer fell on a continuum of 1 to 10, both in its urgency and in what was needed. I felt paralyzed by the immensity of the choices that I faced, and I heartened to Initiation's call. I realized that every crisis, every Initiation, moves one toward evolving consciousness. However, just in that moment I felt too weak to move any further.

Before collapsing in exhaustion, I phoned Janet to describe my ordeal and to tell her that our collaboration seemed to be a guiding light in mobilizing me through this newest Initiation. In some amazing way, the writing that we had begun had provided me with inspiration and instruction. Janet sounded both compassionate in her listening and fascinated to hear of how rapidly my situation had begun to unfold. In our innocence, little were we aware that *fasten your seat belt* time lay just ahead.

The next morning my lethargy grew so great that all I wanted to do was stay under the covers forever and not come out. I would have lingered longer if it had not been for the phone call of a dear friend, Claudia. She was adamant that I begin to seek second opinions about my lip. She insisted that she would stay on my case all day until the job was done. I knew that she would be true to her word, and that I would find it useless to resist.

I placed the appropriate phone calls, made the appointments, and climbed back into bed, not for long. The insistent push of my invisible beloved made clear that there was to be no sleeping on the job. Telepathically I heard, *Go to the tapes.* What tapes? At first, I was perplexed. William responded, *Come with me.*

To my utter confusion I found myself lured to the basement. There I had buried the tapes that I had once used in working with the non-conscious mind. William steered me toward two tapes in particular.

Years earlier I had presented him with two tape options. Now he did the same for me. Curiously enough, the topics ranged from preparing for surgery, to William's tape for physical healing. I held the tapes in my hand, unprepared to listen to either one at that time. I merely retrieved them from the pile and took them upstairs.

As that day neared an end, a sudden impulse filled me. I flashed intuitively on the herbal salve. I had vowed that it was too painful to use again, and it had not produced sufficient physical healing to repeat. Yet intuitively I heard, *Even a ball game has three strikes before a player is called out.* I took this message to mean that one more strike remained to go. Without stopping to question, I slathered the salve on my lip. Suddenly I realized that it would need to remain there for the usual twelve hours. What had I done?

It was almost midnight. I would be unable to sleep, as the intensity of the fire that the salve produced had already begun to sear my lip. I kept thinking that an eruption of Mt. Vesuvius could be nothing compared to this. If it were not for a spontaneous image I received that portrayed this final effort as the tip of the iceberg, I don't know how I could have survived the night.

The pain became great, and the rest of the image indicated that heat had begun to melt the lesion from the inside out. In addition, since the salve outlined the cancer, I was horrified to see that its outline had reached my lower lip as well. This sight frightened me no end, with terror that the cancer could have spread to my lower lip.

Upon composing myself, I recognized that what I saw on the lower lip was merely an overflow of pus from my upper lip. Even so, this time the salve generated deeper blistering and swelling of my lip than ever before. In disbelief I found myself unable to eat, drink, or speak without difficulty. Memories and emotions welled up. I couldn't even express them through the pain. All I could do was record them in my memory and on paper, to explore them later, when my physical body would be more cooperative.

By morning I was a fright to behold. I hesitated to leave the house for any reason. I longed for the sleep that I had lost. That evening I finally received some respite from the pain, and I swooned into a deep slumber. Before long I experienced some of the most multidimensional dreams I had ever had. Later I remembered three of those dreams.

In the first one, as I socialized with a group of friends a bulletin on a door grabbed my attention. Going over to it, I noticed that it was very old, and someone had scribbled on it. I found its message difficult to read or understand. I could see only the words, "This is important." How could that be, when I couldn't even read it? In an aggressive act, I ripped this bulletin off the door and tore it to pieces.

As I returned to my friends and whispered to them what I had done, I asked their opinion as to what I should do next. They offered various suggestions, none of which seemed acceptable. I soon took my leave from them and went straight to the man who had posted the piece of paper. I admitted what I had done, and I offered to make things right by reprinting the page in a clear form. This was fine with him and all was well.

In the next dream, someone who had lost a pair of eyeglasses searched frantically for them. I opened my suitcase and discovered that they, as well as many others, were in there. Perplexed as to how the glasses had gotten there, I wondered whether or not to let people know I had them. I feared that they would suspect me of theft. However, when I did produce the glasses, I was met with rejoicing and relief. No negative repercussions resulted from my having the glasses. There was only gratitude.

The last dream was what I lovingly call a lesson dream. In a lecture hall the topic being discussed was how secrets, held over time, could eat away at one's cellular structures. This damage could result in cancer. As an example, the teacher used two soul mates and how each of them handled secrets. Although they revealed all of their secrets to each other, they held these secrets from others in their lives. This withholding of secrets eventually caused them to be separated in physical form. One dropped his body and the other faced cancer in the lip. Of course, I knew the person to whom the teacher referred. He went on to say that the expression of one's truth is vital to remaining radiantly healthy. Even as I dreamed, I heard this important message and recognized its reference to me.

I woke knowing that my unconscious mind had alerted me to the process that I was undergoing. The meaning of the third dream being evident to me, I focused on the earlier two. As I reviewed them I felt moved to call Janet. Together we explored the dreams' relevance and deciphered their deeper meaning.

Upon closer look, the first dream, the one about a bulletin on the door, reminded us both of the Egyptian mysteries. These mysteries had been ancient, and the scribbling over the bulletin had rendered them illegible. However, these mysteries were important, and somehow the time had come to write them in a clear fashion for all to read. Janet and I chuckled that writing about the ancient mysteries was our job. We were doing well, albeit slowly.

The next dream, the one about the eyeglasses, correlated with the first dream in that eyeglasses symbolize people's perception, which had been lost. However, I was the one who held the container from which to dispense the glasses to those who needed them. As I did so, all were joyous.

We took this part of the dream to mean that the ancient mysteries, and knowledge that consciousness continues beyond physical death, were at hand. I mused to Janet that I appreciated this insight. I wondered what further insights the mysteries of the salve would uproot.

No sooner had I expressed this thought than revelations came to me rapidly. That afternoon a colleague named Lois, who is a nurse and healer, heard of the grotesque demonstration that the salve was

148

manifesting. In her concern, she could not stay away. Lois needed to see it for herself. She came right over with her medical bag to treat my malady.

I comforted her that I had been through the process before, and that I was not surprised or frightened by the outcome. I did confide that this third application of the salve was worse than ever before. I appreciated her support. At that moment my mother invited Lois to join us for dinner. Her invitation seemed innocent enough for a Sunday afternoon. However, we were not prepared for what was about to take place.

The implosion of emotions that the salve had thus far held in abeyance seemed now to rise with a vengeance. Starting seemingly quietly and escalating to fever pitch, the mother daughter conflict of a lifetime came gushing from the depths of our locked in pain. It was immediately evident that both my mother and I had stored an enormous amount of unexpressed rage. The floodgates had now opened. There was no holding back.

All of our polite restraint soon disappeared as the pain of our past betrayal and of our unmet needs poured forth from the mouths of both of us. Dated to as far back as my childhood our memories unleashed themselves, one to the other. In a torrent that seemed to go on forever our sins of the past became exposed before my friend.

Temporarily shocked at witnessing this eruption, Lois appeared uncomfortable. Then in the midst of our seeming insanity, she and I glanced into each other's eyes. Somehow this eye contact became sufficient for her to join our exchange in a facilitating way.

Lois jumped in with her healing gifts, and all of us began to move through our madness with apparent grace. Through her compassion and training, Lois was soon present for both my mother and me. She helped us to reach a resolution.

All of us were left dazed and emotionally spent and humbled by the immense healing that we had just experienced. In under two hours, explosive emotions had awakened from their slumber, had expressed themselves with full intensity and had been revealed into peaceful forgiveness.

What a way to spend the day! We were, as they say, bewitched and bewildered. Each of us gave thanks to the other for a magnificent display of unabashed courage and love.

With laughter the three of us returned to our unfinished dinner. The meal continued with, "Would you like dessert?" Strange as it may seem, out came the fruit, cookies, and casual conversation over what had just transpired.

It was not until everyone had left and I was alone in my bed, reflecting on the enormity of the day, that it hit me. I pondered, *What is in that salve?* Forty years of pain had just been released as if a boil had burst. Would the results last? All I knew for now was that I had experienced my mother's love, and she had felt mine. This love was something that I had longed to feel, and I had almost given up on it. In a mysterious way our emotional healing was a miracle. My appropriately termed basal cell cancer had gone to the base, or so I thought. There would be more to come.

The ensuing week turned out to be most unusual in that it focused on blocked energies within me. The condition of my lip made me unable to work effectively with clients. It became a situation that required a forced retreat.

I felt grateful for the time alone to integrate the rapid revelations that had begun to enter my life. I remained aware of my invisible beloved close at hand. Clearly, he had watched over my sensitive process and begun to piggyback on it. This was especially evident to me on Tuesday of that week as I returned from the dermatologist's office.

Telepathically I heard, *Go to the last segment of "The Guiding Light,"* a daily soap opera that I had taped in my absence. I was not prepared to try to find that program on the tape just yet. Instead I switched on the television and tuned into another show that I watch occasionally. Somehow, static filled the screen. Out of curiosity I clicked channels to see if they were all static. No, just my chosen program. I soon gave in and rewound the tape to the segment that William had insisted I watch.

The message spoken by the characters seemed directed toward me. Imagine my surprise as the opening involved them speaking about passion and love as a fire. In their case, one character felt anxious because the fire had gone out in her marriage. I heard inner laughter followed by the words, *That never happened to us.*

The tape continued, and the next revelation took me deeper. One character told his female friend that her husband was a lucky man because he has a woman who stands by his side no matter what, and would do anything in her power to save him. The implication was, "How many people would give anything for a love like that?" Telepathically I heard, *That's what you gave me.*

From deep within me, tears erupted, tears of guilt for not being able to save William. I felt that he was now absolving me, through the medium of TV. I fell to my knees on the floor and wailed uncontrollably.

Memories of my loss of William, as well as the loss of my father, came in waves that racked my body. *Why, why, do the men I love leave me?* I found myself slithering on the floor like a snake shedding its skin of the theme of aloneness and abandonment. For some unknown reason, my mother came by and witnessed what was taking place. Instinctively she wanted to stop it.

I knew that I needed to go through all of these emotions. I looked up long enough to scream to her, "Get out of my face. It's not you. Don't take it personally. I can't take care of you now. Get out of my face. I have to go through this now for me."

For what seemed like the first time in my life, my mother listened and complied with my request. Later I was to learn that she had heard someone whom she believed to be William saying, *Do it now.* She left immediately.

I moved deeper into my release. All the while, I felt an embrace of love that seemed to be William and perhaps my father saying, *You're not alone. You've never been alone. You 've only been on your own doing a great job, and we're proud of you.* These were words I must have longed to hear and I hadn't known I needed. They were like ambrosia. They soothed the retching waves that rippled through my body. As they did so, I dissolved into the carpet with abandon.

Once peace had returned, slowly I lifted myself to a standing position. I knew that I wanted to allay any of my mother's fears over what she might have perceived. I went over to her, feeling that she might be confused. To my relief, I found her composed and interested only in my sharing. This was unlike the mother I had always known, whose earlier response would have been to accost me with her travails. Instead she listened attentively. Then she began to reveal her own story of the grief she had experienced since my father's passing.

The two of us shared at depths that only widows of beloved husbands know. I felt both a bonding with my mother and a deep compassion for the woman before me. I especially appreciated her for having heard my need, and for exiting with grace.

My mother and I had now found a new way to coexist. In the past, her constant need for attention had led her to ignore my need for privacy. I, in turn, had rejected her and ignored what she needed. This cycle had no beginning and no end. In it, both of us had been losers.

We now forged a new agreement. She could ask for what she needed. If I could respond in the moment, I would. If I were occupied or needed privacy just then, I would ask her to leave. I would go to her when I was ready. This way we both became winners. We hugged and looked at William's picture on her dresser.

Somehow we knew that he had influenced and orchestrated both of us through our roles in this process. We laughed at this knowing. While alive, he had longed to facilitate a healing between my mother and me. However, he had left this task unfinished. He must have found the task easier to handle from his place in the afterlife.

Thankfully, by Wednesday the effects of the salve on my lip had diminished in their severity. I even began to see clients, believing that my emotional intensity had finally subsided. Again, I was wrong.

The next day, as I relaxed in a bath, William's energy appeared and told me, *Listen to "Guiding Light" now.* I didn't want to trust what I had just heard. I thought, *Not again, please not again.* I was not about to get out of the warm water. His voice remained insistent.

Reluctantly I climbed out long enough to find the remote control and turn on the TV, so I could hear it from the tub. Yes, the characters on the screen again mirrored something on which I needed to focus my attention. This time a female character spoke of the sexual abuse that she had experienced in her childhood. She screamed words that eerily matched my own thoughts. So often I had wanted to rip my skin off from the inappropriate touching that I had endured as a child.

With that realization, memories of my own childhood sexual abuse suddenly poured through my body. I, too, had wanted to pull that man's touch from my body. Grateful now to be immersed in warm water, I acted out my need to get rid of any unwanted touching. I scrubbed and scrubbed my skin until it hurt. Then I took time to linger in the warm water, to allow for a collapsing that I sorely needed.

In due time I was able to step out of the tub and pull the drain plug, both physically and metaphorically, on those feelings of unworthiness and damage that I had long held inside. Despite my years of therapy, my NDE, and a lifetime in which I had triumphed over tragedy, I was appalled at the level of shame that had lingered inside of me. This shame was so insidious that it was eating away at my very tissues. In that moment, the fullest realization of my lingering resistance to surgery suddenly gripped me. The mere thought of the lips protecting my vagina being excised brought to a head a much deeper revelation. Yes, long ago those lips had been violated by a man's penis; now they would not be penetrated by a surgeon's knife. Genital mutilation was not an option.

Sexual violation leaves people, myself included, denigrating themselves as "damaged goods." In taking back my power to choose consciously my path of treatment, I had decided that this would no longer be true for me. With all of this awareness I found my cleansing bath to be one that I would remember. My cleansing had truly progressed from the inside out.

The television continued to blare. As I shut it off I realized that my mother sensed something going on. Her curiosity had been piqued, and I shared with her what had just transpired. What happened next could not even have been scripted.

Decades earlier, with hesitation and in trepidation of what my mother would say or do, I had disclosed to her the sexual violation that I had experienced in childhood. At the time, her response was the worst that one could imagine. She had sided with the man who had violated me. This betrayal, long held in my psyche and locked into the cells of my body, now burst forth, dangling the possibility of transformation. I knew that I had reached a defining moment in speaking to her and risking vulnerability, to clear this long held pain. I opted to take the plunge.

She listened as sensitively as she could. I could feel her own trembling as she began to illumine the past even further. I believed that in disclosing the sexual violation that I had suffered after my father's death, I was revealing something of great magnitude to my mother.

She responded as sensitively as she could. Slowly she mustered the courage to confide with me that she, too, had been approached in a sexual way by a man while she had grieved my father's death.

Imagine the shock and the absurdity that my mother and I experienced in that unforgettable moment. First, we gasped in disbelief, then our tension released in a most unusual way. Overwhelmed and stunned, the two of us burst out laughing. Inappropriate as this response may seem, our incredulous disclosure had brought both of us an unexpected closure.

The day ended with a wonderful climax to the saga of the herbal salve. This one came via one of my treasured TV programs. I have long admired Oprah Winfrey, to whom I have related as my role model, mentor from afar, and heroine. Having lived through my own painful past, I had been inspired by her personal story and the transformation that she makes possible for the millions of lives she touches. Her courage, her generosity of spirit, and her creativity in bringing spirituality to the media have consistently moved and enhanced me deeply. To that end I often refer to her show with clients and friends who need certain support that Oprah so brilliantly provides. Indeed, her show has served as a cornerstone in reflecting topics that are relevant to my own progress as well, often seemingly divinely timed.

Especially through my grieving journey, Oprah's program had proved invaluable as one of the pieces that contributed to my own empowerment. I taped her show for faithful viewing, since I was usually with clients when it aired. The VCR remained on and I usually paid no attention to it until later that evening. That day was different.

My invisible beloved became adamant that I view Oprah's program immediately. I noticed that it was almost five in the afternoon, when that day's show would end. What was the point? He persisted, and I surrendered, clicking on the TV.

The song being sung by Lee Ann Womack was titled, "I Hope You Dance." The words were not only motivational, they captured what I most needed to hear. Especially in all that I had gone through during the previous week, experiences that bordered on a life review, the words to this song rang through me. I was especially moved by the message that we have a choice to sit it out or dance.

William had wanted me to choose life and to dance. His laughter and his love would never end. Even now he mouthed the words of the song on which he most wanted me to focus, words about giving faith a fighting chance. I knew that the message was that I must never give up. I had to trust that a higher purpose was at hand.

I also knew that before I could truly be free, I needed to clear the cancer from my lip. The effects of the salve had been monumental, and no significant physical change had appeared. Surgery loomed closer. I began to surrender to its inevitability and to make appropriate arrangements. However, something inside of me wanted first to exhaust all of my inner and outer resources.

I noticed on my bedroom table the two tapes that William had urged me to retrieve. It was time to jump in and listen to them. I began with the one made for William's physical healing. Yes, the non-conscious tapes from which I had turned away had at last begun to call to me. I placed the earphones on my head and settled in, ready to allow my non-conscious mind to take over.

As I listened, something remarkable began to happen. The first voice on the tape was that of Joe, the doctor in California who had created them. His induction, relaxing as always, was followed by an instruction to turn the problem over to the non-conscious mind.

The next portion of the tape would address the physical illness. The voice on that part of the tape was my beloved, William. He had recorded it off the script for himself. What was amazing was that his voice did not take me by surprise. It further confirmed the truth that I had really been hearing him for the past four years. This realization offered me a momentous and powerful affirmation and gift.

The tape continued back to the doctor's voice, and my non-conscious mind lapped it up. The ending piece stirred my emotions. It carried a message that the fear we carry within us is not of our darkness; it is of our Light and the power within us.

This statement concluded the tape series, which left me roused with a palpable energy presence. Crying, I sat upright and felt William by my side, embracing me. Something significant had just happened during the tape session. I felt prompted to go to the mirror. Through my tears I witnessed with awe and appreciation that the lesion on my lip had visibly shrunk. It was still there. However, it was no longer as hard a mass to the touch. This was not my imagination. Something had clearly shifted.

Years earlier, William had listened to his chosen tape and known that the time had come for him to shed his body. Now I listened to my own chosen tape, and I knew that the time had come to claim my body. Gently my invisible beloved had encouraged me to this place.

I still had to face removal of the cancer that remained in my lip. The stage had now been set. I was finally ready. I needed only to decide which path would allow for the transformation. My resistance to surgery had diminished.

What had also diminished was my resistance to using the tapes to explore more deeply the non-conscious mind. I made plans to fly to San Diego, to work again with the doctor who had treated William. This was after saying that I would never ever return to that city in this lifetime, so great had been the pain of those memories. How little we know of "never." Either way, I felt determined to dissolve the cancer in my lip.

I was ready now to live fully and to face the world with the truth that I had known and lived. I had released the agony of the past and cleared the way to a promising new beginning. William had proven to me that he was there for me, both in life and beyond. I was still his priority. He had even demonstrated that if the roles were reversed, as they had been, he would be by my side.

We continued to empower each other playfully. I continued to be moved at the infinite scope of our journey together. He had been my great love and my bodyguard back when the wounds of the past had haunted me. Now those wounds had healed. I was liberated and could finally serve as my own bodyguard. I had grown strong, whole, and, at long last, capable of embracing myself as my beloved.

The inevitable moment had arrived. Full empowerment meant celebrating our journey together with a climax worthy of our love. Even though I had years earlier removed my physical wedding band, the spiritual one remained on my finger. The words that we had spoken for our wedding vows when we had first placed the rings on each other's fingers we now spoke to remove them. "I set you free to be all that you were meant to be."

CHAPTER ELEVEN

Sealed with a Kiss

∞

My flight to California would force me to revisit a past that I thought I had left behind. Anxious and yet eager to see what lay ahead, I knew that I had to make this trip. Listening to the tapes that addressed the non-conscious mind, and hearing William's voice on those tapes had produced a major reduction of the cancer in my lip.

Deep inside of me, I knew that total resolution of that cancer could now be at hand. Taking a chance on this last trip stretched me way beyond my comfort zone. However, the risk felt worth taking.

I arrived on the West Coast not knowing exactly how to reach the doctor's office. Before me appeared a vehicle from a shuttle service called "Cloud 9." Its very name seemed a good omen. I climbed aboard and took Cloud 9 directly to Joe's office.

This doctor had treated William four years earlier. Since then he had relocated to a building that was different from the one where William had received treatments. At least this move meant that I could bypass one encounter with past memory.

When I arrived at Joe's office, he embraced me with a familiarity and affection that released any remaining fears I might have harbored. His demeanor was as I had remembered that of an old fashioned country doctor from the Midwest.

We wasted no time, and we entered his consultation room to begin to delve into my presenting issue. The room itself, furnished tastefully by Joe's wife, held a comfortable reclining chair plus two regular chairs and an easel.

We began by reviewing my answers to the extensive questionnaire that I had completed. My responses revealed a pattern from childhood of narcissistic parenting and birthing trauma. Although the terms themselves sounded ominous, the patterns they described are common in most people and often underlie emotional blockages.

Joe explained how a person's beliefs that are generated from memories can fall into three categories: life-enhancing, life-limiting, and neutral. He made tapes designed to address various issues to shift belief systems. This shift would lead to an upgrade in the current situation as one aligns with one's inner wisdom.

Now we began the experiential aspect of my session. In the dimly lit room, I leaned back in a recliner. Joe handed me a blanket and a set of headphones. Through these headphones he would speak words of instruction as I closed my eyes, ready for the tapes to begin. Joe left the room, shutting the door behind him and leaving me alone with only the sounds that I heard through the headphones. These sounds would soon activate whatever would be mine to experience.

As the session began, Joe's induction guided me deeper and deeper into an altered state. My mind formed an image of an old fashioned inkwell with a quill pen. This was the kind of pen used in ancient writings. Briefly we explored this symbol and the feelings that it generated. Curiously, it reminded me of the multidimensional dream that had followed my bout with the herbal salve. The pen portended a future connection with some kind of ancient writings, even those of Egypt.

That day served as an auspicious beginning for what would unfold during the following two weeks. During that period, I would be absorbed totally, both in my individual therapy and in aspects of that therapy that served as professional training.

Between each day's work I stayed at a quaint inn several miles from the office, and Joe was kind enough to offer me rides. Each morning, starting as early as half past seven, he would arrive at the inn in his white pick-up truck and drive me to his office for a full day of sessions.

At first, we focused on my therapy in clearing the remainder of emotional issues. After we had completed this segment we addressed the remaining issues of guilt, forgiveness, and physical disease. With each shift, I felt that I gradually freed myself from limitations of the past. Knowings that I had held deep within myself began to surface as these limitations lifted.

Despite the intense inner work that I had done prior to working with Joe's tapes, I had previously failed to identify the precipitating event that had triggered the cancer. Now, all too painfully, that event became clear.

158

The last kiss imparted by William at his last breath, just as he passed from this world, had served as that event.

Previously I had been in touch only with the shock value and the power and magnificence of the transcendent qualities of this kiss. What I had failed to acknowledge or even recognize was my anger at being left behind. I had been plagued by emotions that I had recognized as guilt and loneliness. I had not owned my anger. This new revelation helped me at long last to release that anger's hidden energy.

With this release accomplished, Joe and I grew confident that a change in my diseased condition would soon present itself. However, for now the lesion continued to hold on. Still, I had resolved my grief totally. I felt like a new person, truly ready to embrace a new life on my own. Being single actually felt brimming with possibilities.

Somehow this new sensation of freedom transported me in memory to a time before William. I recalled the angel cab driver from a snowy night of two decades earlier. He had reminded me to think marriage only if someone *offered me more than I offered myself.* These words now became my motto.

Now gone was my earlier fear that William would be my only love of this lifetime. I even grew excited about the potential of a new mate. In William I had been graced with an incredible love. Yes, I believe that love lightning can strike twice. This new aliveness inside of me had not been present for years.

In that realization came a stunning new awareness that I had been dependent upon William for my happiness. In fact, I had been more dependent than I was comfortable admitting. I recognized that I had been blessed with his love; however, if truth be told, this love had actually sustained me. Simply put, I had no longer felt adequate on my own. Though passionate and successful in my career, I had accepted the belief that as a woman without a man, I would be unfulfilled. I found it difficult to make this confession to myself. On the surface no one would easily know that I had felt this way. I myself had remained somewhat in denial. The truth became fully evident only by my grief journey being so arduous in its loneliness and pain.

I now grew confident in my ability to become the source of my own happiness. Although I remained passionate about loving and being loved by a man, I no longer felt needy for that affirmation. I merely felt open and curious as to what the future might hold.

At this point my awareness allowed Joe to interface with me regarding consciousness. He stated that all of our experiences are based on our beliefs. My own beliefs regarding death and grief were life-enhancing ones. Therefore, Joe alluded to the possibility that my mind was what had produced my perception of the interactions with William; those that I had experienced since his passing. I listened to Joe attentively, and I felt no resistance to his truth.

Indeed, I affirmed to him that I believed William's essence had supported me. I did not feel attached to that premise. I mentioned the multitude of experiences that I had captured in my writing, as well as opinions that mediums and spiritual photography had validated. These validations didn't make much of a difference to Joe, who told me that consciousness is all, and that energy exists in some way. He went on to add something further that I found equally intriguing, "Once born, energy never dies, and no consciousness is ever lost."

I felt fine with the possibility that my grieving had been facilitated by a wisdom that existed beyond my mind. That wisdom could have been a higher aspect either of myself or of William. Some persons might even dismiss as delusional the communication that I had experienced. In any case, my evolution had moved toward integrating wholeness, functioning at higher levels, and becoming both a more loving self and a more fully contributing member of society.

What remained most important to me was that only good had unfolded throughout this journey of mine. It had become evident to me that I could trust my perceptions. As far as I was concerned, I continued to question if anyone alive knows the absolute truth of what happens after the body dies. Joe and I both laughed as I assured him that I did not depend on or need to have my perceptions really be of William. Joe and I both felt content just to move on from this discourse.

I was now ready to immerse myself in the professional training portion of my visit. Each day would include whatever personal therapy I continued to need, since the cancer remained present. Yet my time also included hours of observing Joe with his patients, reviewing case studies, and reading various materials in depth.

On one occasion Joe handed me his file from William 's treatments. At first, I merely accepted it with gratitude. I intended either to dispose of it properly or relegate it to the "William storage" at home. This would be the old "burn it or bury it" scenario. However, in the quiet of my room at the inn I felt prompted to peruse the file's pages.

William's file revealed a picture even larger than I had imagined. Scanning down the entries, I realized the accuracy of my intuition concerning William's treatment. I also recognized that the complexity of his conflicts had been so deep seated that he would have needed intense introspection to unravel it. In some strange way, both of these revelations brought an added peace to my heart. I knew that both of us had done the best that we had been able to do.

The next day I felt compelled to confront Joe with my findings. To his credit, he easily owned that he had missed one of William's basic conflicts. We continued to discuss William's situation at length. In so doing, we agreed that a multitude of subtle and interrelated issues had made William's journey so challenging.

Suffice it to say that William's issues involved conflicting desires. Joe and I also surmised that perhaps William's ultimate intention had been fulfilled. After all, ascension had been his passion. He had achieved that ascension. William's conscious awareness to our goodbye, and his awakened transition, had left an imprint not soon forgotten.

My two weeks in California seemed timeless. When they drew to a close, I felt renewed, ready to return to New York and move forward in my new life. The cancer in my lip remained visible. However, I knew that I had done all that I could for now. Briefly I considered extending my stay. However, my intuition and my invisible beloved became adamant that I leave immediately. Not until days later would I realize the reason for this urgency. It was early September of 2001.

Joe would have preferred to see a more visible physical change in my cancer before my departure. Nevertheless, he accepted what he saw. What he did do was offer me one last session that veered from the usual program.

In that session, Joe included a guided visualization that would balance the right and left hemispheres of the brain. He then directed the brain's wisdom to ask what else might be needed for full release of my body's diseased condition. What emerged was the message, *Bless yourself and life to the equal intensity of how you cursed it.* Here again was the same message that I had received in Tibet.

Hearing this message, I had nothing left to do but live the recommended advice. I shared with Joe the belief that my inner voice was a taskmaster that would accept no lip service. I used this pun intentionally, for nothing less than true gratitude would produce the physical effect that I sought. Joe concurred. We embraced in fond farewell to await what would happen next. My time with him in California had been enormously gratifying. The cancer had not disappeared, yet the aliveness that I felt had exceeded my expectation.

This time I felt truly on "Cloud 9" when the shuttle picked me up for the return trip to the airport. I expected that my wait before takeoff would be uneventful. However, from the moment I entered the terminal, William grew playfully active. It appeared that he had approved of my therapy and training, and wanted to add his final touches.

Years earlier, the last time that William and I had returned to New York, William had used a wheelchair. Here, upon my return alone, he humorously pointed me in the direction of rocking chairs. What are the odds of an airport having rocking chairs? His laughter abounded, and so did mine.

I rocked and gazed out massive windows, intrigued by the intricate preparation of the airplane that waited just outside. Telepathically I heard, *Go to the newspaper stand.* This directive puzzled and annoyed me, since I was very comfortably seated. I didn't feel the need for a newspaper. William became persistent. I rose and moved toward a tiny shop and purchased USA Today. I soon learned that that was not the reason I had been summoned there.

I found myself perusing the bookshelf of new releases. Among them was John Edward's latest book. Edward is a world renowned medium. I wondered why I had been directed to him. This book seemed like a great one, and with my experiences I felt no need to read it. Once I began to thumb through it, however, I realized why I had been guided toward it. Immediately I found a reference to the scars of grief. As I read, intuitively I heard, *When there is no scarring inside. There is no scarring outside.* I took this message to mean that William wanted me to know that with the inner work I had now done, no scars would remain. I surmised that either the cancer would disappear or the surgery that I needed would leave no marks.

Arriving home in New York I was swamped with client appointments that left me barely able to reflect on my two California weeks. Little did I realize that the next morning would change all perceptions radically for myself, for our nation and for the world.

It was September 11, and along with millions of others I woke to the horror of witnessing events on television as they happened. These were the acts of terrorism on U.S. soil. As with all people, I found both the image of the collapsing World Trade Center towers, and the devastation of such loss of innocent lives, to be beyond comprehension.

Immersed in my own shock and grief over the incredulity of what was occurring, I heard my phone ring. It was a client in her late 80's, living in the Tribeca section of Manhattan. Hysterical, she reported blow by blow to me what she could see from her window. She was convinced that this horror was the apocalypse that both the Bible and the prophet Nostradamus had predicted.

My specialty being post traumatic shock, I did my best to move this client through her trauma. All the while, in the back of my mind I wondered if she could be right. Over the phone I could feel both the immensity of her shock and the pain that surrounded her. In that moment I recognized that I had become fully engaged, both professionally and personally, at my highest level of functioning. Whatever had transpired in California had prepared me for what now lay ahead.

As both a New Yorker and a trained therapist, I began to devote endless hours to counseling grieving clients who had been affected both directly and indirectly by the disaster. Meanwhile I relegated my personal issues to a distant past.

Throughout the days and weeks that followed September 11 my time was filled with offering, to the best of my ability, support to those in need. Therefore, by October I felt moved to see the devastation for myself. A colleague and I ventured to Ground Zero. Our first startling impression could only be described as that of a war zone that spread for several acres. Before us lay shattered steel girders, charred buildings, and white ash. Our immediate response was of pain and sorrow for the lives that had forever been changed by this terrorism.

We bowed our heads in silent prayer for the innocent people who had lost their lives, for those left behind whose world had been torn apart by loss, for the heroes who had exemplified courage, and for those who continued to sift diligently to find and clear the remains of the dead.

I was surrounded by a sight that contained the best and worst of the human spirit. I also became aware of a palpable feeling that radiated holiness. As tears moistened my eyes, I received a mystical vision that filled me with deep reverence. Amid the remnants of indescribable agony that had become a sacred crematorium emerged the phoenix. Symbolically this bird represents death and rebirth. As it soared toward the heavens, it spread its wings and transformed itself into the bald eagle.

I felt humbled by such an intuitive gift of knowing. In my own way I interpreted this vision as a message of hope. From the ashes America would have the opportunity to rise to greater heights than before, touched and more united in its humanity and compassion.

Instead of focusing on the fear and shock engendered by the events of September 11, I believe that the human angels who sacrificed their lives brought us a wake-up call. Such a call is unique for each person. However, the essence of recognizing the fragility of life and embracing its preciousness is common to all. Toward this end, recognizing who and what is important becomes paramount in living life to its fullest. In gratitude for this gift of recognition, we honor and bless the legacy of those who died.

In a synchronistic turn of events, my focus on helping others to heal from the terrorist attacks brought an unexpected change in the cancer in my lip. In the melee I had almost forgotten about the lesion. By now it was October 29 and I could finally recognize the awesome grace that I had received through the darkness of my grieving period. As I shared this realization with Janet, my tears flowed in humble appreciation to the Divine that I had never been abandoned not by God, and not by William.

If anything, in a strange way I had felt a need to heal the cancer on my own. Now, having seen the foolishness of my thinking, I was ready to open to infinite possibilities. I prayed out loud that my experience and this cancer journey be offered for my highest good, that it might contribute in whatever ways could help others.

Indeed, I went as far as promising God that if I could clear the cancer organically without surgery, I would be the mouthpiece for the messages in my story. I would release any fears that had held me back from freely letting go of this trilogy wherever and to whomever it needed to go.

What transpired next exceeded anything for which I had prepared. A peace enveloped me in a knowing that all was well. Without giving it another thought, I continued the process of collaborating with Janet on our third volume.

To our mutual amazement, a physical change in the lesion began to occur before our eyes. A white wax-like substance abruptly surfaced from my lip. We weren't sure what it was.

I did note that this change occurred with an eerie timing, "coincidentally" on the same date that William's cancer had been removed surgically from his testicle four years earlier. I didn't exactly know what this coincidence meant. I just filed it in my mind for possible future reference.

At the first opportunity, I phoned my doctor and described to him what had happened. His reaction could have been alarming in that he surmised that the cancer had become necrotic. I asked exactly what that indicated. He replied that the cancer could have begun to invade healthier tissues. He recommended that I have it checked out immediately. However, I was absorbed in my work and intuitively I felt no urgency. I also heard the familiar laughter of William's presence. I released the matter, deciding to wait until I sensed the need for further action.

What did need my attention just then was gum disease and a tooth extraction that I had avoided since March. I finally visited my periodontist, fearing a deterioration in the condition, since chewing had become an issue.

I expected his admonishment. Instead I received kudos that somehow the problem hadn't grown worse. Knowing me, the periodontist emphasized, "Schedule the surgery when you're ready." I assumed that I would be ready sometime the following year. However, the following day my intuition told me to move on it. This intuitive sense surprised me, and I acquiesced.

I decided to use the non-conscious mind tape to prepare for dental surgery. Again, mysterious ways of the Divine worked their magic. The tape rendered my dental ordeal effortless. It brought me the added gift of illuminating what turned out to be a further understanding of the cancer that had invaded my lip.

I am almost embarrassed to admit that in recounting my ordeal to a friend, I referred to the cancerous lesion as a formidable ally. Wisdom often comes in a slip of the tongue. Hearing "ally," not "foe" as one might expect, captured my attention. This awareness stunned me. Nevertheless, I recognized that the cancer had provided an opportunity for my greatest healing. It had pushed me to face my past, resolve my grief, embrace my future with aliveness, and offer its message for the good of others.

In many ways the cancer had also facilitated my expression through writing. I knew that I could handle no surgical intervention until I had told my story completely. I blessed the cancer for this fact. Intuitively I heard, *Only God/Love in every cell of my body is real. All else is an illusion and be gone.* I wondered what this new message meant, and whether I continued to hold any other allegiance to the cancer.

Quickly I intuited this further message and phoned Joe in California. His question to me was, "What is the symbolic ally for which this cancer is substituting?" I knew the answer. The cancer represented my passion and love, plus the act of holding on to my last physical connection with William. The issue now became whether or not I could bless his transition, honor my presence at that moment, and honor our kiss as a gift without the need to hold onto its vestige. If I could not do all of this, would the cancer have to be cut out from me surgically? I knew the answer and I shared it with Joe. All that remained was to wait and see what would transpire.

My wait was not very long. The next change in the cancerous lesion was triggered innocently by the beauty treatment of lip waxing. I returned home from this treatment only to notice a redness and blistering that had never occurred previously, despite many months of waxing. Could this blistering mean that the lesion had grown worse?

My attending physician was out of town. Without speaking to anyone, I pulled out the yellow pages and called a nearby dermatologist. I hoped that I could see this new doctor instantly. Fortunately, someone else canceled and my appointment would be for the next day.

Upon clinical observation, the new doctor diagnosed basal cell cancer and performed his own biopsy. I was to call the following week for the biopsy results. Disillusioned and disappointed, mentally I surrendered to the surgery that I now saw as inevitable.

I tried to make the best of it, figuring that I would relate to the procedure as a symbolic ritual. I would schedule the surgery either for the end of the year, intending to view the procedure as "out with the old," or plan for the beginning of the New Year as "in with the new." The surgeon's availability would determine my choice.

On the morning before Thanksgiving I woke with the loving presence of my invisible beloved by my side. His energy felt more palpable than it had in months. He radiated excitement and laughter.

Affectionately he addressed me with what would become a prophetic message. *Remember, it's all about love. Listen to your heart. Trust its knowing and not the chatter of the mind. Give and receive love fully. That was our way. Let it guide your way. Happy Thanksgiving. All is well.*

Temporarily I was startled by William's message. Before I could reply he was gone, leaving me with only an etheric kiss and his words. My first thoughts were not necessarily of the magnificence of the experience. Comically, I felt confused to note that he was a day early. After all, Thanksgiving would be the following day. However, with William being out of time and space, I simply felt grateful for his appearance. Its impact did not fully register within me until later in the day.

I phoned for my biopsy report, expecting confirmation of the earlier diagnosis. What I received instead was the pleasant shock for which I had longed. The nurse said, "Everything is fine."

Disoriented, I pressed her. "What do you exactly mean by 'fine'?"

She replied, "It's only sun damage, no malignancy." I exclaimed, thrilled, "What a Thanksgiving gift!"

She agreed, with the words, "Take it as a blessing." Still, she confirmed that the doctor would need to see me on Monday.

I hung up the phone. Waves of elation and relief coursed through me. This was a Thanksgiving imprint of a lifetime. It also marked a turning point, both for William and for me. For William, his Thanksgiving four years earlier had been a beginning of saying goodbye to his body and to his earthly life. For me, this Thanksgiving marked the beginning of embracing my body and my own earthy life.

Then came my euphoric realization that Divine timing had highlighted the supreme message of giving thanks as the core essence of miracles. The words of the Christian mystic Meister Eckhart resonated within me: "If the only prayer you say in your entire life is thank you that would be enough." This moment captured the meaning of his words. The trauma of William's and my last kiss, seared with pain and possibilities, had culminated in a triumph over the last vestige of the cancer that had now cleared.

Quivering with gratitude, I became enraptured with a newfound appreciation for the preciousness of life, for all that was and all that would be. The words of Nietzsche, "What does not kill me makes me stronger," wafted over me. Included in my rapture was a flitting image of the Eight Medicine Buddhas. Could all of this experience somehow relate to a legacy that I could share?

I reflected that my journey with William in such close presence had now reached completion. I know that as he had often emphasized, we will never be separated. I also know that we need to dance in different dimensions for a while. It's time for us both to fly solo until perhaps we reunite. I can accept this separation now.

Surrender to the spiral of love includes an evolutionary expansion. Although I resisted at first, I now embrace destiny in its perfection. Destiny with all of its agony and ecstasy is wondrous to behold in its unfoldment. Fulfillment for me would not be the love story ending in,

'They lived happily ever after." At least, living happily ever after would not include both of us living in the physical.

The repeated message that I had received, *In time truth will be revealed,* had tormented me when I had heard it at William's transition. It had held no meaning for me back then. Indeed, in time a truth has been revealed that is bigger than my human perception could have imagined.

The body does die, and the pain of this loss is real. Ultimately, we never die, and love never dies. We are love's fire. There is no beginning and no end to the infinite vastness of this love.

I still say that the separation that William and I suffered is not what I would have wanted. The words of Cher, consummate entertainer whom I admire for her beauty and boldness, convey my sentiment best. As in her song, "if I could turn back time," I would find a way, I would do so in a heartbeat.

Even with all of my mystical awareness and my ability to experience contact, the love that I shared with William in the physical can never be replaced. I miss the beauty of his physical presence, the tender feel of his touch, the succulence of his kisses, and love's fire in his eyes. My memories sustain me.

My new life has gone beyond any of my earlier expectations of what could be possible. The new felt bliss within me has increased as a fire that can often mirror the Divine reflection that I had shared with William. The empowerment that I now feel entirely within myself rivals William's empowerment of me and does so in a humorous one upmanship way. He had always been my hero and I now had to become my own hero. However, make no mistake. No substitute exists for the pleasure of the physical.

I urge everyone to not take themselves or their loved ones for granted. Never hesitate to express, whether aloud or through actions, your love and gratitude wherever and with whomever you feel it. The simple pleasures of the physical are a gift and a treasure. Once gone they can never be replaced.

No individual knows when their own date with eternity will be. Tomorrow may never come. Embrace the preciousness of each day. Live and love fully in the present. Cherish every moment. It's never too late to begin anew, to make amends, or to seize opportunities that life offers.

Let love, not fear, rule your words and actions. Follow your heart, even if it means that you risk the unknown. To that degree I did so. I have no regrets. While my beloved was on earth I lived an incredibly fulfilling life with him. We had paradise. We did indeed worship, cherish and adore each other and give our hearts until the ends of time.

Now I welcome a new paradise here on earth, with or without William in spirit, as destiny calls. Just as we were a team in life, we continue to enjoy our love in ways that unfold its mysteries beyond what the limited mind can imagine.

My passion for living has been ignited. I have no fear of death.

Am I ready to die? Yes. The mere glimpse through my NDE was intoxicating in love, light, and adventure. Am I longing to die? A resounding, No. Life is a sacred gift to be savored in every moment. Even more, I further celebrate the awesome opportunity that each of us can leave a legacy making a difference that blesses the world.

I have bared my heart and soul from the depths of the truth that I have lived and continue to live. At William's urging, I now admit that gone is my original lament of being rejected by the Light; I now embrace that I returned from the Light. The seeming "curse" of our last kiss has now revealed its blessing in disguise. William had always referred to this kiss as one to build a dream of a new tomorrow with infinite possibilities for love and eternal life.

As I write these words I hear the lyrics of Cher from her song "Believe," changed a bit by my invisible beloved as he initiates it as our new love song. He playfully makes his point by shifting the word "love" to "life": *Do you believe in love after life?* We do. It's now up to you.

Together we offer our story to you, with our love. He has passed the torch on to me with a message, the fire of love that burns within each person is a fire that is enduring and everlasting. It is a spiritual force that illumines a truth beyond human perception that love never dies and neither do we.

This message gives testament to a living awareness of immortality. The accepted myth that death is an end can evolve into awareness of death as a new beginning. I now pass this fire on to you. Let it speak to the destiny that is yours.

Epilogue

Each being on earth pursues a personal journey. In many ways, the purpose of this journey is to discover that we are multidimensional beings, whatever that concept means to you. Those who identify themselves solely with the physical body view death as a permanent loss. Those who are willing to stretch the boundaries of the mind and open their hearts find that myriad possibilities unfold. Our evolution continues as a never-ending mystery.

Life is as a circle. One could say that this circle has no beginning and no end. This concept seems as a paradox, since birth is so often considered life's beginning and death has been feared as its end. Just as each birth is unique, so is each death. As my NDE made clear to me, the only difference between the two is that one is imbued with celebration while the other is immersed in fear. Now is the time to release that fear in whatever form and whatever way best serves one's personal evolution.

In the 21st century, a new Initiation appears to be moving through people's consciousness. More and more individuals are awakening to the possibility that all of us transcend physical form. If so, how can we embrace the emerging awareness of this truth? What does this concept mean to our individual lives?

For me, through my NDE as well as through the communication that I've experienced with my beloved since his passing, life as I once knew it will never again be as limited. Even though the physical and emotional pain of my loss of William had been excruciating, I know from direct experience that here in the physical we are not alone. Our loved ones watch over us and guide us gently as guardian angels.

During the apparent death of our loved ones, they transition to an expanded level of consciousness that exists beyond our physical senses. In most of us, the ability to perceive this level of reality remains dormant. This fact does not necessarily mean that such perception doesn't exist. Believing in the reality of this invisible level requires a leap of faith into an ever expanding consciousness.

We do believe that most people are capable of experiencing contact with deceased loved ones. Such contact occurs in subtle ways that require both attentiveness and awareness. Reaching out to those who have left is facilitated both through dreams and through trusting one's intuitive knowledge. Signs of communication can range from an inner intuitive voice to a physical demonstration.

Our love bonds are never broken. Through his repeated insistence, William's words that we can never be separated gradually took on a more profound meaning. I now accept that the love we receive and the love we give are what continue. That oneness through our hearts' union bridges the portal to eternity.

Our deceased loved ones not only continue in memory and in our hearts, they also live on in our essence. They want us to have happy and fulfilling lives. This same message is heard time and time again through mediums and mystical occurrences. In ways mysterious to us after transition from the physical world, our relationships move to a spiritual reality.

Indeed, throughout contacts I have received from William, his primary emphasis has remained this one. In his relentless support of my moving on personally, he has prodded me professionally to pass this truth along for others: *Love never dies. Only the forms change.*

On a comical note, although our love continues in the eternal realm, William clearly wants me to find romantic love in this physical realm. To that end, my invisible beloved requested something of me that first shocked and later amused me. He acknowledged that since our relationship had transformed [an understatement, to say the least] and had become somewhat confusing in that contact had not ended, divorce would be the appropriate option.

He delivered this message as I was relaxing at a California spa. Jolted by his intention, I found emotions coursing through my body. I felt ambushed. William's loving countenance and laughter quickly assured me of the brilliance and wisdom of his suggestion. He sought a divorce not because he had now achieved his own successful ascension and wished to discard me as an appendage that no longer served his needs. I must confess that this thought had temporarily crossed my mind. Instead, he pointed out that we were already living the reality of death being an illusion on the multidimensional planes. Our wedding vows had proclaimed, *I give you my heart until the end of time,* not the traditional *until death do us part.*

In order to prevent any subconscious attachment on our parts, divorce with love and appreciation for the journey seemed a fitting step. Now was the time, and William reminded me that I was the designer of divorce ceremonies that had even been featured in *The New York Times.* My own slogan was, *Celebrate endings for empowered new beginnings.* This was what William wanted, and we deserved it. I laughed, and then played along with him for my own empowerment. Grounds for our divorce would be "dimensional differences." I would be the one to "file the ending," even though he had suggested it. I would keep all of the community property uncontested.

Typical of William's antics, he responded on Independence Day, July 4, 2005, as I innocently enjoyed a fireworks display with our mutual friends. Sneaking up on me he proclaimed, *Happy divorce with freedom for all!* In that moment, surprised by his presence, I looked up at the next fireworks display and realized that it took the shape of a heart. I had never seen such a symbol before seen in a fireworks display. As my friends noticed the heart shape as well, I whispered to them,

"Wait till I tell you the story of divorce, dimensional style." I heard, with *love forever, goodbye with no regrets. You are not a widow. You are a free divorcee. Have fun and give me a great show.*

I intend to.

Never one to let a significant moment go uncelebrated, I am pleased to say William orchestrated a divorce ceremony as my birthday gift, 2006. Unbeknownst to me, as I walked a beach path near my island home in St. Martin, he beckoned me with laughter. *Look at you, following a well-worn path. That's not your style.* He playfully taunted me as he laughed, alluding to an Emerson quote that was apropos of our life together: "Do not go where the path may lead, go instead where there is no path and leave a trail." Then he motioned, *over here.* He captured my attention to follow his lead and climb over rocks wafted by waves. Only then did I recognize where I was going. I would never have ventured to that spot on my own.

I now faced a rock that was shaped like a pyramid, with waves crashing over it. William had led me to the place where the last time we had been in St. Martin together physically, we had secretly, spiritually wed. Imagine my stunned reaction as I recalled that I now found myself at this place exactly nine years after his memorial, when my hair had caught fire in an eerie initiation. That incident had highlighted the message of his being by my side and passing the torch. Now waves caressed my body in a playful initiation by water as a christening, to signify new life and climactic rebirth.

I felt William's strong arms and loving countenance embrace me. He had delivered a message for my personal life. Now he turned to our legacy, reminding me that my prophecy at his cremation, as mentioned in Book One, had now been fulfilled:

Still shocked, I turned to Willie Mae. In my disorientation, I remarked, "I think I'm getting clues here for something that I'm supposed to share or express. I'm not even sure what it is, maybe a book, a play, or a movie. All I do know is that intuitively something is to come from this. It will probably take live to ten years to complete. At that point I will either have a new life worth living on earth, or my life's ·work will be done. I could go on as well."

Now looking back, over a decade later, I am humbled that my journey took on mythic proportions. Despite the overwhelming despair and bleakness of my future, trusting myself to take the steps that beckoned to me offered the portal to a never-ending journey. Deciphered at last was the answer to the recurring message, *in time truth will be revealed.*

Never before would I have intended or felt deserving of the immense personal and transpersonal blessings that I have received. Never could I have imagined that by not giving up, by trusting in a purpose for my return from the Light, I would find that God would unfold a reality beyond belief.

If someone had told me that the dreams that William and I had so often envisioned, dreams that I was sure had been shattered with his passing, would be fulfilled beyond measure, I would not have believed such things possible.

Despite William's insistence that our last kiss was one to build a dream on, and despite the love letters that came through from him to assure me that his work was "with and now through" me, my brokenness had rebuked his message.

As he had done in life regardless of my resistance, William had pressed on to empower me to greater heights than I could yet see for myself. I am pleased to confess that his efforts have continued in the afterlife. I now embrace the truth that our partnership has evolved in a way that blesses me with our legacy. It has also surprised me with the amazing fulfillment of the prophetic dream that I had as a nine year old child.

In that dream, a feminine force awakened me to the knowing that all of us are infinite beings of Light with a greatness beyond physical form. She placed that knowing in my hands in the form of energy to be entrusted by one person to another at a time when the world would be shifting from denser to lighter vibrations of awareness.

In searching my heart and soul, I am convinced that the time portended in that childhood dream is the time of change that we are currently experiencing. Many recognize that human understanding on our planet is poised to move from the limited perception of an old paradigm, rooted in Newtonian physics based on fear and separation, into a new paradigm that is rooted in quantum physics, based on love and oneness.

Delving into what causes limitation we recognized a gap between the finite self with which each of us identifies, and the infinite self that each of us is becoming. Whereas the finite self traps one in limited physical reality, the infinite self sets one free in a different reality that is boundless. The missing link between these two selves is the art of listening to the whispering of one's soul, trusting its inner wisdom, and taking inspired action. William emphasized that my ability to go within, still my mind, and access inner silence for answers was a key factor in moving through those darkest hours.

Prompted by William, and moved by divine intervention through the Black Madonna, the fulfillment of my dream has come full circle. We now pass into your hands our legacy, dedicated to releasing pain and awakening infinite possibilities in the areas of love and wellness.

Naturally, the first part of our legacy is our Love's Fire trilogy. Book One illumines how listening to one's heart, while honoring mortal boundaries, transcends the forms of love relationships that we have been conditioned to accept. Book Two illumines how listening to one's soul and allowing for divine intervention transcends traditional perceptions of death. Book Three illumines how learning to listen to our own inner wisdom transcends the numbness of conditioned living. Unlike the love story that is told through Books One and Two, Book Three focuses on you. This third book serves as a manual for your personal evolution.

Another significant part, William and I believe, is that wellness is a dynamic state of living that originates in the mind. Often, we commented that the mind is our most precious, untapped natural resource and needs to be the first and not the last place to which we turn for changing our reality.

Our passion together was to enhance quality of life, for ourselves as well as others. His was through using cutting-edge technology, mine was through the application of ancient wisdom, all designed to empower from within. Curiously enough, both ways have their roots in William's cancer journey; one way through direct experience while he was physically alive, the other ways as influences from beyond.

Most significant when he was alive was what we affectionately referred to as the best kept secret for shifting consciousness to awaken our true nature of who we are. Ever since 1997 when we discovered and longed to make this work available to others, I have engaged in and witnessed its development: ground-breaking work in the union of science and spirituality. An endearing and I dare say eye opening quote by Dr. Joe articulates this best: "Prayer done correctly is quantum physics."

Reflecting on my NDE, and as an initiated shaman, I call our signature process a cross between a life review and a vision quest. It is a two day journey of awareness and discovery. It takes one from conception through childhood and basic needs, to life's present situation. Most people have heard that our earlier years are the time when we take on those limiting beliefs that often shape our adult reality. The premise of this unique experience is to restructure the past as if we had already established a foundation of life-enhancing beliefs through safe and supportive parenting. The results are highly individualized and range from subtle to life-changing.

That secret is Dr. Joe's work, L.A.M.P. (Listening to Applied Modern Physics), which is designed to shift core beliefs. Old beliefs that had been based on memories of pain and struggle can shift to a core essence of the natural self, an essence that is based on peace and joy.

One thus moves from conscious efforting to an awakening of the power within oneself. In so doing, one sets the conscious mind free from having to figure out its problem to turning it over to the non-conscious mind, which has the solution.

Ever watchful and promising to take me to my next level, my invisible beloved announced that the first certified presenter's program of L.A.M.P. would be on the anniversary of his passing from this physical realm more than a decade ago. He was determined to have me transform that day and launch a bigger dream for myself and others.

Dr. Joe and I did so on December 7, 2008. Our small group of three people became the first of many presenters who now are qualified to deliver a prelude experience in shifting one to an improved version of themselves. Their focus is on one's present situation and on accessing that part of us that knows the shift that needs to be made. They do so through group experiences as well as individual sessions.

Our first class was a triumphant success. All were empowered and enlightened by Dr. Joe's parting words, "My how my world has changed since I've changed." This profound statement epitomized the truth that as each of us takes responsibility for shifting to our highest and finest self, the world is also enhanced. Each participant understood the awesome and transformational possibility of his or her own commitment. I, in turn, realized how it fulfills my dream of passing on skills to leaders who want to make an evolutionary difference in people's lives.

As if that program wasn't the pinnacle of my work, as I might have imagined, the following year William inspired me to yet another piece of my professional puzzle. Connecting the dots for me of my NDE message and its life review, I, together with Mary, became certified by Dr. Joe to deliver the two day journey. Appropriate to William's style, this was October 18th, transforming yet another anniversary pain, that of our wedding day, into a new triumph.

Our desire is that one of the many gifts we've imparted can make a difference in enhancing your life journey. As they do so, in the true spirit of my childhood dream they are yours to pass on as well. Now, more than ever, our call is to remember the greatness that lies within and the limitless possibilities before us.

Only when our hearts and minds remain open can our multi-dimensional nature reveal itself fully. Opening ourselves to higher levels of perception requires subtle awareness and sensitivity. This process lies within the grasp of each one of us. This opportunity for higher awareness seems to be beckoning with the dawn of the new millennium.

The leap that has begun to occur is a leap into quantum consciousness. This move will take us beyond the limited rational mind, and into more connectedness and oneness with all. The veils that until now have existed between the dimensions have begun to thin. We are poised on the cutting edge of psychological research and technologies to assist in raising our own vibrations. As this change occurs, each of us becomes the highest expression of the God-Self. Every personal evolution contributes to the collective consciousness of humanity in a ripple effect that merges into Oneness.

As we write these words, William is whispering to me a Thank You for keeping alive the message that love never dies and neither do we. He is also encouraging me to remember my plea for God to reveal His/Her plan for me, and to give thanks for all that has transpired. He is reminding me that he has always been just a breath away. When it is my time to let go and join him, he will welcome me with open arms and replace a pain-seared goodbye kiss with a kiss for a new beginning.

At William's prodding, I now know with certainty that my highest evolution comes in being the best and finest me I can be and contributing my gifts to empowering and inspiring the lives of others. In so doing 1 blaze a pathway that I can trust to make a difference for others in their own awakening journey.

On July 4, 2009, William celebrated with me the conclusion of our love story. As I watched a panoramic fireworks display from my back yard, a shooting star came toward me and emblazoned the sky. At that moment I heard William's words, spoken with immense love, *I'll be your guiding star forever. Admit it, you're strong and happy now. You're ready to move on with our love, our legacy, and our message.*

Indeed, I feel a bit sheepish to confess that I know he was right.

That very morning, I had awakened with the words, *True independence is setting yourself free from self-imposed limitations and passing on that living wisdom to others.* Glass of champagne in hand, I now raised it in a climactic toast to my beloved and telepathically beamed, *I'm ready.*

Well, I believed I was ready and did not surmise that William had further intentions. Just as he had successfully transformed memories of our wedding and last kiss, there was one last memory to address before proclaiming this book complete. That day was Valentine's Day 1997, the date our love no longer remained secret, announced publicly as our engagement.

Through a dream he humorously paraphrased his touching words, *Beloved I will love you forever, but my work is finished. My journey is done. It's time now for me to go. It's time to die.*

For me in 2010 he stated, as only he could, *Beloved, I love you forever. Our books and movie are finished. Your journey is beginning. It's time now for you to go out into the world. It's time to fly.*

Inspired by this moving sentiment, I honor the auspicious timing that on December 7, 2010, our first book of the Trilogy, Love's Fire: Beyond Mortal Boundaries, hit Number One on Amazon's Best Seller List in the category of Love and Loss. Only the Divine could have timed it to such perfection to be at the anniversary hour of our last kiss into the Light 13 years ago. Embracing this event and celebrating my beloved's evolutionary partnership seems a fitting tribute for the key message of our legacy; love never dies and neither do we.

Often fueled solely by what I've affectionately termed flying on faith and fumes, I continue to witness the emergence of a life meaning and purpose that I could not consciously have fathomed. Deep within us lies a power to triumph over life issues if we stay open and never give up. All of us discover this power in unique ways that are aligned with our purpose and destiny.

In pursuit of our understanding of this evolutionary change we recognize that the legacy of the Ancient Egyptians can prove illuminating. Janet and I mused on this knowledge and remembered Edgar Cayce's prophecy that the time period in which we now live has seen a return to the pattern of experiences, activities and opportunities that began in Ancient Egypt.

Our further discourses led to revelations that beckoned Janet and me to deepen our research. Although I had told my story to date, we could see that the time had come to glean further the wisdom of the ancients. That wisdom holds practical applications for each person's unique evolutionary journey.

With that awareness, Book Three emerged. One might say that the Initiation of the past whispers to us many secrets that reveal the paradigm shift that has begun to occur for our Initiation into the 21st Century.

Addendum

Never would I have imagined that I would write an update to Book Two, as I thought the story was over. However, when extraordinary events occurred that put the story into a greater perspective, I was moved to write the following words.

My dare to God had been, "to die quickly or awaken my soul's blueprint!" I didn't even understand the words that screamed through me in the darkness and the pain. Little did I realize that God was listening and was going to provide an answer in a uniquely divine way.

In my brokenness I had challenged God, "You want this body. Show me why. I will do nothing self-destructive. I will listen to you and take inspired steps. Show me why I am still here. Show me your purpose." As far as I was concerned, I was done!

Unbeknownst to me, God did indeed have a different plan in mind: and one that would bless humanity as well. Most people have heard that God has a plan for us. I wonder how many take it seriously. God knew better than to reveal it to me, knowing that I would rebuke it.

In my despondent state no way could I have envisioned a plan so great. Just imagine, what if God had announced the following. "You are going to become a best-selling author of multiple books in personal transformation, produce and co-star in a movie (me being camera shy), be inspired to deliver a feminine based spiritual system in Self Awakening, and have your plea for awakening your blueprint upgraded to include others."

My response would have been, "Yeah, right! I can't even breathe through this pain, much less believe that such a miracle beyond probabilities could happen."

Despite my trepidation, as always, I would stay open to God's infinite possibilities. Indeed, all the above and more has come to pass. This bigger picture has prompted the update to Book Two. This addendum is meant to inspire and empower everyone facing any darkness in life. Know that you are not alone, and that divine guidance is available, and navigating you to a destination you cannot foresee. Regardless of the challenge, answers exist that can set you free. A grander soul's blueprint reveals itself, going beyond time and space, limited thinking, and limited beliefs.

Whether you are aware of it or not, we are being constantly guided to become the highest versions of ourselves, so we can be and live our best life. A greater plan is unfolding, and it is imperative to never give up and to never give in. We are all given gifts and challenges in this adventure called life.

I had already been mystically aligned to listen to that voice I affectionately called God. For me, living life was from the inside out. Sadly, most people are conditioned to give their innate power away, and to live their life from the outside in.

As you can see by this book, and especially this addendum, God answered my "why" and went beyond that to create a ripple effect that can bless all. They say God works in mysterious ways. I can honestly attest to the truth of this statement. My burning desire then became, "How could this wisdom and transformational shift be passed on?"

In two separate other worldly orchestrated experiences, I received what we now affectionately call The GPS Code™. This is a spiritually transmitted feminine based system of heart awakening and intuitive problem solving. In many ways it is apropos for the uncertainty engendered by these changing times.

This acronym stands for God/Source Positioning System. As much as I attempted to call it Guidance and Power System, God thwarted me each time and prompted me to say "God." Ultimately, we compromised with the word "God/Source." People uncomfortable with the word "God" could substitute "Higher Power" or any name for the God of their understanding. This is a spiritually based system anchored in the vibrational frequency that "God is Love," and not a religious tradition.

Indeed, what I heard in my NDE, that had stymied me, now was addressed through The GPS Code™. I had been confused as to the implementation of this message, "Challenges, pain, and problems are an inevitable part of life, suffering is optional!" In essence, I know now that it is about shifting from reactive living to responsive living for an extraordinary journey.

One of the undisclosed gifts that I received in the NDE is the chatter of the monkey mind was silenced for the most part. Passed on through the GPS Code™ is the ability to quiet your mind, as well as a simple way to release your reactive emotions so they are expressed rather than repressed or suppressed.

This GPS Code™ process goes beyond personal development and bypasses limited beliefs that keep you stuck. If you're open and desiring to access your authentic nature of self, your divine inheritance and your innate superhero soul powers, this system is for you. There are five steps that are simple and are presented through enlightened entertainment.

We can assure you that by setting your innate GPS, your soul will be in the driver's seat of your own life. As with your car, this system will set your destination to the best solution of your problem, shifting you from self-sabotage to self-empowerment. In the words of Einstein, "When the solution is simple, God is answering."

The despair that I experienced, and the wisdom imparted by the Medicine Buddhas, who urged me to recant my lack of trust in a higher order, have come into full clarity. Their message, "Bless life to the degree that I cursed it," and "What is the legacy you want to leave behind?" has been answered, albeit not in a gentle fashion.

Without going into extensive details, I have been living with malignant skin cancer for over twenty years. Each time it flares up, I heed the guidance of energy medicine and mind/body wisdom and rely on its invisible awareness to propel me to take my next quantum leap. Although challenging each time, nothing prepared me for the third and worst bout imaginable.

Unlike the previous times, the lesion was relentless in its growth and visually frightening to behold. All of my training barely made a difference, and its positioning prominently above my upper lip was impossible to mask.

I was forced to "face" this disease and its momentum as my darkest time. So much so, that my ego cried out that Thomas Moore had it backwards. "It is not the dark night of the soul. Rather, the soul knows its blueprint, it is the dark night of the ego that often does not have a clue!"

Surrendering to the highest plan of my soul through God given guidance was my only option. Ironically, I have taught that the only person you can change and need to love unconditionally is the person you face in the mirror daily. It was my turn through the scariest fire I ever encountered to date.

Deep into the proverbial "rabbit hole" I dived. My mission was shifting the impossible to "I am possible," so as to discover and release the roots of this malignancy. If ever I had to test the spiritual system that had been transmitted through me, it was now. Some days, just getting out of bed and focusing on my work took running The GPS Code™.

The ordeal proved life changing as well as confirming the power of this God given gift. The past family sexual secret, that I thought had been addressed, roared its last vestige, as did the suicidal longings and regrets of

183

dashed dreams. All that had been eating away at my tissues claimed their voice to be released and forgiven. My soul demanded no lip service and no bad mouthing my destiny ever again! The admonition was fully received

I am excited, relieved, and humbled to share that I have vetted The GPS Code™ as my answer to the darkness. Although I had recognized the power of the five simple steps, I was surprised they were the ultimate solution to my having a successful recovery without the need for medical intervention.

Even though I knew that all was in divine order and quantum physics proves that there are no accidents, coincidences, or mistakes, I had remained resistant. I now willingly accept that William and I made a sacred contract outside of time and space that became our blueprint for our contribution to humanity's awakening.

Upon closing, as you may recall, I cried to the heavens for the answer to the question, "Was it free will gone amuck or destiny I cannot foresee?" My resistance and torment of our love story being "happily from the hereafter" instead of "the happily ever after" that I had longed for, has been resolved. I no longer questioned who wrote the script of William saying goodbye to me with our last kiss into the Light.

I have my answer. It is, "Yes," and, "Yes".

Now it is your turn to embrace your destiny to awaken your blueprint. You have the power and the guidance to enjoy the journey of life that is best for you and your highest expression of your possibilities. William and I celebrate passing this torch on, "Love and Life never die, and neither do we."

Apropos to our love story and this update, the end of this writing was July 4th, 2018. Never missing a moment to leave a lingering impression, William slipped his arms around me energetically as I watched the fireworks from the privacy of my home. Emblazoned in the sky, of all things, was a smiling happy face! I stood mesmerized because in his physical life that is how he signed off his love notes to me.

William also seized the moment to congratulate me on my recent healing in such a fun style. Again, he spoke the same words from years ago, *Admit it, you are strong and happy now. You are ready to move on with our love, our legacy, and our message.* Before leaving, he urged me to climax the evening in two ways. I honored both requests.

First, he reminded me of the poem that I penned decades ago. This response came from my heart and soul, when I posed the question of continuing our relationship or abandoning it because of its controversial nature. It empowered me to take the leap of faith that was to become our Love and Legacy. I now also see its relevant wisdom shine through The GPS Code™. We offer my poem for your enlightened entertainment:

What is my task?
This I ask
It is to still my mind,
And listen to the whisperings of my heart,
To laugh easily
And to forgive freely
To release the past
And live the present
To see you in me,
And see me in you,
To know that separation
Is an illusion
For in love,
There is One . . . Inclusion.

He also urged me to toast, as I had years ago, "True independence is setting yourself free from self-imposed limitation and passing on that living wisdom to others."

William emphasized that The GPS Code™ was our fulfillment of that dream. The GPS Code™ was birthed through our collaboration between dimensional planes as our contribution to bringing Light through the darkness.

This transformational system was the culmination of the challenge portended in my NDE, in which I was told that "this is yours to pass on!" I had foolishly thought that I was to create an NDE simulation for others. William laughed and corrected me. My mission was to pass on the wisdom and benefits of having an NDE without the liabilities!

There is a Great Awakening taking place on Earth now. Many have referred to it as the greatest leap in evolutionary consciousness that humanity has ever experienced. Each person who becomes the highest and best version of their true God/Source nature adds to the tipping point of all possibilities!

For those who desire a deeper understanding and fuller experience of The GPS Code™, we are thrilled to take you to your next level.

Please visit https://www.yourgpscode.com/ for a complimentary gift to give you a daily jumpstart routine in empowering your day and evening in just a few minutes. Our desire is for all to enjoy the trip called evolution!

Spirit Face Photographs

Mark Macy, a renowned author and leading researcher in the frontier field of instrumental transcommunication (ITC), receives clear spirit faces on Polaroid film with the help of a subtle energy device called a "luminator."

SOLO PHOTO OF TIANNA

These two photographs were taken by Mark Macy at Wainwright House in Rye, NY, on February 22, 2001, as described on pages 141 and 144-146. Mark Macy has written the foreword to the present volume.

WILLIAM'S FACE REFLECTING THROUGH TIANNA'S

Meet the Authors

Tianna Conte-Dubs, N.D. is a trailblazing blend of mystic, scientist, and international bestselling transformational author. Born with the gift of multi-sensory abilities, Tianna's mystical roots have led to a career spanning over thirty-five years as a trained naturopath, ordained Interfaith minister, initiated shaman, and psycho-spiritual therapist specializing in enlightened self-care and personal evolution. Her passion to integrate ancient wisdom with cutting-edge technology in energy psychology has earned her an international reputation as a "physician" to the soul. After a Near-Death Experience in 1995 and having escorted her beloved into the Light through a transcendent kiss, Tianna is uniquely qualified to bring a deep intuitive knowledge of human consciousness, life, death and transformation to the eternal journey. Her expertise in relationships focuses on training others to live life with passion, purpose, and pleasure. Affectionately referred to as the "spa shaman," she is a living embodiment of the power to transform sacred wounding into personal and professional triumph. Her dedication to passing on this wisdom has resulted in the formation of two companies whose intention is to enhance the quality of life for all people. She is director of Infinite Possibilities Productions and Visionary International. She is the producer whose story is featured in a spiritual documentary, Awaken Your Riches, inspired by Think and Grow Rich, and co-stars in Dying to Live. Formerly, she was on the board of directors of Wainwright House. Currently, she is in private practice, and founder of the GPS code in collaboration with her beloved William in spirit. Her legacy purpose is now sharing the GPS code with the world to empower people in accessing their divine guidance and living their life to the fullest while enjoying the ride. Tianna travels, lectures, and participates worldwide with shamans and spiritual masters to pioneer ways and opportunities for people to explore the evolutionary power of love-based living.

William. The world's authentic ghost writer extraordinaire. His relentless pursuit of the truth pressed his beloved wife, Tianna, to express the fullness of their eternal love journey. Before his transition William worked as an international business entrepreneur and interfaith minister, specializing in healing and prosperity consciousness. His passion was to provide tools and support to set people free from self- imposed limitations. He continues to do so in the afterlife through "divine intervention." His mission is still with and through mystical collaboration with Tianna. His promise to Tianna of fulfilling her ultimate childhood dream and NDE has been fulfilled through his collaboration in the GPS code for humanity's awakening.

Janet Cunningham, Ph.D. is an internationally known specialist in regression therapy, trainer, transpersonal counselor, seminar leader, and author of ten books. She has explored how psychic abilities manifest. In so doing, she has helped some people to develop their abilities and others to become more grounded in physical reality. Her esoteric and practical nature allows her empathic abilities to sense beyond the personality into one's soul…and the various subtle energies of one's unconscious being. Dr. Cunningham is president of the International Board for Regression Therapy (IBRT), a certifying body. She is also a member of EARTH, (European Association for Regression Therapy), past- president of the International Association for Regression Research and Therapies, Inc., a networking organization. She served on the faculty of the Professional Institute for Regression Therapy in California and trains practitioners in regression therapy as co-founder of the World Regression Institute. After supporting several co-authors to write their stories and share their knowledge, Janet founded Heritage Authors®, a family-operated company created to "preserve the memories" and Stories of the Tablet, a branch which encourages people to share their spiritual journey in books and DVDs. Janet empowers people to discover their soul's purpose for this lifetime. She has also documented the ancient Egyptian spiritual beliefs as a model for consciousness. Dr. Cunningham has conducted training sessions and workshops throughout the world and led tours to spiritual sites, including Egypt, China, Thailand and Turkey.

Other Works by the Authors:

By Tianna Conte-Dubs

Love's Fire: Beyond Mortal Boundaries with Janet Cunningham

Love's Fire: Initiation into the 21sf Century with Janet Cunningham

Your GPS Code: Guidance, Solutions and Freedom God's Way
by Dr. Tianna Conte

Compilation Books: Contributor with various authors

The Change: Insights into Self-Empowerment

The Voyage to Your Vision

Hey, Did You AHA that?

My Big Idea Book

Are YOU the Missing Piece: Don't Leave a Hole in the World

My Journey My Journal

Gratitude Journal: Creating Moments of Gratitude Every Day

By Janet Cunningham

A Tribe Returned Illustrations by Orazio Salati

Inner Selves: The Feminine* Path to Weight Loss (*for men and women who validate their intuitive nature)

Weight Loss Breakthroughs, 4 audio cassette tape album workshop - or
2 CDs

Caution: Soul Mate Ahead! With Michael Ranucci

Weight Solutions: The New Body-Mind-Spirit Approach with Judith Valentine, Ph.D.

Survival on a Wing and Prayer with Gail Lionetti

Love's Fire: Beyond Mortal Boundaries with Tianna Conte-Dubs

Love's Fire: Initiation into the 21st Century with Tianna Conte-Dubs

Sisters' Memories with Judith Bums

The Upward Spiral: Breakthroughs to Joy (fiction)

www.JanetCunningham.com

www.HeritageAuthors.com

For those who want to pass on the "fire" through these products, we offer our Thank You with savings: 10% discount on three of the same products. Larger discounts available on quantity orders. Please inquire.

INFINITE POSSIBILITIES PRODUCTIONS
2005 PALMER AVE. #181
LARCHMONT, NY 10538-2421
PHONE: 800-711-5903

www.LovesFireTrilogy.com

Infinite Possibilities

The vision that Tianna and William had for Infinite Possibilities, founded in 1993, was one that would promote people, projects, and products that raise awareness, expand consciousness, and lift humanity. With William's passing, that dream seemed to end as well. Tianna had no desire to continue without him. Unbeknownst to her, William had other plans. This included Tianna retaining the position of CEO, despite her protestations. William affectionately refers to her as Chief Evolutionary Officer while he co11tinues as Chief Enlightenment Officer . . . and so it seems to be.

With William's expanded awareness and Tianna's gifts at bridging the dimensional worlds, Infinite Possibilities is dedicated to its original vision. In that light, we offer:

- ➤ seminars in spa settings
- ➤ private sessions and retreats
- ➤ products for stress-free pleasure
- ➤ quantum technology

Anyone interested in pursuing any of the information related to people and products mentioned in this trilogy may feel free to contact Infinite Possibilities.

Playfully, Tianna and William believe a great read deserves a great beverage! We invite anyone interested in a stress free pleasure coffee (that reduces inflammation and weight) to send a self addressed, stamped envelope to Infinite Possibilities for a free packet or visit the link below for info on how you can become a new you and prosper too.

www.secrets.newyoupro.com

Tianna and William also believe in world travel as a means for new experiences and new possibilities. Anyone who is interested in receiving a complimentary travel voucher, please inquire how that can be made possible. Email *tianna@infinitepossibilitiesproductions.com* or call 800-711-5903

Invitation: R-Evolutionary™ Circles-----

We believe in the ripple effect of consciousness of the power of one person awakening to their own Light, passing it on for the fulfillment of all. We personally invite you to be part of our ongoing community of like-minded people who are dedicated to personal evolution.

- ➢ We offer Tele-classes on relevant topics for discussion with the authors and surprise guests.
- ➢ Occasional VIP tickets to related Workshops and retreats.
- ➢ Advanced notice with special bonuses on future products and events.

RSVP of your interest by contacting us toll-free by phone: 800-711-5903

E-mail:

tianna@infinitepossibilitiesproductions.com

Follow Tianna on Social Media

https://www.twitter.com/DrTianna
http://www.facebook.com/gpscode
https://www.facebook.com/tianna.conte.77
https://www.linkedin.com/in/drtianna

Follow Janet on Social Media

http://www.twitter.com/drjcunningham
https://www.facebook.com/janet.cunningham.750
https://www.linkedin.com/in/janet-cunningham-109b084

Or please visit our websites:

www.yourgpscode.com
www.InfinitePossibilitiesProductions.com
www.spiritualitymadepractical.com

www.ingramcontent.com/pod-product-compliance
Lightning Source LLC
Chambersburg PA
CBHW031251090426
42742CB00007B/406